Immigration Detention Inc.

"Who knew that hatred driven by racism could be so lucrative? Hiemstra and Conlon's *Immigration Detention Inc.* answers this with a resounding and meticulously researched exposé of the political and economic forces driving the expansion of immigrant detention. This book is essential reading for policymakers, activists, and anyone concerned with immigration justice and the deeply rooted connections between public and private sectors."
—Ravi Ragbir, immigration activist and co-founder of New Sanctuary Coalition

"A vital and troubling look at the grotesque practices of the privatized immigration detention industry, whose soaring profits are dependent on inflicting extreme suffering. This book is a microcosm of what ails America in an era of rampant capitalism and exclusionary nationalism."
—Reece Jones, author of *Nobody is Protected* and *White Borders*

"*Immigration Detention Inc.* provides the most thorough breakdown of the immigration enforcement industrial complex that I have ever read. With meticulous research and analysis, Hiemstra and Conlon not only delve into the everyday horrors people face in detention—including horrible food and faulty medical care—but also reveal the tentacles of power and finance behind immigration control. In other words, if you want to know what's really going on, and what you might do about it, you will find no book more important than this one."
—Todd Miller, journalist and author of *Build Bridges, Not Walls* and *Empire of Borders*

"In this shocking exposé of conditions in U.S. immigration detention facilities, Conlon and Hiemstra reveal the high costs of privatization—most obviously for those who are detained but also for the wider U.S. society. Much of what is described is unfathomable: rotting food; failure to treat basic medical problems; gynecological procedures undertaken without consent. Such matters are not exceptional, they are 'business as usual', the system working as designed. As states around the world turn with ever greater enthusiasm to immigration detention, this book offers a stark warning of all that will be lost in the process."
—Mary Bosworth, Professor of Criminology, University of Oxford and author of *Supply Chain Justice*

Immigration Detention Inc.

The Big Business of Locking up Migrants

Nancy Hiemstra
and Deirdre Conlon

First published 2025 by Pluto Press
New Wing, Somerset House, Strand, London WC2R 1LA
and Pluto Press, Inc.
1930 Village Center Circle, 3-834, Las Vegas, NV 89134

www.plutobooks.com

Copyright © Nancy Hiemstra and Deirdre Conlon 2025

The right of Nancy Hiemstra and Deirdre Conlon to be identified as the authors of this work has been asserted in accordance with the Copyright, Designs and Patents Act 1988.

British Library Cataloguing in Publication Data
A catalogue record for this book is available from the British Library

ISBN 978 0 7453 4946 6   Paperback
ISBN 978 0 7453 4947 3   PDF
ISBN 978 0 7453 4948 0   EPUB

This book is printed on paper suitable for recycling and made from fully managed and sustained forest sources. Logging, pulping and manufacturing processes are expected to conform to the environmental standards of the country of origin.

Typeset by Stanford DTP Services, Northampton, England

Simultaneously printed in the United Kingdom and United States of America

EU GPSR Authorised Representative
LOGOS EUROPE, 9 rue Nicolas Poussin, 17000, LA ROCHELLE, France
Email: Contact@logoseurope.eu

Contents

Acknowledgements   vii
List of Figures and Tables   xii
Abbreviations and Acronyms   xiii

Introduction: Immigration Detention Inc.'s Deep Dependencies   1

1 **Probing U.S. Detention's Unhealthy Growth**   10
    The spread of immigration detention in the United States   12
    The business of detention   19
    Facilities of focus and major contractors   21
    Researching detention's inner workings from the outside   29

2 **"Meatballs that smell like fecal matter": When Bad Food is the Business Model**   38
    Cut-throat competition in the "corrections" food industry   39
    What's (not) on the plates   48
    A system based on bad food, working as designed   59

3 **"Cost Containment" and Litigation: The Institutionalization of Medical Neglect**   62
    Issues with detention medical care   63
    Competitive contracting: litigation, influence, cost over care   72
    The ICE Health Services Corps and "public" health   79
    Issues that add up to the institutionalization of medical neglect   81

4 **Starved for Profit: How Migrants Become Captive Consumers and Coerced Workers**   83
    Detention conditions that drive demand for high-cost commissaries   85

The high cost of relying on commissaries	86
Commission rates and county contracts	88
Keefe, private equity, and profiting from detention	89
Captive consumers, exploitable labor, and "voluntary" work programs	93
Saving on labor costs	95
Pushing back against the cycle of exploitation	97

5 The Accountability Industry: Rubber-stamping Bad Care — 104
- National Detention Standards — 105
- ICE inspections — 107
- Accreditations for sale — 114

6 Breaking Unjust Detention Dependencies — 124
- Webs of dependence: Private companies — 124
- Webs of dependence: Local governments and communities — 127
- Lobbying and revolving doors — 130
- Breaking the webs depending on detention — 133
- The deceptive appeal of "Alternatives to Detention" — 140
- What now? — 144

Afterword: Chaos and Cruelty in the First Month of the Second Trump Administration — 151
- Implications for "immigration detention inc." — 153
- Private companies continue to drive detention — 157
- Sorting fact from fiction in the frenzy to expand detention and deportation — 158
- Fighting and ending "immigration detention inc." — 161

Notes — 163
Index — 206

Acknowledgements

Our research—and this book—began with two deceptively simple questions: who benefits from the U.S. detention system, and how? Now, more than a decade on from our first attempts to address these questions, we know that, in many ways, the answers are anything but simple, as this book demonstrates. So, too, the process of researching and writing this book has not been straightforward or without challenges. We have been generously supported by remarkable communities and we are grateful to all those who have inspired, contributed to, engaged with, and encouraged our work.

We want to first acknowledge individuals who, as migrants, have been—or currently are—detained, as well as their families; some of whom we know and have interacted with, others whose experiences we've learned about in the course of this work, and all who are unjustly locked up as grist for the myriad players that benefit from detention.

In bringing the depth and reach of detention's avarice into focus we are motivated and humbled by the many advocates and activists who have worked and continue to work relentlessly to counter the detention machine in our region of research, including Will Coley, Alina Das, Amy Gottlieb, Camille Mackler, Kathy O'Leary, Sally Pillay, Ravi Ragbir, Rosa Santana, Katy Sastre, Father Tom Sheridan (RIP), Whit Strub, Amy Torres, Gabriela Viera, Chia-Chia Wang, Will Westerman, Karina Wilkinson; and our deep apologies to those we have failed to mention.

We are thankful for excellent research assistance from CUNY graduate student Marlene Ramos, Stony Brook undergraduate students Moud Adesah, Jeanette Blanchette, Nic Grima, Megha Kanabar, Aakanksha Kirtane, Mercedes Odinmah, Raisa Rahman, Evelyn Lopez Rodriguez, Briana Rosenberg, Cassandra Skolnick, Pramiti Yashroy, and Syosset High School student Jessica Yao. Special thanks to Cassandra for the two maps of detention facilities and sustained pursuit of online sources.

For assistance framing and interpreting our public information requests, many thanks to Claudia Valenzuela of the Heartland Alliance, Jesse Franzblau of the National Immigrant Justice Center, Sue Long of the Transactional Records Access Clearinghouse, Austin Kocher at Syracuse University, and investigative reporter Matt Katz. We owe special thanks to NIJC and TRAC for their significant collections of documents. Detention Watch Network has long been a vital reference point and resource, we are inspired by and draw on the organization as a key source of information, initiatives, and organizing to end detention. We recognize, too, the county employees tasked with filling our public information requests through the years.

We were honored to dialogue with other presenters and participants at the Elizabeth Detention Center: Past, Present, and Future symposium in October 2023, organized by Ulla Berg and Carolina Sanchez Boe, and hosted by the Department of Latino and Caribbean Studies at Rutgers University, NJ. We benefited from the exchange with scholars and groups who work in the U.K., U.S., and Australia at the Carcerality and Resistance workshop, May 2024, held at the University of Edinburgh, and organized by Cetta Mainwaring along with her amazing team.

We have presented different aspects of this work over the years at conferences and events that are too numerous to list in detail. We are very appreciative of the many opportunities we've had to share and discuss our ideas at meetings of the American Association of Geographers; Canadian Association of Refugee and Forced Migration Studies; Critical Geography; Eastern Sociological Society; Royal Geographical Society with the Institute for British Geographers; and the Carceral Geographies conference.

Our gratitude to Jonathan Darling, Reece Jones, and Todd Miller for generously giving publishing advice.

Sincere thanks to Ben Platt for expert editorial guidance, and the patience to coach two stuffy academics toward less stuffy (we hope!) tone and language, and for helping us to clarify what has significance and draw out what's interesting, all with buoyant reassurance.

We are also grateful to the Pluto Press team. Thanks to editor Neda Tehrani for early guidance on our project, and later David

ACKNOWLEDGEMENTS

Castle and Robert Webb. Jeanne Brady showed great patience during the copyediting process and Dave Stanford with the proofs. Thanks to Melanie Patrick for the creative cover design. We appreciate the U.S. marketing team Lily Brunson and Patrick Hughes, and the U.K. marketing team Sophie O'Reirdan and James Kelly. Thanks, also, to Jonila Krasniqi and Emily Orford.

For Nancy: To Deirdre—I learn so much from your probing questions, sharp insights, and theoretical acumen. Our partnership is an essential pillar in my scholarship, and we have seen each other through a lot of life events! It continues to be an honor to do this work with you.

I am grateful to be part of several different writing groups and partnerships that force me to make forward progress, no matter how overwhelming things get. I thank Mary Jo Bona and Kristina Lucenko for constant cheerleading, writing spaces, and feedback; the Feminist Geography Writing Group for incredibly consistent writing forums; Jenean McGee for early morning writing zooms, and Jenny Strandberg for twice-yearly writing retreats.

I've engaged in fruitful conversations that boosted my brain and somehow enriched this book with so many people, including Ulla Berg, Emily Billo, Geoffrey Boyce, Andrew Burridge, Kate Coddington, Gioconda Herrera, Emily Kaufman, Austin Kocher, Kenneth Sebastian León, Jenna Loyd, Lauren Martin, Cetta Mainwaring, Emily Mitchell-Eaton, Alison Mountz, Joseph Nevins, Sarah Tosh, Katie Wells, Jill Williams, and huge apologies for whoever I am leaving out due to my end-of-book brain fog!

I am deeply proud to be part of Stony Brook University's Women's, Gender, and Sexuality Studies Department, with always supportive and encouraging colleagues. Special mention to Liz Montegary and Jackie Donnelly for doing all the behind-the-scenes stuff that keeps things running these last few years. I am thankful to students in my Stony Brook classes for their persistent curiosity and commitment to learning and action.

Invitations to present various components of this work provided critical opportunities for developing ideas. I thank Joseph Nevins and the Department of Geography at Vassar College (2023), Ricardo Santos and SUNY Nassau College (2022), and the Social Anatomy of a Deportation Regime working group at CUNY

(2019). Funds supporting this project in various ways have come from Stony Brook University's grants for Faculty in the Arts, Humanities, and Social Sciences (FAHSS), and the Union of University Professionals.

I am wildly fortunate to have unwavering and constant family support. My parents Roger and Janet Hiemstra have been relentless supporters of my career and writing since the very beginning. They've also provided critical advice, feeding, and childcare throughout the years. To Sean: your unflagging support is my anchor, and your steadfast belief in my research endeavors helps me to move forward with determination and confidence. This book would not have been possible without all that, plus your willingness to bend schedules and take on extra parent duties to give me writing time. To Kian and Saskia: working on this book has meant missing a lot of activities with you, and sometimes being unfairly grumpy when I am with you. Hoping that a more just world can exist in your future keeps me going.

For Deirdre: collaborating with Nancy in this research and as co-author is an immeasurable honor. You infuse our shared work with your verve, critical sensibility, extraordinary organization, and lucid style; my thanks for your continually generous brilliance.

Colleagues at Saint Peter's University, NJ helped get this project off the ground, with special thanks to David Surrey and Anna Brown. I'm grateful for engagement with colleagues at University of Leeds: thanks to Clare Woulds and the School of Geography for support and research time, and to comrades in the Social Justice, Cities, Citizenship cluster and Leeds Migration Research Network for stimulating intellectual exchange. I'm thankful for funding received to support this work, including a Faculty Research Award from Saint Peter's University and an International Research Mobility Award from University of Leeds.

Ideas and feedback shared with colleagues at invited workshops have been very generative throughout this project. I'm thankful for invitations to present facets of this work at Refugee Tales (2016) and the Global Politics of Border Externalization and Offshoring workshop (2024) at Sheffield University, and organized by Lucy Mayblin, Joe Turner, and Ipek Demir. Thanks, also, to Arshad Isakjee, Thom Davies, and Tesfalem Yemane whose work, alongside Lucy and Joe, on the Channel Crossings Project, resonates deeply. I'm grateful to Francesca Esposito, Federica de Cordova, Anna Maria Meneghini, Mary Bosworth, and Andriani Fili for the opportunity to contribute to the seminar Interrogating the Border-Industrial complex (2024) at the University of Verona and co-organized by Border Criminologies, University of Oxford.

Colleagues, mentors, and friends who inspire and support are many. I'm very grateful to David Bell, Sasha Brown, Andrew Burridge, Kate Coddington, Darlynne Devenny, Elizabeth Cullen Dunn, Deborah Gambs, Nick Gill, Mary Gilmartin, Myles Gould, Alex Hall, Cindi Katz, Austin Kocher, Martin Lemberg-Pedersen, Hannah Lewis, Jenna Loyd, Lauren Martin, Dominique Moran, Alison Mountz, Dusana Podlucka, Joseph Robinson, Paul Routledge, Jonathan Turner, Jen Turner, Louise Waite, Jill Williams, and Nichola Wood. There are scores more peoples' names stashed in notebooks, to you all, stacks of thanks.

And, foremost, enormous gratitude to my family near and far, *go raibh mile maith agaibh go léir*. To Stephen and Sadie, especially: your steady encouragement; great patience and generosity through my all-engrossing (pre)occupation; plain-speaking wordsmithery; discerning edits; always welcome, though sometimes under-appreciated, reminders of the value of whimsy and laughter; and your resolute commitment to making the world gentler, are simply—which is also to say, not straightforwardly—all that really matters.

Figures and Tables

FIGURES

1.1	Average daily detained population, 1979–2024	16
1.2	ICE detention budgets, 2005–24	20
1.3	Map: The six detention facilities in our study	22
1.4	Map: NY and NY metro area detention facilities in our study	22
1.5	Page from 2013 Bergen County IGSA with ICE showing ICE's redactions	32

TABLES

1.1	Major contracts for facilities in our study	24
2.1	Food contractors and value of contracts for facilities in our study	40
2.2	Price per meal and contract value in bids for Bergen County Jail's 2015–19 food contract	44
3.1	Medical service providers for facilities in our study	73

Abbreviations and Acronyms

ACA	American Correctional Association
ACLU	American Civil Liberties Union
AGS	Akima Global Services
ATD	Alternatives to Detention
BCJ	Bergen County Jail
BI	Behavioral Interventions, Inc.
CALEA	Commission on Accreditation for Law Enforcement Agencies, Inc.
CCA	Corrections Corporation of America, now renamed CoreCivic
CCR	Center for Constitutional Rights
CCS	Correct Care Solutions, now Wellpath
CDC	Centers for Disease Control and Prevention
CDF	Contract Detention Facility, one type of detention facility, owned and operated by a private company
CFG	CFG Health Systems
CHS	Correctional Health Services
CMC	Correctional Medical Care
DHS	Department of Homeland Security
DWN	Detention Watch Network
ECCF	Essex County Correctional Facility
EDR	Employee Dining Room
ERO	Enforcement and Removal Operations, agency within ICE
FOIA	Freedom of Information Act
FOIL	Freedom of Information Law
GAO	Government Accountability Office
GDCS	GD Correctional Services
HCCF	Hudson County Correctional Facility
HRF	Human Rights First
HRW	Human Rights Watch

ICE	Immigration and Customs Enforcement, agency within the DHS
IGSA	Intergovernmental Service Agreement
IHSC	ICE Health Services Corp
INS	Immigration and Naturalization Service (ICE's predecessor)
ISAP	Intensive Supervision Appearance Program
KCN	Keefe Commissary Network
MTC	Management & Training Corporation
NCCHC	National Commission on Correctional Health Care
NDS	National Detention Standards
NGO	Nongovernmental Organization
NIJC	National Immigrant Justice Center
NSA	National Sheriff's Association
NWIPC	Northwest ICE Processing Center
OCCF	Orange County Correctional Facility
ODO	Office of Detention Oversight, agency within ICE
OIG	Office of the Inspector General of the DHS
OPRA	Open Public Records Act
PBNDS	Performance-Based National Detention Standards
QCCH	Quality Choice Correctional Health
RFP	Request for Proposals
SPC	Service Processing Center, one type of detention facility owned by ICE
TRAC	Transactional Records Access Clearinghouse
TVPA	Trafficking Victims Protection Act
USMS	U.S. Marshals Service
VMBG	Valley Metro Barbosa Group
VWP	Voluntary Work Program

Introduction: Immigration Detention Inc.'s Deep Dependencies

"My job is to keep taxes at a minimum and to bring in revenue," explained New Jersey's Essex County executive, Joseph DiVincenzo, in 2018.[1] Beneath this seemingly banal statement, however, was a harrowing reality: DiVincenzo was explaining why the county could not *afford* to stop detaining immigrants in its jails on behalf of the federal Immigration and Customs Enforcement agency, or ICE.

ICE money, about 5 percent of Essex County's total revenue, was crucial to the county's budget.[2] This point was made clear at a 2018 meeting in Essex County when one community activist asked an elected official, "If I take my kids to the zoo, am I supporting—are we visiting something that was built using money from $117 per night per detainee?" The county leader responded that ICE money (that is, the dollar amount paid by the federal agency to the county for imprisoning each migrant per day) "is certainly part of" what pays for Essex County Parks, including the zoo.[3] Detaining immigrants—the message was unambiguous—helped pay for this suburban county's version of the American Dream.

The county did not stop detaining immigrants for ICE until it secured a contract to jail inmates from another county.[4] Revenue, after all, did have to come from somewhere.

The U.S. federal government has the biggest detention system in the world, paying more than $3 billion per year to lock up around 40,000 immigrants every day across the country. Some of that money is paid out at the local level as in Essex County, New Jersey, where it plugged holes in the fraying budgets of schools and parks and police departments. Most of the money, however, ends up in the hands of private companies, who provide food and medical services, laundry and transportation, staff and facilities: all to imprison immigrants.

Every year, the amount of money paid out for detention continues to grow. If you follow the money and the entities that coalesce around it—as we do here in *Immigration Detention Inc.*—you'll soon see that the whole country is entangled in a web of dependency on detention. Countless companies, state and county governments, and even unintentionally implicated individuals—like the parent mentioned above asking about their local zoo—are benefiting, in various ways, from the federal government's decision to criminalize migration, incarcerate migrants, and do so using overwhelmingly private companies and subcontracted services. You'll see, too, that once money is involved, it is terrifically difficult to change course. Local governments and communities become dependent on detention for critical income, compelled to remain involved.

Yet that is far from rock bottom. Because, in fact, as this book shows, the people detained in these facilities are starved, sickened, and exploited as a matter of routine operation. In the six facilities we investigate, as well as in many others like them across the country, costs are cut and massive savings are made by denying those confined in detention centers access to adequate food, medicine, sanitary conditions, and more. Migrant detainees routinely report food infested with insects, bacteria, or even excrement; being denied medication or doctor's visits; even being required to purchase "luxury" items like shampoo, soap, and ibuprofen, as well as phone calls.

These detainees are imprisoned in county jails and state prisons as well as in privately run detention facilities. This happens even though immigration detention is a civil legal process, not a criminal one.[5] Detention supposedly allows the Department of Homeland Security, through ICE, to exercise and administer immigration enforcement. In other words, the purpose of detention is to check, verify, and confirm immigration status. Immigration detention is not supposed to be punitive. But in reality, it is indistinguishable from criminal incarceration, holding detainees in harsh, prison-style conditions that create unchecked opportunities for avaricious authorities to prey on criminalized migrants.[6]

And the results are catastrophic. Since 2011, there have been 112 documented, preventable migrant deaths in detention.[7] Incarcerated individuals are 6.4 times more likely to end up with a food-related illness than people outside prison settings.[8] Detainees' limited options to mitigate detention's abusive conditions mean working for 12 cents per hour while paying in-store commissary prices up to six times more than prices outside. And veneers of accountability, window-dressed with rubber-stamp inspections and accreditations, are, effectively, "for sale" annually with price tags under $20,000, a paltry sum compared to the income from immigration detention contracts.

The revenue that contractors pull in is colossal: GEO Group, ICE's largest detention operator, earned $1.05 billion, almost 44 percent of its total revenue, from ICE contracts in 2022 (some of these for electronic monitoring). The same year, CoreCivic made over $550 million, 30 percent of its total revenue, from contracts with ICE.[9] And this doesn't even begin to take account of the myriad other players who benefit or are financially involved in immigration detention: contracted service providers, supply networks, local governments, and connected government agencies.

Immigration Detention Inc., therefore, has two primary goals. The first goal is to reveal the lived consequences of seemingly innocuous economic speak like "bring[ing] in revenue" or focusing only on "the bottom line." The second goal is to show the alarming depth of financial dependence on depriving immigrants of their freedom.

Since detaining immigrants brings financial rewards, on which corporations *and* counties now depend, there has been a concerted push to incarcerate more immigrants. Over the last four decades, the number of immigrants imprisoned has skyrocketed, even when the number arriving was the same as or less than in previous years. The push to lock up ever greater numbers of migrants is rooted in the messy connections between government at different levels—from local municipalities to federal agencies—and prison corporations, which have lobbied Congress to pass laws that mean more immigrants wind up behind bars.

As more and more human beings have been locked up in worse and worse conditions, ever more profit is generated for those doing the imprisoning.[10] It's a vicious cycle, one in which many of us are implicated. And it's only accelerating.

Through our investigations of detention food provision, medical care, commissary stores, detainee labor, and the accountability industry, we show how the U.S. detention system spins out complicated networks of political and economic dependence. We emphasize that those who have a stake in continued detention—and are eager to see more of it—include *both* private and public entities. The participation of private companies, guided explicitly by capitalist profit-making goals, is not so surprising. But we show that public entities, like local governments and connected government agencies, are also caught up in and driven by these same logics. And for all those involved, success is measured in dollar signs, which means that all players are rewarded for bad detainee experiences. Stakeholders provide services that leave detainees chronically hungry and make them sick, sell them overpriced items to survive, and take advantage of their labor, all while saving on costs and maximizing profit.

We also show that detained migrants are not alone in being affected by detention expansion and the incorporation of ever-increasing numbers and types of businesses. In fact, the political and economic dynamics at the core of immigration detention also inflect public life. Locking up migrants is now taken as an accepted norm and an inevitable response to migrant arrivals. The dynamics we detail in this book have altered society's moral compass. *Immigration Detention Inc.* is therefore both the book's title and our shorthand—as "immigration detention inc."—for the web of sickening, corrupting dependencies that are woven as more and more private and public entities are pulled into—and benefit from—detention operations.

Indeed, detention may be one of the few issues that has bipartisan support, popular with both Republicans and Democrats across administrations and layers of government. As the U.S. detention system has grown aggressively for more than four decades, detention has come to be understood and accepted as a necessary part of any response to immigration—whether it be considered a "crackdown" or "humanitarian relief."

This book comes at a pivotal moment in the United States and more widely, too. In the last several years, there have been some swings in the total number of migrants who are locked up in U.S.

detention centers on a given day. The most recent "low" figure of 13,258 was reported during the global COVID-19 pandemic. Since then, the population of migrants detained has steadily climbed, and, at time of writing in January 2025, stood at around 39,000 individuals imprisoned in one of roughly 150 facilities around the country. But the U.S. appears poised to vastly expand its detention system even more, and quickly.

With recent increases in reported numbers of migrants arriving at U.S. southern borders, "crisis" talk and "get tough" proposals have dominated political rhetoric, policy implementation, and public attention. Immigration was a central issue of the 2024 presidential election. Increasing detention capacity was part of President Joseph Biden's efforts to decrease migrant arrivals in the run-up to the election. At the same time, Donald Trump's plan for mass deportation was arguably key to his successful campaign. His advisors have signaled that ballooning detention capacity—and the use of private contractors—will be critical to realizing the plan. Without a doubt, "immigration detention inc." is booming in the United States.

With the world's largest system for incarcerating migrants, other countries look to and follow the lead of the United States. As the Global Detention Project reports, immigration detention is "flourishing nearly everywhere [including] deepening institutional entrenchment in destination countries, as well as its spread—at the urging of the world's wealthiest countries—to places where [...] safeguards are non-existent."[11] So, the analysis that *Immigration Detention Inc.* provides is significant far beyond its U.S. focus.

In fact, detention has become a nearly universal response to unauthorized international migration. Instead of addressing the root causes—massive global inequalities, laws that make it impossible to migrate legally, and reliance on cheap migrant labor—states build detention regimes. For example, Australia's notoriously harsh detention system relies on private companies to isolate asylum seekers in remote facilities, many offshore and even in other island countries. Until ruled illegal, the United Kingdom's Conservative government was planning to offshore asylum-seeking migrants to Rwanda in a U.K.-funded detention center. The Italian and Albanian governments recently signed an agreement that the Italian government will fund detention centers in Albania to lock up migrants who arrive on Italy's shores.

New detention systems springing up around the world are propelled by the same public-private dynamics and money-making logics that underpin the U.S. system. Detention will become ever more normalized unless we can expose the crude logics and sever the connections between detention infrastructures and political and economic gain.

Chapter 1 examines how the United States arrived at the point where it has the dubious record of the world's largest population of migrants who are "locked up," with mushrooming spending to expand this gargantuan detention system. Immigration detention is about web widening—that is, integrating more and more entities into the business of detention by sweeping increasing numbers of primarily Black and brown bodies into the net of confinement and control. Big prison corporations, like GEO Group and CoreCivic, are known to have a stake in immigration detention. In this book, we focus on six facilities in New Jersey and New York to home in on the many additional players that are engaged in and financially benefit from detention.

A cloak of secrecy surrounds the entities that are involved with immigration detention, so our investigation has required developing strategies to circumvent barriers to information. We draw on many different sources: from documents acquired via public information requests, government reports, and in-depth journalism, as well as interviews and conversations with people who see the inside of detention centers and who speak directly with detainees, such as lawyers, volunteers in visitation programs, and formerly detained migrants. After laying out the wider social and political context of "how we got here" and the research approach the detention system necessitates, subsequent chapters dive into the wide range of stakeholders—including subcontracted companies, local governments, and various government agencies—that are sucked into the U.S. detention system.

The first industry in the web of dependence that *Immigration Detention Inc.* digs into is that of food provision. In Chapter 2, we break down the process of how food companies obtain contracts with the county jails that detain immigrants. When county governments decide who wins a food contract, cost is nearly always the deciding factor, with the lowest bidder inevitably winning. Competition between companies is intense and cut-throat. Company strategists want the contracts because they are highly lucrative. They know that in a detention environment, the customer is not who actually eats the food; the customer is the facility operator trying to pay as little as possible to feed detainees. Food companies can also count on loose rules about and sham oversight of what they actually serve. They are free to pinch pennies to maximize profit. The result is meals that are so routinely awful—and often disgusting—that they leave detainees hungry and even sick.

Chapter 3 explores detention medical care and the institutionalization of medical neglect. The U.S. healthcare system is known for its bloated costs and dizzying minefields of bureaucracy. In detention, there are bureaucracies, of course, but added to these are contracting battles marred by litigation, attempts to influence decisionmakers, and the degradation of care. Wellpath, part of a private equity firm and with a giant role providing detention medical services, has scooped up contracts to become the largest company in the detention and jail healthcare industry. The recent history of lawsuits brought against Wellpath includes over six hundred cases about the inadequate services provided, ranging from "indifferent care" to "cruel and unusual punishment."[12]

Chapter 3 also goes deep on the ICE Health Service Corps (IHSC), the government-run agency with an oversize role in detention medical care. IHSC's "cost containment" approach, like private providers, is driven by a principle of weighing cost over care.

In Chapter 4, we delve into how revenue and savings multiply for detention stakeholders through the combined effects of in-facility stores and detainee labor. Commissaries are a high-cost lifeline for detained migrants. The benefits of turning detained migrants into what we describe as "captive consumers"—where the miseries of detention compel detained migrants to accept their own exploitation—pile up even more when detention "voluntary work" programs are added to the mix.[13] To stave off chronic hunger, quell untreated pain and illness, and to try to make conditions bearable, detainees are driven to do work that keeps facilities running. Cooking, cleaning, and laundry work are coveted jobs, deemed a "privilege," for which detainees receive the shocking sum of one dollar per day.

We review recent efforts to put a stop to this cycle of privation, detainee demand, and mistreatment, and highlight how all the entities that benefit from detention—contractors, local to federal government agencies, and private equity investment firms—pit and play against each other in an effort to protect and continue to benefit from this harmful cycle.

The appalling depth and reach of the detention system is apparent when we look to mechanisms that are supposed to provide oversight of the detention system and hold facilities and contractors to account. Chapter 5 delves into the illusion of accountability in this system. Carefully composed National Detention Standards provide a veneer of quality control that is proven to be largely fictitious. Inspections processes are deeply flawed and superficial, whether they're completed by government or subcontracted businesses. Attempts to redress violations through enforcement are ineffective, at best. In the three years from 2015 to 2018, for instance, ICE issued just two facilities with financial penalties and instead waived 65 documented violations. And grievance procedures for locked-up migrants are also riddled with problems.

Accreditations add to the illusion. For a price, accrediting agencies offer contractors and facility operators the appearance of high standards and responsible care, while helping to minimize legal liability. But the accreditations process is rife with conflicts of interest, and every aspect is monetized.

Chapter 6 first traces how the immigration detention system's networks of dependence stretch out beyond the industries and agencies already covered, to pull in an even wider array of people and businesses, all who come to have a stake in detention. We consider how financial dependency generates moral acceptance, as individuals, households, communities, and counties come to rely on detaining immigrants.

This chapter then turns to questions of "What next?" There is already an impressive range of individuals and organizations working to break down the dependencies that detention generates. We consider the important work that is being done and outline

INTRODUCTION

additional strategies—informed by what we have learned through this project—for dismantling the U.S.'s increasingly deep and troubling dependence on detention.

An Afterword, written just one month into President Donald Trump's second term in office, catalogs the chaotic and cruel actions taken in the unfolding efforts to implement the new administration's mass deportation plan. Taking stock of some of the fast-paced developments to date underscores a constant, which is the massive and rapidly growing revenue generating opportunity unlocked by "immigration detention inc."

Immigration Detention Inc. makes clear that the only crisis of immigration is one the United States has made for itself. We also raise the alarm as the U.S. has embarked on another huge expansion of its detention system, and as we see the emergence of a global system of detention in response to increasing human mobility. But the book also offers a path forward, revealing how we can break the tangled webs of dependency and bring an end to the devastating political, economic, and moral embrace of immigration detention. And the way to do so starts with the exposure and elimination of impulses and opportunities to generate revenue and seek profit by locking up migrants in the United States' sick, sickening, and exploitative immigration detention system.

1
Probing U.S. Detention's Unhealthy Growth

At the beginning of 2025, the Immigration and Customs Enforcement agency (ICE) was detaining around 39,000 people in the United States.[1] Detainees are held in a vast but piecemeal network of roughly 150 facilities,[2] a network which has the capacity to detain at least another 14,000 people (as was demonstrated in 2019). While detention facilities are concentrated near the U.S.-Mexico border, they are also located around the entire country, in nearly all fifty states and most U.S. territories. Detaining immigrants is at the core of the United States' approach to border and immigration enforcement. In fact, the country has the largest, most sprawling system of immigration detention in the world.

The country's increased investment in detention in the last three decades is astounding. In 1994, the U.S. had a detention capacity of just 6,785.[3] Today's immense system—more than five times that size—comes with a serious price tag: $2.8 billion was allocated in the U.S. national budget to pay for detaining immigrants in 2023.[4] The 2024 budget allocated $3.4 billion for a capacity of 41,500. The pace of detention expansion is picking up.

All this money goes to a hungry knot of companies and local governments that make the vast detention system possible. The network of stakeholders spirals out far beyond detention center owners and operators. Detained individuals require sustenance, health care, opportunities to communicate, and other basic necessities. Many, many providers are eager to step in, drawn by the financial opportunities available.

Indeed, the increasing involvement of private companies precisely mirrors the growing detention system and increasing budget allocations. In 2005, only 25 percent of ICE detainees (then under

20,000 per day) were in private facilities.[5] In 2023, this was up to almost 91 percent.[6] As the numbers detained in private facilities have expanded, detention costs keep going up. Private companies are not simply functioning to increase capacity for ICE. Instead, these companies now *drive* the laws that are made to detain more and more migrants, and, of course, push for bigger and bigger budget allocations for detention.

Prison companies consistently spend a lot of money lobbying policymakers at local, state, and federal levels, to support laws and policies that expand detention capacity. Consider CoreCivic and GEO Group, the two companies that have benefited the most from ICE's detention of migrants in private facilities. In 2023 alone, CoreCivic lavished a reported $1,680,000 on lobbying around detention, while GEO Group's efforts cost $1,250,000.[7] And that money was well spent: researchers have found clear links between politicians' support for harsh immigration laws, detention, and receipt of campaign donations from private prison companies.[8]

This book reveals that these webs of financial dependence feed the continued and expanding use of detention. We argue that these webs generate value—and make money—from immigrants. And they do so by feeding migrant detainees less food of worse quality, giving them less medicine and fewer visits to doctors, and charging them astronomical prices for necessities like toothpaste, antacid, and phone calls to family members and lawyers. In short, companies contracted to operate in detention centers increase their economic gains by providing *less* than they should.

Perhaps worst of all, these same immigrants often *work* within their detention centers, giving the companies practically free labor. Indeed, many migrants are desperate to do so, since they need money inside just to get by.

This book identifies and traces many of the financial relationships that enable these immigration detention centers to operate. After all, if these companies and local counties *couldn't* profit from immigrants, they'd have far less incentive to lock them up in the first place.

We expose these abuses by taking deep dives into key detention industries, drawing on case studies of six specific detention facilities to do so. In this chapter, we introduce these detention sites, and we explain how we got around the many roadblocks to researching detention.

First, however, let's take a brief look at the history of the U.S.'s massive immigration detention system. In 1994, the system's capacity was less than 7,000. How was the current capacity of over 50,000 reached less than three decades later?

THE SPREAD OF IMMIGRATION DETENTION IN THE UNITED STATES

The widespread, regular use of immigration detention is relatively new in the contemporary United States. But throughout its history, the U.S. government has repeatedly detained and forcibly moved individuals who fall outside particular ideas of American identity.

A handful of examples of these disturbing ideas about who was, is, or is not considered American include slavery and fugitive slave laws, the removal of Native Americans from ancestral lands and their confinement on reservations, Chinese exclusion laws of the 1880s to early 1900s, the "internment" of 120,000 Japanese immigrants and Japanese American citizens in the 1940s, and forced "repatriation" to Mexico of roughly one million Mexican immigrants and Mexican American citizens in the 1950s. Indeed, from the opening of New York City's Ellis Island Immigration Station in 1892 to the present day, the United States has shown a remarkable propensity to appropriate or construct camps, facilities, and transportation systems to isolate and expel whole groups of people.

Immigration detention cannot be tied to any one political party; it is a popular enforcement strategy with both Republicans and Democrats. The specific reasons cited by politicians for building systems of confinement and forced mobility of immigrants vary, but there are common underlying threads through time.

First, targeted groups nearly always fall outside dominant, race-based ideas of U.S. national identity, as indicated in the examples above. Immigration laws, and how they are enforced, have consistently tried to restrict citizenship as a privilege for primarily white residents, disproportionately impacting people of color. Second, targeted groups are depicted as endangering American security, with (usually non-white) immigrants framed as criminals, morally depraved and otherwise deficient, or a threat to national sovereignty and safety. Third, the confinement and expulsion of some (but not all) immigrants tend to benefit employers by weakening the position of immigrant laborers in terms of wages, job security, and safety. While the U.S. economy has famously always relied on immigrant workers, business leaders have consistently pushed for immigration policies that give them flexibility and control of the workforce.[9]

While these three threads are woven into the construction and expansion of today's immigration detention system, additional factors come into play.[10] Starting in the 1960s, the U.S. initiated profound changes to its immigration policies. The 1965 Immigration and Nationality Act abolished the national origins quota system, in place since the 1920s, which had strictly limited the migration of all but those from Northern and Western Europe. At the same time, increasing instability in countries of Latin America and the Caribbean—tied to Cold War maneuverings, including U.S. influence and interventions—spurred new patterns of human mobility to the United States. Also, in response to Cold War geopolitics and an evolving global human rights agenda, the U.S. began shifting policies to grant asylum to migrants from a wide array of countries.

The result was growing numbers of non-white immigrants in the United States, and in more areas of the country. These changing demographics became increasingly apparent in the late 1970s and 1980s, at the same time as the U.S. economy entered a long downturn. Despite evidence to the contrary, pundits and politicians often blamed economic woes on new immigrants. Terrorist attacks in the 1980s and 1990s, some linked to immigrants, fueled national security fears. Collectively, these factors led to rising public unease about immigration, scapegoating and criminalization of racialized immigrant groups, and anti-immigrant laws and policies in local, state, and national forums.

Importantly, too, policymakers started to embrace the idea that detaining immigrants—more than just containing them prior to deportation—worked to *deter* future immigration. The general logic of deterrence holds that punitive actions and heightened enforcement will discourage potential migrants. Today, deterrence remains a common justification for detention and deportation, despite the fact that decades of these policies have yielded little real proof that they do actually discourage migration in the long term.[11]

It is against this backdrop that the contemporary detention infrastructure began to take shape (see Figure 1.1). In the early 1980s, public panic rose over escalating Cuban, Haitian, Mexican, and Central American immigration. In response, Republican President Ronald Reagan adopted a new policy of detaining more asylum seekers from these places. Reagan also required the U.S. to permanently keep available 10,000 detention beds. Existing government-owned detention facilities, most on the U.S.-Mexico border, were quickly overcrowded. To increase capacity, the Immigration and Naturalization Service (the INS, the precursor to today's ICE) contracted space with private prison operators and local governments.

And here is another key shift behind the expanding detention system: a new view of immigration detention as an opportunity to generate revenue and create jobs. In the past, the U.S. government had relied on private operators for *temporary* detention space (for example, in the early twentieth century through the 1950s, the government detained migrants near the U.S.-Mexico border in privately owned hotels).[12] But in the 1980s, the private prison industry—already building infrastructure for the largest incarcerated population in the world—eagerly stepped in to accommodate rising detention numbers. In this, they were led by the Corrections Corporation of America (CCA, now renamed CoreCivic) and the Wackenhut Corporation (now renamed GEO Group), which remain the most profitable and largest in the industry to this day.

At the same time, larger shifts in the general economy put local economies in dire straits. Deindustrialization led to increasing unemployment, and the federal government decreased economic support for state and county governments. While immigration enforcement has always weakened the position of immigrants in the labor market, suddenly one enforcement strategy emerged as a source of revenue itself. To local governments and communities struggling financially, contracting out space for immigration detention plugged holes in household and county budgets.[13]

Together, prison corporations and local governments seized on immigration detention as an area for expansion. And so, under Reagan, prison corporations' army of lobbyists collaborated with political representatives from places looking to host prisons, driving new policies and laws that made more immigrants detainable. With both corporations and municipalities impatient for profit, they worked the system to invent new reasons—never previously codified into law—to detain immigrants.

The result of this collaboration was, first, the 1986 Immigration Reform and Control Act. This new law had the desired effect: for the first time, *criminal* penalties for not following immigration laws were imposed, resulting in larger numbers of detainees. Next was the 1988 Anti-Drug Abuse Act, which invented the "aggravated felony," a legal category for crimes that, when committed by non-citizens, mandate detention and usually deportation.[14] Another surge in detention capacity followed in 1989, when Republican President George H. W. Bush introduced a mandatory detention policy for any asylum seeker whose claim was denied.[15] Then, in 1994, Democrat President Bill Clinton laid out a new border strategy called "Prevention Through Deterrence," which included expanding detention capacity, under the false yet popular idea that harsher punishment of migrants would discourage more immigration.[16]

In 1996, two laws were passed that solidified the legal framework for today's detention system, and immediately began to further extend its capacity: the Illegal Immigration Reform and Immigrant Responsibility Act, and the Antiterrorism and Effective Death Penalty Act. These greatly expanded the categories of immigrants subject to mandatory detention and deportation (including legal residents), while significantly adding to the list of deportable acts. It also became much harder to fight deportation.

And, right away, private companies and local governments were standing by, eager to provide the new detention capacity required. By the end of Clinton's administration just a few years later, detention capacity was up to almost 20,000.

Following the terrorist attacks of September 11, 2001, the rhetoric of "homeland security" infiltrated almost all aspects of public policy and life, and immigrants were increasingly demon-

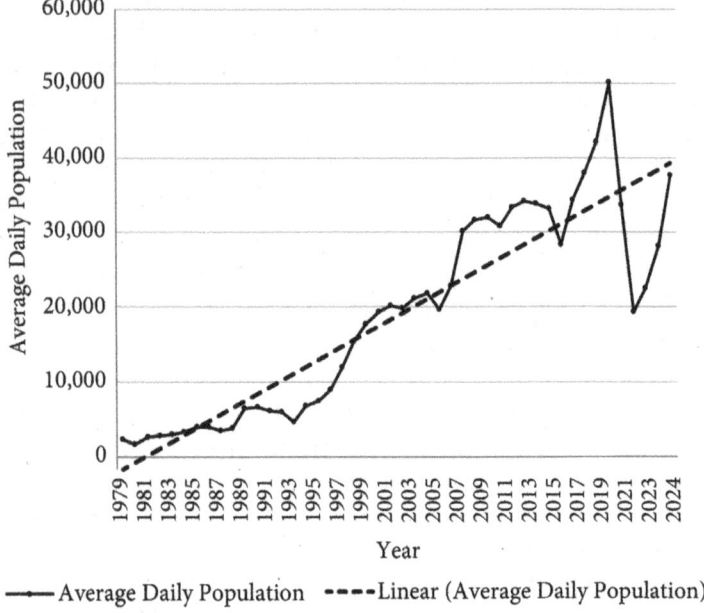

Figure 1.1   Average Daily Detained Population, 1979–2024[17]

ized. Detention became central to the U.S. government's response post-9/11. Propelled by racialized tropes of bad non-white immigrants who did not fit into ideas of American identity, lobbying by prison-related companies, and the dominance of policies oriented around "deterrence," the legal infrastructure and physical capacity for detention gained even more momentum.

A framework for *indefinite* detention was established through the 2001 PATRIOT Act, as well as a number of legal decisions that followed. The Homeland Security Act of 2003 created the Department of Homeland Security and replaced the INS with the scaled-up, bigger-budget Immigration and Customs Enforcement (ICE) agency. The 2004 Intelligence Reform and Terrorism Prevention Act mandated that ICE increase detention capacity by 8,000 *each year* from 2006 to 2010. Other laws and initiatives set ever higher deportation goals, involved local law enforcement agencies in immigration policing, and loosened categories of "detainable" and "deportable" immigrants to include groups previously off-limits as too vulnerable, such as families, mothers, and children. During Republican President George W. Bush's tenure, detention capacity reached 30,000.

Detention and deportation remained central to U.S. immigration policy under Democrat President Barack Obama, from 2008 to 2016. The administration gave more power to ICE field officers and local officials to detain non-citizens, especially through agreements with local law enforcement agencies such as 287(g) and the Secure Communities program. Perhaps worst of all, beginning in 2009, Congress included an annual "detention bed quota" in yearly funding bills, requiring that ICE make sure that there was a standing nationwide detention capacity for at least 34,000 individuals. Even this was not enough for some: ICE officials and representatives from states with the most detention capacity pushed to interpret this quota as requiring the beds to be *filled* and not just *available*. Consequently, "guaranteed minimums" were written into ICE contracts with private detention operators and local governments. These contractual clauses are condemned as "local lockup quotas" by anti-detention activists, who argue that these clauses influence decisions about who to detain and for how long.[18]

Policymaking in the Obama era continued to be driven by the idea that harsh and harmful enforcement policies deter future immigration, despite the continued lack of evidence to support this assumption. This thinking shaped the Obama administration's response to rising numbers of parents and children fleeing north to escape violence in Central America. Coinciding with this, the use of facilities to detain families increased. To facilitate expansion of family detention, the Obama administration relied largely on private companies. These policies were introduced at the same time as incarceration rates in the criminal justice system slowed; consequently, the private prison industry increasingly viewed detaining immigrants as providing a path for continued profit.

By 2017, when the openly anti-immigrant Republican Donald Trump became president, the immigration detention system was already detaining nearly 40,000 people daily. Under Trump, ICE went after more settled immigrants, intentionally separated and detained parents and children, and narrowed the criteria for granting asylum. The Trump administration openly embraced detention, working quickly to further increase capacity to 52,000. They added forty facilities to the detention system through fast-tracked contracts with private companies and some local governments, by lowering detention standards and contracting without competitive bidding. In August 2019, amid a summer surge in migrants and the use of temporary camps, detention numbers reached their highest ever: 55,654 (see Figure 1.1).[19]

Then, in early 2020, immigrant detention facilities and prisons were among the first institutions hit by the COVID-19 pandemic. Without appropriate medical and hygiene protocols—compounded by facility operators' indifference to preventing the spread of the disease—rates of infection and death among inmates and detainees were shockingly high.[20] When news of the alarming conditions leaked to the public, efforts were made to drastically reduce numbers of incarcerated and detained individuals. The U.S. immigrant detention population shrank to under 20,000 by the fall of 2020. Eighty-one percent of these immigrants were held in private detention facilities.[21]

When Democrat Joseph Biden became president in January 2021, around 15,000 people were in detention facilities. But as the pandemic subsided, the number of immigrants arriving at the U.S.-Mexico border escalated quickly, and the Biden administration responded predictably. In addition to continuing many of the Trump administration's policies, the Biden government prioritized detention and relied heavily on private prison companies to do so.[22] By September 2023, the number of people in immigration detention had reached 35,000, with around 90 percent of those detainees in privately-operated facilities.[23] At the end of 2024, the daily detained population had reached 39,000 once again.[24]

The Biden administration was also planning for more expansion of detention capacity. In June 2024, for instance, ICE put out a request for privately-operated detention facilities in New Jersey, where much of our research is based. The proposed expansion would give New Jersey the capacity to detain roughly 2,500 migrants.[25] In May and September 2024, ICE officials issued "multi-state requests for information," looking to increase detention capacity in 15 states in the Mid-west and on the West Coast.[26]

With the November 2024 election of Donald Trump as president for a second term, the U.S. is readying to enact an unprecedented "mass deportation" of immigrants. Trump's openly anti-immigrant campaign rhetoric framed immigrants as a threat to American security, identity, and way of life. He blatantly invoked racist dog whistles, and blamed immigrants for all manner of problems. Trump appointees promise to target immigrants on a scale not seen in a century. They have signaled that detention will be central to their plan of action, both because of their unquestioning belief in the false logic of deterrence and to facilitate their aggressive deportation agenda.[27] Private prison corporations' stock has skyrocketed since the election.[28]

This brief history chronicles how U.S. immigration detention has grown steadily and exponentially since the 1980s to reach the enormous system it is today. Detention has been a politically popular strategy—across party lines—for publicly "handling" immigration, justified by racialized ideas of national identity, myths of deterrence, and a tendency to scapegoat immigrants for all sorts of economic, social, and political issues. Goals of financial gain propel detention growth, with the incarceration industry at the center of the ongoing expansion.

THE BUSINESS OF DETENTION

The role of private companies and financial dependence in the continued extension of immigration detention in the U.S. cannot be emphasized enough. Federal government spending on detention has ballooned with every subsequent presidential administration since the 1990s, climbing from around $8 million in 1994[29] to $2.8 billion in 2023. The 2024 budget included $3.4 billion to detain 41,500 people daily (see Figure 1.2).

While the United States still imprisons more people than any other country worldwide, the building of new prisons has slowed in the last two decades. This is largely due to decreasing incarceration rates as a result of changing criminal laws and penalties. President Joseph Biden's 2021 order to phase out private contracts for prisons also contributed to decreasing prison build-up.[30] In the face of stalling prison growth, immigration detention offers sta-

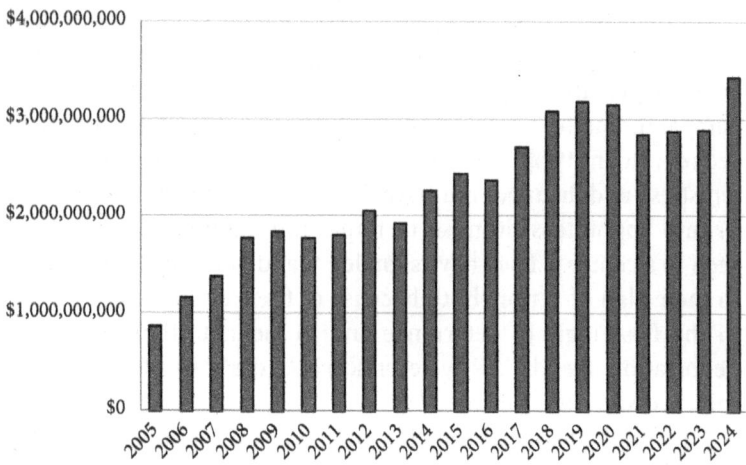

Figure 1.2   ICE Detention Budgets, 2005–24[31]

bility and new opportunities for the "correctional" industry. The biggest companies in the incarceration industry are GEO Group and CoreCivic. As noted in the Introduction, in 2022, GEO Group took in $1.05 billion from ICE contracts, nearly 44 percent of its total earnings, while CoreCivic made $552 million from ICE, or 30 percent of its earnings.[32]

There is a long history of a "revolving door" between government and private prison companies, and this employment pipeline has extended to immigration detention. Frequently, individuals move from positions in which they are responsible for setting or enforcing laws around detention to positions in which they personally profit from those laws. A high-profile example is John Kelly, who served in the first Trump administration as both Secretary of the Department of Homeland Security and Chief of Staff, and oversaw rapid expansion of U.S. detention capacity, particularly for detaining unaccompanied minors. Four months after he left the White House, he was employed on the board of a company that profited from child detention, Caliburn International.[33]

Not only is the U.S. now the global leader in incarcerating individuals, it also leads the world in detaining immigrants, though it is far from the only country that centers detention in its response to immigration. The reasoning underlying the U.S. detention system drives the growing use of detention in many countries. This includes countries that, like the U.S., are immigrant destinations, such as Australia, Canada, Italy, South Africa, and the United Kingdom, as well as transit countries for migrants, like Algeria, Guatemala, Mexico, Turkey, and Tunisia.[34] The potential for financial gain is a factor in all these developing detention regimes. The use of detention will only continue to grow worldwide, unless we can sever economic dependence on detention infrastructures.

As mentioned above, while large prison corporations play a central role in the U.S.'s massive detention system, there are many stakeholders who benefit or are somehow dependent financially: other types of companies, local governments, and connected government agencies. This book focuses on these other players. We now introduce the six facilities in our study and begin to identify some of the companies integral to detention's daily operations.

FACILITIES OF FOCUS AND MAJOR CONTRACTORS

The vast capacity of the U.S. detention system is currently achieved through a cobbled-together network of at least 150 facilities around the country.[35]

To trace the expanding webs of economic relationships woven into this system, we focus on six facilities in the states of New Jersey and New York (see Figures 1.3 and 1.4.). The six facilities are, in New Jersey, the Elizabeth Contract Detention Facility, Bergen County Jail, Essex County Correctional Facility, and Hudson County Correctional Facility; and in New York, the Buffalo Service Processing Center and Orange County Correctional Facility. Some are government facilities, one is a private facility, and one falls somewhere in between.

By tracing the money and power behind these detention facilities—in two states far from the U.S.-Mexico border, where media attention is often focused—we reveal larger national policy trends and major corporate and government actors in the business of immigration enforcement. The local and regional contexts that led to the incorporation of these six facilities into the United States' detention system include factors discussed above: post-industrial

IMMIGRATION DETENTION INC.

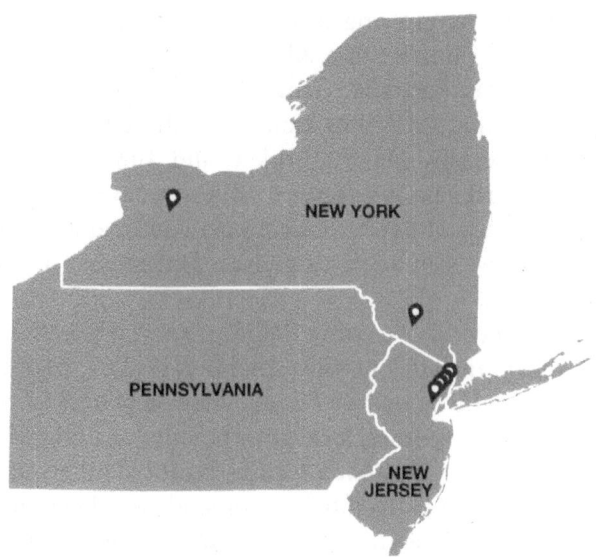

Figure 1.3 Map: The six detention facilities in our study[36]

Figure 1.4 Map: Greater NYC area detention facilities in our study

recession, neoliberal vacuums in state and federal support, and political maneuverings. With moves for criminal justice reform at the federal level and in some states, jail populations are decreasing in many places. Both private companies and county governments see immigration detention as a viable alternative to fill empty space and maintain revenue streams.

The fact that the economic seduction of detention is not tied to conservative and Republican leadership is clear, too. All six facilities are in two states controlled by Democrats. The three New Jersey county jails are also under Democratic leadership.

Our selected facilities include examples of the three primary ownership and contracting arrangements used by ICE.[37] One type of facility is owned by ICE, called a Service Processing Center (SPC). SPCs used to be owned *and* operated by ICE, but today the operation of all SPCs is contracted out to private companies. The Buffalo Service Processing Center, one of the facilities we focus on, is one of twenty SPCs. A second type of facility is a Contract Detention Facility (CDF), which is entirely owned and operated by a private company. The Elizabeth Contract Detention Facility scrutinized in our project is an example of this arrangement. The third type of facility is a local government jail, contracted by ICE through an Intergovernmental Service Agreement (IGSA). IGSA-contracted facilities in our study include the Bergen County Jail (New Jersey), Essex County Correctional Facility (NJ), Hudson County Correctional Facility (NJ), and Orange County Correctional Facility (New York).

Since we began this project in 2012, changing laws and practices around detention have meant that the uses of some of the facilities has changed. After a law aiming to ban detention in the state of New Jersey passed in 2021, the three New Jersey county jails in our study—Bergen, Essex, and Hudson—stopped detaining immigrants for ICE. We still trace the operation of these facilities to the present day. The continued contracting of the same service companies in these facilities—even though they aren't currently holding ICE detainees—shows how the business of immigration detention is one and the same as the business of criminal incarceration. And tracking what happened to detainees previously held in these facilities contributes to our call to dismantle the system entirely, discussed in Chapter 6.

Here we provide brief profiles of these six facilities, including contracting relationships central to their operation. Collectively, these profiles provide a solid sampling of major players in immigrant detention: from county governments to prison corporations to companies selling specific services for confined populations. Clearly, no matter what the ownership structure of a detention facility is, private companies are deeply involved in its operation (see Table 1.1).

Table 1.1 Major contracts for facilities in our study

Facility	Contract Type	Food Service	Healthcare Service	Commissary Provider
Bergen County Jail *Hackensack, NJ*	IGSA: ICE (U.S. Marshalls) & Bergen County	Aramark	County provides	Keefe
Buffalo Federal Detention Facility *Batavia, NY*	Contract: ICE & Akima Global Services	Akima Global Services	ICE Health Services Corps	Trinity Services
Elizabeth Contract Detention Facility *Elizabeth, NJ*	Contract: ICE & CoreCivic	CoreCivic	ICE Health Services Corps	Keefe
Essex County Correctional Facility *Newark, NJ*	IGSA: ICE & Essex County	GD Correctional Services	CFG Health Systems	Keefe
Hudson County Correctional Facility *Kearny, NJ*	IGSA: ICE & Hudson County	GD Correctional Services	Wellpath	Keefe
Orange County Correctional Facility *Goshen, NY*	IGSA: ICE & Orange County	Aramark	Wellpath	Keefe

Buffalo Service Processing Center

The Buffalo Service Processing Center in Batavia, New York, opened in 1998. It is also called the Buffalo or Batavia Federal Processing Center. Its detainee capacity is 650, with a guaranteed minimum (the number of beds a facility is contracted to maintain available for ICE) of 400. The detainee population as of May 2024 was 537. The 2023 average length of stay was 61 days. This facility can hold both women and men (though it appears no women have been detained there since 2021).[38]

The Buffalo facility was owned and operated by the federal government for only about a decade. In 2009, an outside company, **Valley Metro Barbosa Group** (VMBG), was contracted to provide food service and some staff, eventually expanding services to include security, commissary, laundry, and land transportation. VMBG operated the Buffalo facility until 2014.

Akima Global Services (AGS) won the Buffalo contract in 2014. AGS still runs the facility today, including food service, in a contract worth over $28 million per year.[39] AGS is an Alaska Native Corporation with headquarters in Herndon, Virginia.[40] AGS also runs the Krome Service Processing Center in Miami, Florida.

Other companies and government entities fill in the services that AGS doesn't provide at the Buffalo detention facility. Detainee medical services are provided by ICE's **Health Service Corps** (IHSC). Commissary services are contracted to **Trinity Services**.[41]

Elizabeth Contract Detention Facility

The Elizabeth Contract Detention Facility is in Elizabeth, New Jersey. As of January 2025, it was the only facility in the state detaining immigrants for over 24 hours, with a capacity of 304 immigrants, and a guaranteed minimum of 285. In 2019, the average population was 289, with 260 men and 28 women. During the pandemic, numbers went down significantly to under 80 (74 men and 3 women), but immediately started climbing back up. In May 2024, the detainee population at Elizabeth was 226.[42] The 2023 average length of stay was 17 days.

The Elizabeth facility first opened in 1994, when Esmor Correctional Services leased the property—originally built as an industrial warehouse in 1974—from Portview Properties and converted it to an immigrant detention center. Detainees were held there in abysmal, abusive conditions, sparking protests by detainees in 1995 that culminated in a "riot" that drew national attention.[43] An INS investigation accused Esmor of gross mismanagement and neglect, canceled the Esmor contract, and closed the facility.[44]

Just one year later, in 1996, the Elizabeth Detention Center was reopened, but now under the management of the **Corrections Corporation of America** (CCA), which changed its name to **CoreCivic** in 2017. Despite the new contractor, conditions have remained notoriously bad. Fighting against both activists and the 2021 state law banning detention, CoreCivic has kept the facility open. The property is still owned by Portview Properties, which is part of the Elberon Development Group. Under activist pressure that brought public attention to their involvement with CoreCivic, in 2020 Elberon sued in an attempt to end its contract with CoreCivic. The lawsuit was unsuccessful.[45]

CoreCivic snuck in a two-year contract renewal for Elizabeth with ICE just before the 2021 state law went into effect. The contract was set to expire in August 2023, and the law prohibited renewal of any detention contracts in the state. But CoreCivic filed a lawsuit arguing that the New Jersey law was unconstitutional because it interfered with the federal government's ability to use private companies to enforce immigration laws. The Biden administration supported CoreCivic's claim, and in September 2023, they won their case. ICE renewed CoreCivic's Elizabeth contract for $19.9 million per year. This legal decision has upended activist efforts in other states to ban detention at the state level (discussed further in Chapter 6).[46]

CoreCivic is responsible for general operation of the facility, including security, cleaning, maintenance, and food service. As with the Buffalo facility, medical care is provided by the **ICE Health Services Corps**. The commissary is currently operated by **Keefe Commissary Network**.

Bergen County Jail

Bergen County Jail (BCJ) is in Hackensack, New Jersey. Built to house criminal justice system prisoners for the county around

1965, it was remodeled in 2000 and again in 2009. The facility's total inmate capacity is 1,236. Most records indicate that BCJ began housing immigrant detainees in 1996, through an IGSA with the U.S. Marshals Service (USMS). The number of detainees BCJ housed for ICE periodically increased, going up to 290 daily spots in 2016. In Bergen's mid-pandemic (August 2020) ICE detainee numbers were 167 men and 17 women, with the average length of stay of 69 days. BCJ stopped detaining immigrants for ICE in 2021 with the passage of New Jersey's state detention ban. Per Bergen's last ICE contract, they received $120 daily per detainee.

BCJ's food service is currently provided by **Aramark**, and medical care provided by various subcontractors. **Keefe Commissary Network** has the commissary contract, and **Global Tel*Link** provides phone service to all inmates and detainees.

Essex County Correctional Facility

The Essex County Correctional Facility (ECCF) is in Newark, New Jersey. The facility opened in 2004, with a total inmate capacity of around 3,000. ECCF began housing up to 500 detainees for ICE in 2008, and in 2011 the number of detainee beds was raised to 800.[47] ECCF had a guaranteed minimum of 700. The actual detainee population fluctuated between 500 and 800 until the pandemic; in June 2020, at the height of the pandemic, a report listed the ICE detainee population as 362. The facility detained men only. The average length of stay in 2020 was 123 days. ECCF phased out ICE detention over a few months after the passage of New Jersey's state detention ban in 2021. As per the 2017 ICE contract, Essex County was receiving $117 per day per detainee.

Essex County contracts food service for the jail to **GD Correctional Services** (Aramark also held the facility's food contract at one point). Medical care is contracted to **CFG Health Systems**, commissary to **Keefe Commissary Network**, and **Global Tel*Link** provides phone service.

Hudson County Correctional Facility

The Hudson County Correctional Facility (HCCF) in Kearny, New Jersey, opened around 1992. It first began housing immigrant detainees in 1996. In 2002, the USMS and the Immigration and Naturalization Service (INS, ICE's predecessor) gave Hudson County $7 million to expand and renovate the jail to include detention space for a total of 512 prisoners (both USMS and INS prisoners).[48] After the renovation, the jail's total inmate capacity was 2,100, with 476 beds reserved for male and female ICE detainees. The highest number detained at HCCF was over 800 in 2016. After 2017, the detainee population gradually decreased, a decline likely tied to Hudson County's 2018 decision—in response to activist pressure—to terminate its ICE contract by the end of 2020. While county leaders reversed this decision in November 2020, the pandemic had brought detainee numbers down to 68 in August 2020, and then the state ban led to the end of ICE detention at HCCF in 2021. Until then, Hudson County was getting $120 per day for detainees housed there. The average length of stay in 2020 was 76 days. Activists had long noted that the jail's location, in an industrial area near transportation hubs, exposed inmates to health risks and made access by family and supporters very difficult.[49]

The HCCF contracts food service with **GD Correctional Services** (previously with Aramark), **WellPath** for medical services (previously with CFG Health Systems), and **Keefe Commissary Network** for commissary operation. **Global Tel*Link** provides phone service.

Orange County Correctional Facility

The Orange County Correctional Facility (OCCF) in Goshen, New York, opened in 2001. Its total capacity is 778 inmates. The OCCF started housing ICE detainees in 2008, agreeing in its IGSA to hold up to 120 male and female detainees. Orange County currently receives $133.93 per day for each detainee. Since New Jersey county jails stopped detaining for ICE in 2021, OCCF and the Elizabeth CDF are the only ICE detention facilities in the greater NYC area. In 2022, OCCF cut the number of ICE detainees it holds to 56 men and 24 women, citing staffing shortages,[50] but some detainees claimed the transfers were made to punish and silence those on a hunger strike to protest inhumane conditions.[51] In May 2024, the detainee population at OCCF was 67.[52]

OCCF contracts with **Aramark** for food. The medical service contract is with **WellPath** (technically it is with NY Correct Care Solutions Medical Service, which became part of Wellpath in 2018). The commissary contract was held for years by **Aramark**, but in April 2020, the contract was taken over by **Keefe**. **Global Tel*Link** provides phone service to inmates and detainees.

This book explores the contracting relationships that sustain immigration detention in these six facilities, as well as the knotted dependencies they create. Subsequent chapters dive into the ever expanding array of stakeholders sucked into the business of locking up immigrants, as well as how a cost-cutting mindset leads to abysmal conditions for those detained. But many detention industry players, including ICE, don't want the public to know about their bottom line or common operating procedures, so this research has required developing strategies to circumvent barriers to information.

RESEARCHING DETENTION'S INNER WORKINGS FROM THE OUTSIDE

According to existing U.S. law, immigrant detention is not intended as a punishment.[53] Instead, detention is supposed to be administrative in purpose, meant to hold detainees while they wait for resolution to their immigration status. But detention is certainly experienced as punishment, and expressly articulated as such by policymakers and detention operators. All facilities in the U.S. detention system are operated as carceral facilities. Detainees are frequently confined in jails and prisons that house criminal justice system prisoners. The companies contracted to provide services in detention centers are the same as those contracted for prisons and jails.[54]

It is notoriously difficult to obtain information about what goes on inside carceral facilities. These are, by definition and design, meant to lock people up and they seem to lock up information about inner workings, too. Uncovering details about immigrant detention centers is even more challenging. Academics like us are rarely permitted entry for the purposes of research.

A lot of the information we seek—about the money involved in detention operations, contracts, and how facilities are run— is actively concealed from the public. As such, anyone trying to obtain information about detention must learn to work around roadblocks thrown up by ICE, other government agencies, and private companies. For us, this entailed using a variety of sources to build a powerful archive of documents and accounts that expose relationships fundamental to the running of detention facilities.[55] We start with our efforts to collect documentation.

Public records requests

Organizations and individuals have long struggled to obtain documents related to detention policies, operations, and costs. Given this challenge, laws intended to protect the public's right to know are essential tools for any investigator. The federal Freedom of Information Act (FOIA) 5 U.S.C. § 552 grants the public the legal right to access government records. State laws also allow members of the public to seek records from state and local government agencies.

In 2013, we filed two FOIA requests with the ICE FOIA office.[56] In one request, we asked for any agreements that ICE made with other entities regarding use of the facilities in our study, including agreements with county governments (for use of a county jail), and contracts with private companies contracted to run a facility (for the Buffalo facility: Akima Global Services; for the Elizabeth Detention Center: CoreCivic).

The other 2013 request was for documents regarding the subcontracting of specific services required to operate a facility, including food, medical care, commissaries, communication, laundry, security, transportation, cleaning, and maintenance. (Here, we take deep dives into the first three services: food, medical, and commissary.) This second request also applied to documents pertaining to the daily workings of facilities, including handbooks given to detainees about facility rules and procedures, commissary price lists and records, detainee work assignments, and facility schedules.

ICE typically responds to attempts to obtain information with delay and evasion, as we experienced. FOIA law requires requests to be answered within 20 business days, but this time limit is routinely broken. It took 14 months for ICE to respond to our 2013 requests—and only after we repeatedly called, emailed, and informed the office of our intent to pursue legal action. Additionally, the format and content of the files received was confusing and frustrating. For each of the 2013 requests, we were sent huge PDFs on CDs: one was 385 pages, and the other 788 pages, with no explanations of the order or what was contained, and no searchable metadata. It took weeks to go through the files and catalog what was there.

So, even when our 2013 FOIA requests were technically "filled," extracting information was time-consuming and tedious, while the documents received for different facilities were wildly inconsistent. What we were given apparently depended on what individual facility employees tasked with handling FOIAs chose to send in response to the central ICE FOIA office's request.

Another tactic that ICE and private companies use to conceal information is redacting: removing or covering up parts of released documents. Federal FOIA law and state public records laws allow for particular "exemptions" in records releases, intended to protect personal privacy, operational procedures, and companies' ability to compete in the marketplace. Such exemptions are used extensively and excessively. The documents we received from our two 2013 requests were substantially redacted, including nearly all dollar amounts, numbers related to facility capacity and currently detained, names and work contact information for people in leadership and management positions, and information about routine facility operation (see Figure 1.5).

Obviously, the fact that significant chunks of information are concealed in the documents we are able to access is frustrating. These omissions make it difficult or impossible to learn—from these documents, at least—how money is spent on detention, operations and conditions inside detention facilities, who is responsible, and who benefits.

It has since become even more difficult to extract information from ICE. In January 2019, we submitted another FOIA request for a much smaller range of documents than requested in 2013, and for only one facility (Buffalo). Our experience this time around

IMMIGRATION DETENTION INC.

	ORDER FOR SUPPLIES OR SERVICES SCHEDULE - CONTINUATION				PAGE NO 2	
IMPORTANT: Mark all packages and papers with contract and/or order numbers.						
DATE OF ORDER 01/11/2013	CONTRACT NO. USMS #50-06-0023				ORDER NO HSCEDM-13-F-IG013	
ITEM NO. (A)	SUPPLIES/SERVICES (B)	QUANTITY ORDERED (C)	UNIT (D)	UNIT PRICE (E)	AMOUNT (F)	QUANTITY ACCEPTED (G)
	The purpose of this task order against USMS 450-06-0023 is to provide adult detention and transportation services for ICE detainees at the Bergen County Jail. Funding in the amount of ▓▓▓▓ is provided for CLIN 0001. Funding is not provided for CLIN 0002 at this time. The task order and funding period of performance is January 1, 2013 through February 28, 2013. Additional funds may be applied to future invoicing. This action is associated with requisition 192113FNY3112001C The total value of this task order increases: From: ▓ By: ▓ To: ▓ Exempt Action: Y Period of Performance: 01/01/2013 to 02/28/2013					
0001	MANDAYS FOR BERGEN COUNTY JAIL Funding period of performance: 01/01/2013 thru 02/28/2013 Rate ▓ X 7,552 beds = ▓ As a result of this change, the overall contract value is increased: From ▓ By: ▓ To: ▓ As a result of this change, the overall quantity is increased: From: 0 By: ▓ Continued ...	7552	EA		▓	
TOTAL CARRIED FORWARD TO 1ST PAGE (ITEM 17(H))						

Figure 1.5 Page from 2013 Bergen County IGSA with ICE showing ICE's redactions

demonstrates how ICE is taking much longer to fill FOIA requests. We received an answer to the 2019 request three-and-a-half years later, in August 2022, and we filed an appeal of that request in October 2022, which (as of January 2025) had still not been filled, despite our regular email inquiries.

Other researchers and journalists have documented the increasingly lengthy times for FOIA responses. Some delay is due to a surge in FOIA requests beginning in the first Trump administration, but it goes hand in hand with a growing disregard for transparency that both preceded and succeeded Trump's first term. There are also numerous accounts of ICE FOIAs only being filled when legal action is taken. Additionally, document types that we received from the 2013 requests appeared to be off-limits in 2022, such as commissary price lists, detainee handbooks, and detainee work program information. Ninety-seven of the 133 pages in the file received in 2022 were completely redacted—nearly 75 percent of the file (which is why we filed an appeal).

Private companies have shown that they are willing to put significant resources into preventing the public from seeing their detention contracts. For example, Detention Watch Network (DWN) and the Center for Constitutional Rights (CCR) fought a lengthy court battle—from 2013 to 2019—to obtain records related to guaranteed minimums in detention contracts. Their efforts were resisted by GEO Group and Corrections Corporation of America (CCA, now renamed CoreCivic), which claimed the requested information was shielded by FOIA exemptions related to protecting competitive company information and plans related to law enforcement actions. Supported by ICE (under *both* the Obama and first Trump administrations), the U.S.'s two largest incarceration companies filed repeated motions and appeals all the way to the Supreme Court.

Eventually, CCA and GEO Group were forced by the courts to release most of the requested information.[57] But this legal battle shows the lengths to which private companies involved in detention will go to try to prevent the public from knowing about the work that they do and the money involved, and, also, that this obstruction often has the full support of the federal government.

After realizing that obtaining the documents we sought at the federal level from ICE could be ineffective, we decided to investigate further at the state level. We used New Jersey's Open Public Records Act (OPRA) and New York's Freedom of Information Law (FOIL) to submit requests directly to counties in our study that detain immigrants for ICE: Orange County in New York, and Bergen, Essex, and Hudson Counties in New Jersey. We submitted multiple rounds of requests to these counties in 2014, 2019, 2021, 2023, and 2024. At times, we submitted large requests (like our 2013 FOIA requests) to all four counties at once, and other times just to a single county for a specific category of document.

For the most part, county government agencies have been much more responsive to our requests. They generally stick to requirements specified by law about time to respond, and provide the range of documents requested without issue. County employees responsible for filling our request have politely emailed or called to clarify documents we seek. We have requested and received documents like detention contracts with ICE (Intergovernmental Service Agreements, or IGSAs), county contracts with private companies for services in the facilities (like food, medical, commissary), detainee handbooks, and commissary lists and records. Through the requests to the New Jersey counties, we also acquired records of meetings of elected county officials who vote for facility contracts and services.

Notably, there are stark contrasts between what ICE redacts and what county agencies redact. While the county-provided documents do contain redactions, these are much more limited than in the ICE responses. For example, redactions by county OPRA and FOIL officers tend to focus on a single number or name. In comparison, ICE officials tend to redact entire passages and even pages, especially in more recent requests. Sometimes we have obtained the same exact document from both ICE and a county agency, to find the ICE copy heavily or entirely redacted, and the county copy with few or no redactions. These contrasts indicate stark differences in approaches to the information that should be "protected" from public knowledge.

We also draw on documents obtained by others through public records requests. The National Immigrant Justice Center (NIJC) runs the Transparency and Human Rights Project, hosting an online archive of documents related to detention contracting—primarily contracts, IGSAs, and inspection reports—collected by their and other organizations and individuals (for example, we have shared our gathered documents). The Transactional Records Access Clearinghouse (TRAC) at Syracuse University regularly submits FOIA requests to numerous federal government agencies, including ICE, and produces summary reports and graphics. TRAC also maintains the FOIA Project, which keeps track of lawsuits filed pertaining to FOIA requests. Local immigrant rights organizations and journalists doing in-depth investigative reporting have also shared documents they obtained through public records requests.

Additionally, we have found useful documents in ICE's online "FOIA library" of records previously requested, which ICE is legally required to maintain. Prior to 2018, ICE inspection reports were only obtainable via FOIA. Successful litigation by NIJC led to the release of some reports, and in 2018 Congress began ordering ICE to release reports within three months of an inspection being conducted. Several other government agencies that inspect detention facilities, with varying degrees of reliability, supply reports which are also available online.

ICE is required by law to conduct inspections. These ICE inspections have a reputation for being inaccurate and infrequent, more meant to serve as a "rubber stamp" than to actually detect issues to be addressed. Therefore, when an ICE inspection report *does* actually note a problem or detainee complaint, we find it significant, and likely representative of far larger issues than actually included in the report.

Filling in the gaps

To cover information voids caused by the difficulty of getting documents from government agencies and private companies, we draw from a variety of other sources. Many organizations generate reports about detention facilities and companies for the purposes of anti-detention campaigns, through visitation programs, or while supporting detainees and their families. National and international organizations regularly publish findings about various aspects of detention, for example, the American Civil Liberties Union, American Friends Service Committee, Detention Watch Network, Freedom for Immigrants, Human Rights First, Human Rights Watch, and the National Immigrant Justice Center. Local and state organizations in New York and New Jersey compile data about specific facilities.

We also rely on the work of journalists who do in-depth reporting on particular facilities or companies, from local to national outlets. These organizations and individuals sometimes publish information specifically about the facilities in our study. We also draw on reporting about facilities not in our study, but operated by the same companies. Because corporations often have company-wide policies and operational playbooks, it is likely that those companies operate similarly across all their detention contracts.

Various forms of government and legal records can be useful. County government officials often have public meetings in which detention-related matters are discussed; records of these meetings may be available as minutes, transcripts, or recordings. Congressional entities also generate reports of use, including testimony provided to committees in charge of oversight of immigration enforcement, the nonpartisan Congressional Budget Office (which is funded by Congress), and investigations by the offices of individual members of Congress. Public filings of lawsuits and legal decisions are another source of information about detention. As we detail in subsequent chapters, there is a huge volume of litigation around detention, including lawsuits filed by detainees and their families (or organizations representing them) regarding conditions of detention and rights violations, and by companies suing over lost contract bids.

Additionally, we can glean important information from publicly available materials about businesses. Companies sometimes post useful details online, meant to attract new customers, inform investors, or simply provide a public face. Investment analysts post profiles of individual companies. Marketing analysts produce regular reports assessing the strengths and weaknesses of particular industries, including those involved in detention like food provision and carceral industries. Employment websites often list available job opportunities with certain companies, and employee-facing websites contain reviews of working conditions with companies or at particular locations.

For this project, we also conducted a limited number of interviews. Ideally, we would speak directly with immigrant detainees, who have first-hand knowledge of what happens inside detention centers. But it can be exceedingly tough to speak directly to detainees. While detained, opportunities to communicate with people outside are tightly restricted, and often prohibitively expensive. Detainees can also be hesitant to communicate for fear of reprisals by facility operators or ICE. But the majority of detainees only leave behind such restrictions when they are deported, which would require tracking them to countries outside the U.S. Detainees who are released and remain in the United States may fear that talking to researchers could hurt their immigration case or residency status. Or they may simply not wish to talk about their detention experiences, and as researchers, we are hesitant to ask former detainees to rehash potentially traumatizing memories.

Still, we have been able to talk to other people who see the inside of detention centers and who speak directly with detainees, such as lawyers, volunteers in visitation programs, and journalists. We also rely on other accounts that include detainee testimony, such as news stories, inspection reports, and immigrant rights groups' reports.

The cloak of secrecy around immigration detention makes this kind of piecemeal, creative approach essential. To be sure, much information remains hidden. Even so, we have gathered enough puzzle pieces to trace the major flows of money running through this industry and to get a sense of the lived realities behind them.

But for everyone, the extreme difficulty in accessing information about the money involved in detention should raise red flags: what are players in the detention industry so determined to conceal? This book exposes detention's hidden webs of financial entanglements, and how they drive political and cultural responses to immigration. The next chapter pulls back the curtain on the carceral food services industry.

2

"Meatballs that smell like fecal matter": When Bad Food is the Business Model

On July 24, 2018, inspectors arrived at the Essex County Correctional Facility in New Jersey, to assess conditions for ICE detainees. While this in itself wasn't unusual, what was different was that the inspectors arrived unannounced; and, as such, they actually found and reported problems. These inspectors, from the Department of Homeland Security's (DHS) Office of the Inspector General, instead of the internal ICE office that usually does inspections, recorded serious issues with food handling and safety, sanitation, and the quality of food served to immigrant detainees. Because ICE inspections are often more of a "rubber stamping" exercise, the fact that this inspection documented anything at all was worthy of note. But what really made this visit singular was just how bad they found the Essex County facility, which at the time housed 797 male ICE detainees.[1]

The inspectors discovered "open packages of raw chicken leaking blood all over refrigeration units," as well as "slimy foul-smelling lunch meat." Moreover, they actually listened to the detainees themselves, and documented their concerns. Specifically, the inspectors reviewed complaints filed by detainees, recording comments like "it's becoming impossible to eat [the food]. It gets worse every day. It literally looks like it came from the garbage dumpster"; and "For dinner, we were served meatballs that smell like fecal matter."[2]

The bottom line? The food was disgusting, with the potential to make detainees really ill. Such accounts are quite common throughout the U.S. immigration detention system. Here, we showcase the routinely awful food served in detention facilities.

Crucially, we reveal that bad food in "corrections" facilities is not a mistake. Instead, bad food *is* the business model. This is because companies contracted for food service in these facilities are disincentivized from delivering quality meals. In other words, crappy food for incarcerated consumers is a strategic business decision.

In fact, these companies are so successful that food service contracts for carceral facilities are highly competitive. The competing companies know they can count on flimsy contract boundaries and little oversight to get away with lousy food in order to maximize profit.

What this means for detainees is that food service can be so deficient, in both quality and quantity, that they frequently suffer chronic hunger and sickness. Hardships are deliberate: after all, why else would jails demand, in their contracts with food service companies, to provide *better* food for their guards?

CUT-THROAT COMPETITION IN THE "CORRECTIONS" FOOD INDUSTRY

Regardless of who owns a facility (and whether it's for detaining migrants or incarcerating U.S. citizens), food service is supposed to be decided through a competitive contracting process. At the Buffalo Service Processing Center and the Elizabeth Contract Detention Facility—which hold only immigrant detainees—food services are included as part of larger umbrella contracts for the running of the entire facility. Buffalo is operated by Akima Global Services, and Elizabeth by CoreCivic; we briefly profiled these two companies in Chapter 1. Food at the four county jails in our study is provided by companies whose contracts are for food service only (see Table 2.1).

Major food service players

While Table 2.1 shows the current food contractors at the four county jails, these companies' grip on a particular facility is far from secure. By digging into the recent food-contracting history for these jails, we get a glimpse at the fierce jockeying that takes place for these contracts, as well as the astounding amounts of money at stake. We are also introduced to the two biggest compa-

Table 2.1 Food contractors and the value of contracts for facilities in our study

Facility	Bergen County Jail (NJ)	Essex County Correctional Facility (NJ)	Hudson County Correctional Facility (NJ)	Orange County Correctional Facility (NY)	Elizabeth Contract Detention Facility (NJ)	Buffalo Federal Detention Center (NY)
Food contractor	Aramark	GD Correctional Services	GD Correctional Services	Aramark	Core Civic	Akima Global Services
Contract value *meals provided at $1.35–$2.25 per meal	$9.07 million 2021–26 *$1.8 million/year	$15.8 million 2024–26 *$7.9 million/year	$46.9 million 2024–29 *$8.9 million for second year	$4.8 million 2023–25 *$2.6 million for second year	*bundled with facility contract	*bundled with facility contract

nies in the corrections food market in the United States: Aramark Correctional Services and Trinity Services Group.[3] Aramark currently has the food contract at both Bergen County Jail and Orange County Correctional Facility. But until only 2023, Trinity Services Group had the Orange contract. In the recent past, Aramark also had the food contracts at Essex County and Hudson County Correctional Facilities, but lost the contracts after a competitor out-bid them. A strong regional competitor—if minor compared to Aramark and Trinity—GD Correctional Services now has the food contracts at both the Essex County and Hudson County Correctional Facilities.

Aramark Correctional Services, headquartered in Philadelphia, has been a major food provider for the U.S. corrections industry for decades. In bid documents, Aramark indicates it has nearly fifty years of experience providing food to the corrections industry and serves around 550 facilities.[4] Bergen's current contract with Aramark for food services was signed in 2021 and is worth up to $9.07 million for five years (2021–26), or $1.8 million per year, to provide food for the inmate population (including detainees) of 825 plus staff working in the jail and another facility. In 2021, Bergen County Jail paid Aramark just $1.35 per meal per inmate.

Aramark's two-year (2023–25) contract with Orange County Correctional Facility is for $4.8 million.

Trinity Services Group, with headquarters in Oldsmar, Florida, claims to provide food services to over 400 correctional facilities and 300,000 inmates. Trinity does not currently serve facilities in our study, but it is an important player in carceral food. The company's website states that it is the "largest contractor dedicated to the Corrections Industry."[5] (Both Aramark and Trinity also provide commissary services to jails; Trinity runs the commissary at the Buffalo facility.) Trinity had the food contract at Orange County Correctional Facility from March 2018 to March 2022 for a total of $4.91 million and then renewed for a year for another approximately $1.04 million. For Orange's roughly 700 residents, that came out to between $1.28 and $1.38 per inmate meal, depending on the number of meals served.

GD Correctional Services (GDCS), which currently has the food contracts at both Essex County and Hudson County Correctional Facilities, is comparatively more of a regional company. It is based in Verona, New Jersey, less than twenty miles from the Essex County Correctional Facility. In contrast to Aramark and Trinity, GDCS—according to its website—serves only 15 correctional facilities, though the website proudly claims, in large font, that GDCS "currently maintains over 80% of the New Jersey correctional food service market share" and employs over 300 people.[6] Like Aramark and Trinity, GDCS is constantly jockeying for new contracts; the website reports that the company's growth strategy is to seek "opportunities in the region surrounding New Jersey entering into the [sic] Pennsylvania and New York"; according to their website, in 2017 and 2018 GDCS won new contracts in two Pennsylvania jails.

Essex County currently has a two-year contract with GDCS, from January 2024 to January 2026, for $15.8 million or about $7.4 million per year, providing food for around 2,400 inmates plus staff. On its website, GDCS narrates its origin story as beginning with a contract at the Essex jail in the early 1990s. GDCS then lost the ECCF contract to Aramark in 2004, regaining it in 2010. ECCF inmates are fed by GD Correctional Services for $2.43 per meal (per GDCS's 2024 contract). Hudson County contracted food service with Aramark until 2017, when GDCS won a three-year contract, worth $15.1 million, to feed 2,300 inmates and 675 staff. In August 2020, the contract was renewed until September 2023, for an additional $16.5 million. Hudson County Correctional Facility inmates were fed for $1.96 per meal by GD Correctional Services in 2020. GDCS's contract with Hudson was renewed in 2024 for five years, at a total contract value of $46.9 million, with a first year amount of $8.5 million, increasing each year to reach $10.2 million for the fifth year.

As mentioned in Chapter 1, the Bergen, Essex, and Hudson facilities are not currently holding ICE detainees among their inmates, since the 2021 New Jersey ban on contracts between state agencies and ICE. Still, these facilities' contracting processes and decades-long detention operations, together with the three other facilities we scrutinize, are emblematic of continuing, system-wide practices and economic relationships. And the food service providers involved continue to hold contracts at other ICE detention facilities.

Bidding wars and cost cutting

From the fraught food service histories of these four county jails, we see that companies are always eager to win (or win back) another facility's contract. As a result, they are constantly submitting bids for open contracts—and trying to underbid their competitors. The bidding process is similar in all of the counties we investigate in terms of what jails request, what information contractors provide, and how winning bidders are chosen.

While bidding and evaluation processes seem mundane, the over-arching obedience to a cost-benefit logic is important for understanding why *bad* food *is* the business model in detention. To this end, it's worth explaining the process in some detail. First, when a particular contract is coming open, the appropriate county office issues a Request for Proposals (RFP). RFPs set out the parameters of a contract, and explain the information that bidders must include in their proposal as well as the criteria that will be used to evaluate bids. RFPs are generally made publicly available for a few weeks before bids are due, but the exact duration of the open bidding period depends on the county.

Next, counties evaluate and compare the received proposals. Specific implementation of the evaluation process varies; some counties work through evaluation committees, while others appear to be reviewed by a particular office or official. For example, before Bergen County awarded its 2015 contract for food service at the jail to Aramark, the three submitted bids were evaluated by a committee of five members made up of officers at Bergen County Jail and the County Sheriff's Chief Budget Officer. Committee members were tasked with scoring each bid according to three criteria, which were then tallied to give each vendor an overall score.

Finally, counties decide which bidder is awarded the contract. In the documents we reviewed from Bergen and Essex Counties, this involved a simple yes or no vote on a resolution at a meeting of the elected board of county commissioners (called "freeholder" boards in New Jersey until January 2021). In all cases in the four counties in our study, county officials' decisions followed the recommendations of the committee, office, or official that evaluated the submitted bids.[7]

Cost is clearly the most important criterion in the awarding of food service contracts. The lowest bid—based on the least amount that the county must pay per meal to feed its inmates—wins. This is plainly evident in the records we've reviewed of bid evaluations and county leaders' decision-making processes. Take, for example, how Bergen County Jail's 2015 food contract bids were assessed. Three companies submitted bids: Aramark, GD Correctional Services, and CBM Managed Services. Aramark already had the food contract for Bergen, and ultimately won it again. As mentioned above, each bid was scored according to three criteria, which were weighted differently: experience and past performance (30 percent), personnel qualifications (30 percent), and cost (40 percent). Obviously, points awarded in the first two categories were equal, so cost was given the most weight. Thus it was cost alone that really put Aramark on top in the bid evaluation process.

We see more evidence that contract decisions are regarded as rational and undisputed economic calculations in the records of county officials' decisions. In 2013, for example, Essex County decided to extend GD Correctional Services' food contract, and issued a Memorandum to that effect. Under "Reasons for Recommendation," the Memorandum states that "The Correctional Facility must feed its patients [sic] and this contract fulfills this need"; under "Alternatives," it states "There is no alternative except to bid this service and award to the lowest responsive/responsible bidder." Likewise, in 2015, when Bergen County awarded the food contract to Aramark, the recorded justification for the decision was that "Nutritious meals are required to be provided to the inmates at the Bergen County Jail [...] that are prepared under sanitary conditions and that are prepared in an efficient and cost-effective manner."

To county leaders, then, cost (along with, apparently, efficiency and sanitation) underlies any contracting decision. There are no mentions of food quality or detainee satisfaction and health. Because the lowest bids nearly always win, pennies per meal make a difference, as is evident in the competing bids for the Bergen jail's food contract in 2015, presented in Table 2.2.

Table 2.2 Price per meal and contract value in bids for Bergen County Jail's 2015–19 food contract

Food contractor	Year 1: price per meal	Year 2: price per meal	Year 3: price per meal	Year 4: price per meal	Year 5: price per meal	Total value of contract bid (million)
CBM	$1.25	$1.30	$1.36	$1.42	$1.67	$9,850,611.24
GDCS	$1.52	$1.52	$1.52	$1.55	$1.60	$9,767,067.12
Aramark	$1.30	$1.34	$1.38	$1.42	$1.46	$8,729,094.72

As Table 2.2 shows, small differences add up. Aramark's winning total bid comes in at nearly $1 million less than GDCS's and $1.1 million less than CBM's. Food service providers eager to obtain and keep jail and detention facility contracts try to shave as many pennies off each meal as they can. They know it can mean the difference between getting a contract or not.

But while it's pennies to the county, it's sickness and disgusting food for detainees.

Industry consolidation, stability, and profit

Companies involved in detention and prison food operate within a dizzying arena of corporate consolidation. Two of the companies recently contracted for food service at the four county jails—Aramark and Trinity—are actually nodes in much bigger corporate networks.

For example, Aramark Correctional Services is part of the massive Aramark Corporation. If you've bought meals at large institutions, like universities, hospitals, or national parks around the U.S. and Canada, you're likely to have eaten Aramark food. Aramark Corporation is a U.S.-based company that provides a range of services—food, uniforms, housekeeping—to businesses, schools, medical facilities, and recreational parks in 19 different countries. Aramark provides food service to around a hundred facilities that detain immigrants for ICE.[8] Similarly, Trinity Services Group is actually the "T" in TKC Holdings. The "K" is Keefe Group, which provides commissary and other services to prisons and detention centers, which we discuss in Chapter 4. TKC Holdings is backed by H.I.G. Capital, which also owns prison medical services contractor Wellpath, discussed in Chapter 3.[9]

Both the fierce jockeying for jails' food contracts and the aggressive gobbling up of the companies who obtain those contracts show that correctional food service is an important cornerstone of the larger food service industry. We examined market research and industry analysis reports intended to inform investment decisions to help us understand why.

The market research company IBISWorld's Food Service Contractors industry report lists "Correctional Facilities" among the top six "First Tier Buyers" in the food service industry supply chain. In concrete terms, this means carceral facility food contracts are viewed as critical, for investment purposes, for the larger food industry.[10] The report goes on to identify Aramark as one of three "Major Players" in the food service industry. No wonder, then, that IBISWorld describes correctional facilities as a "niche market" that "can be extremely lucrative and very competitive."

A principal reason why corrections food companies are so important to the larger food service industry is that they provide financial stability. As the IBISWorld report explains, in general, the food service contractor industry experiences significant market swings; consequently, many operators try to serve different kinds of facilities, in order "to have steady revenue streams despite short-term economic trends." Correctional facilities are a desirable market because they "provide stability from year to year and are not subject to the whims of the broader economy due to the non-discretionary nature of such operations."[11] So, while a downturn in the economy may lead to people spending less money at places like parks and stadiums, there will *always* be a supply of prisoners and immigrant detainees to help keep these corporations in the black. And, as discussed in Chapter 1, they use lobbying to ensure that more and more people are—and will continue to be—locked up.

The detention and incarceration market is one where corporations find both stable income and cost savings, that can help to make up for losses in the broader market. Highlighting this, the IBISWorld report showed a downward revenue trend in 2020, largely due to closures from the COVID-19 pandemic. And yet "a promising trend" for the food service industry is also flagged: "To the industry's benefit, during the current period, demand for outsourced catering services from correctional, health, educational, recreational and sport facilities has increased steadily."[12] From a business standpoint of rational economic decision-making, corporations involved in detention food offer security.

From the food industry's perspective, then, it is a plus that the United States consistently incarcerates so many people. And, similarly, even more stability is provided by how the government consistently centers detention in its immigration policy.

What happened in New Jersey jails in 2017 is a good example of the stabilizing role of detention from a crude and purely business perspective. After New Jersey passed bail reform laws in 2017, the number of criminal justice system prisoners in the state's jails dropped significantly. But at the same time, the ever-rising number of detained immigrants offered a counterweight to declining prisoner populations. Consequently, food service contracts—along with other jail contracts—did not have to be drastically cut.

Immigration detention, then, helps to insulate the food industry from downturns when events like the COVID-19 pandemic occur or when laws around policing and incarceration are reformed.

Corrections food not only provides stability to the food industry; it is also extremely lucrative. One reason for this is because deep cost savings on labor are built into the food industry business model. While the biggest cost for most operators is labor,[13] in corrections food contracts, free (or close to it) inmate or detainee labor is *guaranteed*.

Contracts that we examined promised food service providers specific numbers of inmate or detainee workers to contribute to food preparation, serving, and clean-up. Usually the contracting facility—not the food service company—pays imprisoned detainees, but only between $1 and $3 per day: rates far below what a food service company would have to pay non-inmate workers.

For example, the 2017 Hudson County Correctional Facility's call for food service bids notes that the successful bidder must provide 31 full-time employees to sufficiently staff food services at the facility, but it goes on to note that the outsourced business's staff will be supplemented by 30 to 35 inmates, per shift, each day. This means that roughly half of the food service workers are free to the contractor—a huge saving in wages.

Inmates are often desperate for any way to earn money. They also are not unionized. We discuss the phenomenon of detainee labor more in Chapter 4, but our point here is that access to cheap, captive, desperate labor is part of the food industry business model, and part of why corrections contracts are so sought after.

Another reason is that the "customer" in corrections food is the facility operator, not who is being fed. And what this "customer" cares about is spending as little money as possible while also abiding by federal and state minimum requirements for inmate food, passing inspections, and keeping their ICE contract. Keep in mind that most inspections entail automatic approval, with serious problems rarely identified or fixed, as we cover in detail in Chapter 5.

As a result, corrections food service providers effectively serve a captive audience, one that has no real recourse to demand better food. Providers don't have to worry about cooking to order, make food appealing, or offer a variety of real options. Instead, they can purchase and cook in bulk, buy whatever items are currently cheapest, and serve without attention to ethics or aesthetics. In short, they can focus on maximizing profit and still make their customer—the facility operator—happy.

The competitive bidding process—and the language of "no alternatives," "efficient and cost-effective," and "lowest responsive/responsible bidder"—mean that detained migrants are fed for between $1.35 and $2.43 per meal. Exactly what is considered or included for meals at these costs is worth scrutinizing.

WHAT'S (NOT) ON THE PLATES

Winning contracts are not written so that food in detention will be enjoyable, satisfying, or even filling for most detainees. They are written with bare-bones subsistence and minimum calorie counts in mind. But even these absurdly low standards for food service are frequently flouted. Consequently—and not surprisingly—detainees are routinely hungry. Even worse, the food actually sickens them.

"Adequacy" and chronic hunger

Requirements in food service contracts are written to meet the National Detention Standards (NDS). First issued in 2000, the NDS were revised in 2008, 2011, and 2019 (we elaborate on the NDS and accountability measures in Chapter 5). Most contracted food providers are supposed to meet some version of NDS requirements regarding food service, including policies and procedures about sanitation, food handling, storage, menu options and variety, staff/worker training and hygiene, regular cleaning and self-inspections, and security. Yet while the NDS are quite minimal, facilities often don't follow them.

At the top of the "Food Service" section of all iterations of the NDS is some version of this statement: "Every facility will provide detainees in its care with nutritious and appetizing meals, prepared in accordance with the highest sanitary standards." While this sounds like a good foundation, food service guidelines also tacitly acknowledge that providers are simultaneously spending as little as possible to feed detainees. The 2011 NDS, for example, state that "The FSA [Food Service Administrator] shall base menu selections on *the best nutritional program the facility can afford meeting U.S. minimum daily allowances*" (emphasis added). This instruction from the federal government recognizes that facilities follow tight budgets and, consequently, doesn't expect them to do more than necessary. The 2000 version of the NDS frames this by stating "All meals are provided in nutritionally *adequate* portions." So, minimum standards can allegedly be met if detainees are able to *just* get by on what they are fed.

In facility contracts and inspection reports, the ideas of minimum daily allowances and adequacy are interpreted as minimum calorie counts. At the Buffalo Federal Detention Facility, the daily average calorie count for food provided by the contractor Akima Global Services, as listed in a 2020 inspection report, was supposed to be 3,015 calories. However, journalists who toured the facility in 2018 reported that the daily calorie count was only 2,500 to 2,800.[14] Similarly, Hudson County's 2017 Request for Proposals for food service providers requires a weekly average of 3,400 calories per day, seemingly indulgent compared to the Buffalo facility. It is significant that this statement of calories per meal is only an *average*. It means that the calorie total can be less for some meals, as long as the vendor can demonstrate that they have made up for the lower calorie count at other meals. Hudson County officials do want to make sure that this flexibility isn't abused; in answer to a GD Correctional Services' question regarding the call for bids, the Hudson purchasing agent clarified that no daily average can be below 2,900 calories. Still, that 500 calories allows vendors a lot of leeway in what they serve or do *not* serve. For example, an entire meal of chicken, rice, and a vegetable is about 500 calories.

Let's dig deeper into these required calorie counts. A person's caloric needs vary by age, sex, height, weight, and physical activity. According to the USDA (U.S. Department of Agriculture), the estimated daily needed calories to maintain their current weight for adult women ranges from 1,600 to 2,400 calories, and for adult men 2,000 to 3,000.[15] To drill down a bit more here, the recommended calorie intake for a moderately active male between the ages of 19 and 25 is 2,800 per day. For a moderately active male between 26 and 45 years of age, it is 2,600 per day. The majority of male detainees in U.S. detention fall between 19 and 45 years old. Food service providers at detention facilities routinely serve between 2,500 and 2,900 calories per day. However, even for detainees who are served food that, in theory, provides enough calories to meet the minimum requirements, they may often be compelled to skip it because it is poor in quality or spoiled. Many detainees lose weight.

Another way to comprehend what "adequate" food means for detainees is by looking at sample menus and required portion sizes. In Hudson County's jail, where the required daily calorie count for inmates is higher than some of the other facilities we have investigated, the 2017 RFP (request for proposals) states that inmate breakfasts should include: "Such foods as fruit, 100% fruit juice, breads and cereals, and 3 oz. of a protein source such as eggs, meat or a suitable substitute." Requirements for inmate lunch and dinner are "Such foods as HBV protein, starch, hot vegetable, soup, dessert, bread, salad and dressing, coffee, cold drinks including milk and appropriate condiments." Other requirements in the same RFP state: "Chicken 1/4 are required at a minimum of 4 times per 6 week cycle; casseroles [...] at a maximum of 18 times per 6 week cycle; beef patties [are permitted] a minimum of 6 times per 6 week cycle." When we put all these details together what's shown is that actual meat on the menu is fairly rare.

Acceptable portion sizes for vegetables and other foods are equally sparse. For instance, the Hudson RFP specifies that a hot vegetable portion is a half-cup. Four ounces of fried potatoes is a "sufficient" starch portion. An acceptable hamburger portion is 4 ounces. Even the original quarter-pounder beef patty, which was 4 ounces, now weighs in at 4.25 ounces.[16]

What is clear is that for some eaters, at least, these minimum portion sizes are likely to be reduced diet rations. And, because food service contractors are aiming for "adequate" provision and little more, it is unlikely that extra or second helpings are routinely served.

Hudson's 2017 RFP also notes that snacks are not provided every day; instead, the provider has the option to provide snacks up to three times a week. What's more, even what constitutes a "snack" for an inmate is barely enough to make up for the supposedly "adequate" portions at mealtime. As the RFP states, in an infantilizing manner, a snack might consist of something like "cookies and milk, half sandwich and milk, or fruit and beverage."

The bottom line is that—even as detention food service providers technically meet detention standards and the terms of their contracts—most detainees are chronically hungry. A recurring complaint among detainees is that they simply do not get enough food to eat.

Even so, ICE inspectors repeatedly determine that detainees' complaints are not valid simply because what they are served meets NDS and contract requirements on paper. At the Buffalo detention center, for years inspectors have routinely registered complaints about food quantity. We looked at reports going back to 2008 where an inspection recorded that "several detainees complained about small food portions." This was refuted, in the report, when inspectors "randomly selected and viewed 11 food trays served to detainees and found the food portions were adequate." Another report, by ICE in 2010, noted that "Many detainees told ODO [Office of Detention Oversight] food portions at BFDF [Buffalo] are too small." However, the report dismissed detainees' views stating that "ODO verified the daily calorie counts for the meals are adequate."

The specific food service company doesn't matter. At the time of the above inspections in 2008 and 2010, food service at the Buffalo facility was contracted to Valley Metro Barbosa Group. But portion size came up again in 2017 and 2020 inspection reports, after food service at the facility had been taken over by Akima Global Services. Echoing detainees' complaints over a decade earlier, the 2020 report noted that some interviewed detainees "stated the food portions are small and inadequate." And, shrugging off inmates' direct experiences once again, under "Action Taken," the report noted that inspectors from "ODO interviewed the food service director (FSD) and reviewed menus with corresponding nutritional analysis. All menus have been certified as nutritionally adequate by a registered dietitian with the daily average calories listed as 3,015."

In effect, "adequate" means that chronic detainee hunger is accepted—and dismissed—by inspectors, as well as being standard in food service provision.

Far from "appetizing"

Making barely adequate food even worse, detention food is also severely lacking in quality. We come back to the statement at the top of the Food Service section of the 2000 NDS checklist: "Every facility will provide detainees in its care with nutritious and appetizing meals, prepared in accordance with the highest sanitary standards." Nutritious, appetizing, sanitary. Food service is also supposed to follow a 35-day menu cycle approved by a dietitian to ensure variety, and providers should publicly post the menu. Additionally, facilities are required to serve detainees at least two hot meals per day.

Again, this sounds like a good foundation. But when the customer isn't eating the food and there is no real oversight, there is a lot of room for loose interpretations, loopholes, and outright violations.

A 2012 independent report on detention at Hudson County Correctional Facility found food was the dominant complaint among detainees, who said that "it was often unappetizing and that there was very little variety."[17] The same year, a report on Essex jail tallied complaints filed by detainees—from information obtained through public records requests—and found that 27 percent of all complaints had to do with "food quality and special diets."[18] The report went on to note "particularly when the menu includes meat, [detainees] said that they receive 'purified liquid' or 'red sauce,' which is passed off as meat."

A 2018 report by Human Rights First on immigration detention at the Elizabeth, Essex County, and Hudson County facilities stated that "Individuals at all three facilities reported significant weight loss due to poor food quality. One individual at Hudson claimed to have lost 15 pounds during only three weeks of detention."[19]

The DHS Inspector General's 2019 report about the Essex jail reviewed complaints filed by detainees in a seven-month period, from January to July 2018, and found approximately 200, or 12 percent of the total, were kitchen-related.[20] As we quoted in this chapter's introduction, complaints included comments about food that had an appearance similar to garbage, smelled like fecal matter, and was impossible to eat.

Detainees' complaints also indicate that guidelines about variety are routinely flouted. Food service is supposed to follow five-week menu cycles, and to post these menus for detainees to see. But reviews of complaints highlight that facilities either don't post menus or don't stick to posted menus. For example, the previously mentioned 2012 independent report on the Essex jail included detainee complaints that they rarely received the food listed on the menu.[21] ICE inspection reports that do note complaints about variety are usually followed by an account of how the inspectors investigated the claims: often by reviewing existing 35-day menus at the facility and finding that they contain sufficient variety, *not* by actually observing what was served over time. ICE inspectors take the available menu and food service supervisors' statements as proof of reality, instead of considering what detainees tell them.

What's more, the National Detention Standards allow operators to make substitutions to the dietitian-approved menus. These substitutions may mean the use of red sauce instead of actual meat—in other words, not really following a menu.

Detainees often suffer from how food service is scheduled. The NDS include guidelines about the timing and conditions for serving meals. For example, the 2011 standards require that "Dining room facilities and operating procedures shall provide sufficient space and time for detainees to eat meals in a relatively relaxed, unregimented atmosphere," and "The dining room shall have the capacity to allow each detainee a minimum of 20 minutes dining time for each meal." However, it is evident that these guidelines are not consistently followed; in some cases, facilities' written policies directly contradict them. The 2018 Human Rights First report on Elizabeth, Essex, and Hudson jails found that, "Detainees at all three facilities also reported that they experienced significant time pressure to eat. Any food or drink remaining after the granted time expired was thrown away."[22] Additionally, according to the NDS, "Food shall never be used for reward or punishment." And yet, the use of food as a reward is *written* into the Hudson County Correctional Facility food contract, which states that snacks are to be provided only three times per week, "as an incentive for good behavior."

According to the NDS, no more than 14 hours can pass between meals served, and yet facilities routinely reach (or come close) to that maximum gap between dinner at night and breakfast the following morning. For example, mealtimes listed in the 2013 Elizabeth Detention Center Detainee Handbook are 6:45 am, 11:45 am, and 4:45 pm, leaving a 14-hour gap between dinner and breakfast. Meals are served at the Buffalo detention center at 6:30am, noon, and 5 pm (as listed in a 2013 ICE inspection report), a 13½-hour gap. The contract for food service at the Hudson jail states the mealtimes as 6am, 11 am, and 5pm for dinner, a 13-hour gap. The Orange County Correctional Facility serves breakfast at 6:10 am, lunch 11–12:30 pm, and dinner 5–6 pm, potentially a 12-hour gap. Fourteen hours—even twelve—is a very long time, particularly if meals barely meet minimum calorie counts.

Indeed, a frequent complaint from detainees is that there are long periods in which they simply have no access to food. A New Jersey lawyer we interviewed explained: "Something we heard repeatedly [...is] that the food is particularly bad that they offer, the hours of meals are very challenging, so time between dinner and breakfast the next day is very long." In essence, detainees are compelled to fast on a daily basis.

Facilities are required to provide special meals due to religious beliefs or medical needs. After their requests are approved by a facility chaplain or food service director, detainees should have access to a "common-fare menu." But this menu is only a 14-day cycle, and hot entrees only have to be served three times a week. Facilities' food services are also required to provide meals to meet special medical diets as determined by a health professional. However, these requirements are routinely ignored.[23]

For example, a 2010 ICE report on the Buffalo facility noted two detainee complaints that they were not receiving special diet meals, one for a kosher diet and the other due to an egg allergy. The 2012 independent report on detention at Hudson found religious diet needs poorly served:

> [...] one person interviewed, who is Rastafarian and requires a vegan diet, reported having been able to eat nothing but rice and beans or peas since being detained for over a year and a half.

As a result of the poor diet, he was losing hair and nails and had to be given a multi-vitamin by medical services. When he was unable to take the vitamin due to an allergic reaction to one of the ingredients, he was told that no other vitamin could be provided.[24]

Detainees requiring but not receiving special medical and religious diets became even more of a problem amid pandemic lockdowns, as noted in numerous independent reports and also highlighted by complaints recorded in ICE inspection reports.

Sickening food

Prison and detention food that leaves the people who eat it hungry is enough of a problem, but for detainees and inmates the situation is even worse because such food actually makes them sick. A 2017 study by the Centers for Disease Control and Prevention (CDC) found that inmates at correctional facilities are 6.4 times more likely to get food-related illness than non-inmates.[25] The CDC study identified *salmonella* and *clostridium perfringens* as the major specific causes of sickness from food in prisons, with bad chicken products the worst.

These disturbing findings are true for the facilities in our study. The 2012 report on Essex jail included an account from a member of a visitation program, who said that "detainees often contracted parasites and other stomach problems after a couple of months in ECCF."[26] The 2019 report about the unannounced DHS inspection of Essex disclosed, "Detainees stated the food was of low quality and consuming it caused vomiting and diarrhea, common symptoms of food poisoning." It also quoted one detainee grievance with a startling admission: "I have a stomach infection because of it and the nurse herself told me it was caused by the food"[27]

Precisely to avoid making consumers sick, food service operators are supposed to follow common-sense practices around food handling, storage, and preparation.[28] They are also supposed to conduct regular, weekly inspections of all areas, and follow established cleaning schedules. But clearly, such procedures are often not followed, and even blatantly disregarded.

There are repeated reports of spoiled food, unsafe food preparation practices, and unsanitary conditions. Sometimes, these seem relatively minor, such as in a 2007 ICE inspection report about detention at Bergen jail, which noted inappropriate securing of a kitchen knife, poor cleaning of food preparation surfaces, and use of expired food items. But many of the reported conditions are truly revolting, and obviously immediately dangerous to detainees' health.

"Individuals at all three facilities reported that food, particularly meat and rice, is often raw, spoiled, or expired," according to the 2018 Human Rights First report on the Bergen, Essex, and Hudson facilities.[29] The 2019 DHS report on Essex quoted earlier detailed raw, bloody chicken leaking in the refrigerators and slimy, obviously spoiled lunch meat. The report went on: "Although this mishandling of meats can spread salmonella, listeria, and E. coli, leading to serious foodborne illness, we observed facility staff serving this potentially spoiled meat to detainees." The DHS inspectors at Essex also noted, "During dinner service, we observed facility staff serving detainees hamburgers that were foul smelling and unrecognizable," and the report included alarming photos illustrating what had been observed. The report also cited expired and moldy bread being stored "to be used for making bread pudding once every 2–3 weeks."[30] Similar observations have been reported at detention facilities elsewhere.

Improper food temperature is a common issue in detention and prison facilities. This is not just a problem of inconvenience or taste; it is, above all, an issue of food safety and detainee health. If not maintained at a sufficiently cold temperature, uncooked food can spoil; if cooked food has been kept too long without refrigeration, it can poison the eater.

A 2011 ICE inspection of Hudson jail noted that "Ten of the 24 detainees (42 percent) reported the food trays were served cold and they requested a microwave oven to reheat their food." The 2012 independent report on conditions at Essex stated that many detainees complained of cold food.[31] This issue became more acute after COVID-19 lockdown rules were put into place, meaning that food had to be distributed to multiple housing units and then inmate cells instead of served in a central location. A 2020 ICE inspection report for Hudson during pandemic isolation protocols stated that a common detainee complaint was that "Hot foods were cold when delivered in the housing units."

Issues to do with sanitation also lead to problems with rodent and insect infestation. A 2007 ICE inspection report of the Bergen facility noted that "evidence of rodent infestation was observed in the dry storage area." The 2018 Human Rights First investigation recorded, "one individual at Elizabeth reported that he has received food with worms or maggots in it."[32]

Not even access to water is guaranteed. The 2011 NDS were the first standards to state that "Clean, potable drinking water must be available," which led to the inclusion of drinkable water in inspection criteria. But obtaining water safe to drink has been a problem at detention facilities in our study. The 2012 report on Essex detention noted that lack of access to clean drinking water was a recurring problem. The 2018 Human Rights First report found water to be a problem at both Essex and Elizabeth: "Several detainees at the Elizabeth facility reported that the water from the drinking fountain has an obvious white coloration, with two people describing it as 'pure bleach.' Detainees at the Essex facility stated that they often run out of water in the units and that the water from the bathroom tap is undrinkable."[33] During the pandemic lockdown when water was brought to detainees' cells, a December 2020 ICE inspection of Elizabeth again noted potable water as an issue, both in terms of water quality and quantity. A former Bergen detainee told a reporter that one issue at that facility was "no clean water to drink."[34]

Knowing good food from bad

Local officials and people who work in jails and detention facilities do understand that the food inmates and detainees are served is crap. Throughout this chapter we've seen how detainees voice concerns over and over while investigations repeatedly shed light on how ghastly and sickening the food is in detention. These problems are highlighted and compounded when we consider that not only do officials recognize that detainees are provided with poor food, but that some officials even insist on it.

The reality is that some contracts knowingly distinguish between good and bad food by precisely spelling out the different requirements for food provided to facility employees than that provided for inmates. Distinctions about what counts as "adequate," "appetizing," or acceptable are stipulated in differentiated costs per meal for facility staff and for detainees. For instance, the 2017 bid documents and contract between Hudson County and GD Correctional Services lay out very carefully—and with quite a bit of detail—how the food service provided to the Employee Dining Room (EDR) *must* be different from what is available to inmates. Specifically, it must be *better*.

In the Hudson jail food contract, requirements and examples for detainee food take up roughly one page. In contrast, two full pages describe in depth the requirements for what must be served in the EDR. For example, earlier we discussed the minimal requirements for inmates' meals that are set out in contract documents. And we know that food actually prepared for detainees frequently flies in the face of these base requirements.

In contrast, for facility employees, the food contract clearly states that choice, variety, and even specific brand-name products must be made available. For instance, it's noted that grilled meats must be served at all meals in the EDR, and there must be a choice between two entrees every meal. For employees, "the same meat (i.e. chicken, beef, pork) cannot be served as the only meat option more than 3 times within a 7 day period." Also, the EDR is required to offer a salad bar stocked with a minimum of 15 items, and a separate sandwich/sub-station at every meal. Detainees may get an occasional treat at a meal of a small square of cake, with snacks only occasionally provided. Meanwhile, for employees, there must always be four different desserts available, and a soft-serve ice cream machine always in operation.

The Hudson contracting documents also specify particular brands that patently differentiate between employees and inmates. For instance, name-brand products required for employees include such items as Kellogg's, Post, or General Mills dry cereals, whereas inmates receive generic bulk dry cereal. Employees can dine on Thumann's or Boar's Head cold cuts and Chicken of the Sea or Bumblebee canned tuna; at the salad bar, they'll find Wishbone or Kraft salad dressings. Meanwhile, for the inmates, Chunk Light tuna is the only offering and options for salad dressings are non-existent, because they don't have a salad bar.

When it comes to mealtimes, staff schedules provide a three-hour range across meals in contrast to inmates who are given rigid times and a mere twenty minutes or less to eat at each meal. In short, for employees, it's recognized that what makes a decent food service includes quality products, a varied menu, and lots of different, daily options.

These differences are far from trivial. They demonstrate that those running detention centers understand what is reasonable and acceptable and, when it comes to migrant detainees, they choose to do otherwise. This reality occurs even though it directly contradicts National Detention Standards, which state that "The staff dining room shall offer the same food items as the detainee dining room." Such overt disavowal of the NDS plainly shows that knowing good from bad is built into the business model for detention food service contracts, and migrants, as the recipients of detention's inadequate and often sickening food, pay the biggest price.

A SYSTEM BASED ON BAD FOOD, WORKING AS DESIGNED

Minimum calorie counts, small portion sizes, infrequent light snacks. Food in detention is shaped by requirements of "minimum daily allowances" and "adequacy," and what food service providers can "afford" in contracts won by submitting the lowest bid. The system is based on making money off of detainees, and set up in such a way that chronically hungry and sick detainees are part of the business model. In explaining why incarceration food makes inmates sick, an investigation published in *The Atlantic* identified the common practice of outsourcing corrections food, and, specifically, the "systems of perverse incentives in play: The more cheaply prisoners can be fed, the more money can often be made by the people charged with their care."[35]

The corrections food industry does well because, ultimately, there is great potential to make a lot of money, yet without having to substantially respond to the complaints of those who eat the food. In other words, contractors can under-provide with little accountability. Very few ICE contracts have been lost due to NDS violations or bad inspection reports regarding food, certainly none for the detention facilities in our study. Even detention facilities found to have numerous violations of the NDS—repeatedly—face no real consequences.

For example, the June 2020 ICE Essex inspection report noted that various problems found in the 2019 report had not been resolved; this was mentioned as a statement of fact and not as a red flag that demanded action. Indeed, shabby inspections are part of the detention system. Food contractors can cut corners on quantity and quality, with little fear of negative consequences. *The Atlantic* article also points to a faulty inspection process, which varies depending on if the facility is run by a county, a state, or the federal government, making "it easy for violations to slip through the cracks," rarely resulting in consequential penalties.[36] By occasionally noting hard-to-ignore violations, inspections provide a veneer of legitimacy, thereby allowing a system that runs on sick and hungry detainees to continue.

Identified problems to do with food—no matter how appalling they are—rarely stop a contract from being signed. In contracting and bid evaluation documents for the six facilities in our study, we have never seen evidence that food service violations to the NDS (as recorded in ICE inspections, journalistic accounts, or NGO reports) are considered by county officials awarding contracts.

In minutes or other accounts of county officials' meetings regarding food contracts, there is *no* discussion of the quality of the food service among competing contractors. When the Essex jail's contract was open for bids in 2010, there were two bidders: GD Correctional Services and Ahtna Technical Services. GDCS won the contract by offering meals at roughly 25 percent less than their one competitor; GDCS bid $1.43 per meal, and Ahtna bid $1.95 per meal. County records show no discussion of what a 50-cent difference in price per meal means, nor is there any mention of the many recorded detainee complaints regarding food, or even why so few companies opted to compete for such a potentially lucrative contract.

WHEN BAD FOOD IS THE BUSINESS MODEL

Detainees' experiences simply don't figure into decisions at all: there is *no* consideration of complaints, standards violations, or companies' problematic histories within a jail or detention center, or at facilities elsewhere. For example, when Bergen County renewed its contract with Aramark in 2015, nowhere in the bid evaluation documents was it noted that Aramark was repeatedly found in violation of NDS in past ICE inspections. Instead, for county decision-makers, food service in detention is just another agenda item to be decided based on rational economic logic and a calculus that, all too often, produces sickening consequences. Detainees—their experiences, rights, and needs as humans—are absent from the county's decision-making process.

In the next chapter, we consider how this "less care, more profit" business model plays out in medical services for detained migrants. We focus on facets of "immigration detention inc." that we have not yet discussed: how litigation over contracts is pervasive, and efforts to influence contracting decisions are relentless. The cost-over-care approach to medical care further contributes to literally sickening detainees.

3

"Cost Containment" and Litigation: The Institutionalization of Medical Neglect

On March 25, 2020, New Jersey's Bergen County Jail became the first ICE detention facility in the U.S. to report a case of COVID-19; the day before, a young man had tested positive for the virus.[1] Just over two weeks later, on April 10, 2020, New Jersey set another record: the nation's highest number of confirmed coronavirus cases among detained migrants.[2]

At the local and national level, during the first phase of the pandemic, ICE left detained migrants exposed and sick. In an analysis of the first wave of the coronavirus pandemic between May and August 2020, for instance, a Detention Watch Network (DWN) report estimated that detention facilities contributed an additional 18,524 COVID-19 cases in the New York/New Jersey region. Overall, across the U.S., almost half a million COVID-19 cases can be attributed to ICE detention facilities during this period. This puts the total number of COVID-19 cases whose spread can be connected to detention in the U.S. above the total number of cases for countries including Germany, France, and Canada for the same period.[3]

New issues—such as management and control of infection, as well as treatment of those infected—were exacerbated by preexisting issues in these facilities and conditions of confinement in general. Even before COVID-19—as part of the routine provision of medical care in the system—detention facilities were what the DWN report called "hotbeds of infection."[4] Dozens of articles and reports have long documented severely inappropriate and insufficient care. Protests inside and outside detention facilities

"COST CONTAINMENT" AND LITIGATION

have attempted to draw attention to facilities' consistently poor-quality care.

In fact, in recent years, medical care in detention has only deteriorated, and poor care seems to become ever more normalized.[5] The most profound evidence of this is the alarming, steady number of deaths in detention. Between 2011 and 2018, there were 71 documented deaths in U.S. detention. From 2019 to 2023, there were 41 deaths in detention, including a 2020 spike due to COVID-19.[6]

It is not supposed to be like this. The U.S. Constitution guarantees medical care for incarcerated and detained individuals,[7] and the United States is a signatory of international covenants promising to provide medical care to prisoners.[8] But examining the care provided to detained migrants, we see that, in reality, the U.S. immigration detention system has institutionalized medical neglect.

This chapter first offers an overview of the many recurring problems in detention medical care and the devastating impacts for detainees. It then explains how these problems stem from the pervasive objectives of limiting spending and making money, instead of providing good care.

ISSUES WITH DETENTION MEDICAL CARE

It is well-established that the medical care provided to detained immigrants is subpar and even atrocious. All six of the facilities in our study have been the subject of plentiful and consistent complaints about medical care, and we focus on evidence concerning these sites. We also incorporate findings from reports about other facilities run by the private companies we investigate or by the ICE Health Services Corps.

Every detention center is supposed to have the facilities and capacity to properly manage detainees' medical care. Their experiences, however, show that there are profound problems with all aspects of medical care in immigration detention. Even simple medical care—the sort that is easily accessible and routine outside of detention—is often difficult or impossible to obtain.

Accessing treatment and medication

Medical care is difficult to access from the moment individuals enter the detention system. Every facility is supposed to conduct a detailed health screening of each detainee upon admission, an "intake assessment." But these screenings are often incomplete or skipped entirely, resulting in consistent failures to identify and treat medical conditions.[9]

Then, treatment of chronic and pre-existing conditions is routinely neglected. A diabetic woman did not receive her regular blood transfusions and dialysis treatments for five months while detained at Hudson jail. Once released, she had to be hospitalized to deal with the resulting deterioration in her condition.[10] One detainee "complained that he was not receiving proper medical care for his back and ankle pain because medical staff refused to let him use his own ankle braces, which were stored with his property" because the metal in the braces was deemed a security risk.[11] Another report noted "inadequate and dangerous monitoring and treatment of detoxification from alcohol or drugs," which can contribute to short- and long-term health problems and even death, as routine.[12]

Prescribed medications are often not given to detainees. If they have medication with them when detained, it is usually taken away upon entering a facility.[13] The 2018 Human Rights First (HRF) report on care for detainees at the Elizabeth, Essex, and Hudson facilities recounted how a detainee named Ali had his "blood pressure medication […] taken from him and he was told he would receive a substitute shortly as his medication was 'too expensive.'" Ali's elevated blood pressure was left untreated for the week it took the facility to procure medication. A woman with epilepsy, Angela, "reported that she was denied her medication upon entering detention. It wasn't until after she had a seizure that she was given medication, and it was only a fraction of her usual dosage."[14]

Detainees who become sick while in detention are similarly restricted from receiving appropriate treatment. The first roadblock is the very procedures that detainees must use to ask for medical care. An inmate or detainee who needs care has to submit a medical care request. In most facilities, the requests are pieces of

"COST CONTAINMENT" AND LITIGATION

paper submitted to a locked box (though some facilities have implemented digital medical request systems). Inspectors at the Bergen County facility in 2010 and 2012 found that there were no sick call forms available, and it was unclear in which box slips should be submitted. A 2017 investigation of detention medical care identifies additional "barriers to care" at various facilities, such as having to get up very early to place sick calls, translated instructions not available for non-English speakers, and no information in any language (including English) about how to even ask for a sick call.[15]

Then, detainee requests for medical care are often not responded to in a timely manner.[16] According to written facility policies, detainees who submit requests for care should receive some type of response within 24–48 hours. If someone is sick or in pain, 24 hours—let alone 48—is a long time. Yet even these stated timeframes are frequently ignored, leaving detainees waiting far longer. One man held at Hudson was not seen until a month after his request, leaving him with excruciating abdominal pain.[17]

Facility staff, whether willfully or unintentionally, often act as gatekeepers. The process of requesting medical care is mediated by any number of individuals who might delay or deny care.[18] "There is a certain medical staff member who conducted the sign-up for unit sick calls," notes a 2017 inspection of the Buffalo facility, "who does not provide sufficient time for the sign-up and displays poor communication skills." While the response to a submitted sick call is supposed to be managed by a medical professional, security personnel—not necessarily trained to assess medical needs—are often those who detainees must ask for medical care. For example, at the ICE-owned Buffalo facility, the ICE Health Services Corps is responsible for the provision of medical services but Akima Global Services is contracted to run the facility; this includes managing the sick-call request system and bringing people to and from the medical unit. So, it is Akima staff—trained only in basic first aid and CPR—who make decisions about granting access to medical services.

Most alarmingly, there is evidence that medical care requests are sometimes ignored entirely. In 2019, CNN conducted an in-depth investigation into the care provided by Correct Care Solutions (CCS, now Wellpath), looking into documented issues at 120 sites in 32 states. CNN spoke with employees who described how medical requests had been hidden and shredded.[19]

Even when a detainee manages to meet with medical services staff, there can be additional barriers. Often, decent translation is not available for detainees who do not speak English.[20] Medical providers are supposed to offer certified translation services or use a call-in translation service, but they often don't. A 2017 report gave the example of a Spanish-speaking man with suicidal ideation and severe hallucinations who was moved between Bergen, Hudson, and Orange County facilities. Psychiatric care at all three facilities was provided only in English. Occasionally, a correctional officer or fellow detainee translated for the man, a violation of a patient's right to privacy that he said made him uncomfortable.[21]

Personnel can also discriminate and harass in ways that impede care. The 2018 report on the Elizabeth, Essex County, and Hudson County facilities noted, "Many detained immigrants, particularly non-English speakers, endure frequent racist comments, harassment, and discrimination from medical and correctional staff."[22] A collective of organizations supporting detainees at the Buffalo facility alleged repeated racial discrimination by staff in 2022.[23]

Staff responses to medical care needs can, quite simply, exhibit outright cruelty. The 2018 HRF report included this account:

> "Jaime" is an asylum seeker suffering from a severe gastrointestinal condition since entering detention about five months ago. According to Jaime, the medical staff are not performing adequate tests or treating his condition. Instead, he feels they neglect his condition and place him in segregation as a form of punishment for speaking out about the inadequate care. He told us that one officer at the facility even said, "Fuck your problems. Fuck your bleeding. Don't make problems for me." Jaime described the attitude in the facility as, "'If you get sick here [...] we will torture you.' I was tortured."[24]

Insufficient and inappropriate care

The medical care that detainees do receive is frequently insufficient and inappropriate, often to the point of medical neglect. A common

"COST CONTAINMENT" AND LITIGATION

grievance is that the only treatment for any medical issue or complaint is ibuprofen or acetaminophen. The 2018 Human Rights First report on detention at the Elizabeth, Essex, and Hudson facilities summarized, "Many detained individuals reported that pain killers, mainly ibuprofen, are provided for symptoms ranging from stomach aches, chest pain, and in one instance, severe back pain after a fall by an elderly man. It appears that ibuprofen is offered not as a complement to, but rather as a substitute for, physical exams, x-rays, or other testing."[25] Other examples of subpar care abound. The report noted, "At the Hudson facility, we observed one woman using a bra as a sling for a clavicle fracture after being told that proper arm slings were a 'suicide risk.'"[26]

Problems with staffing are routine in detention facilities—both insufficient numbers and unqualified, poorly trained personnel. Reports have repeatedly documented system-wide evidence of "provision of healthcare by unlicensed or under-licensed personnel."[27] One investigation noted chronic use of licensed vocational nurses (LVNs), who are supposed to work only as support staff for more trained medical staff, managing medical units on their own.[28] Medical staff have been found to not know how to use diagnostic machines during critical medical events.[29]

Issues also arise when a detainee must leave the detention facility to receive needed medical care. A recurring problem is extended delays in accessing care off-site.[30] For example, one report examined the case of an immigrant detainee at the Hudson County jail who was diagnosed with rectal cancer after enduring a three-month wait to be taken to a specialist.[31] Another gave the example of a man's request to seek attention for a malfunctioning pacemaker, which was repeatedly denied.[32]

Mental health care

Detention itself—the conditions, the treatment, the uncertainty—contributes to intense stress, and can negatively impact detainee mental health. But mental health care in detention is a disaster. "Adequate Mental Health Care is Often Unavailable or Difficult to Access, or Leads to Worsened Conditions": so reads a major section title of the 2018 Human Rights First report on conditions in the Elizabeth private detention center, and Essex County and Hudson County Correctional Facilities.[33]

The lack of mental healthcare professionals is particularly deplorable.[34] Then there are issues with medications related to mental health: sedatives are over-used while invasive drugs are incorrectly prescribed. Often, medications correctly prescribed to control mental health conditions—like PTSD or bipolar disorder—are not supplied.[35] One report included the account of a detainee at the Orange County Correctional Facility who was deprived of medications for his diagnosed schizophrenia, and yet he was repeatedly given medications contra-indicated for schizophrenia. Such misuse of medication continued, despite self-harming by banging his head against a small window so hard he required stitches. Even then, the medical service's solution wasn't to correct his medications, but to put him in segregation or restraints.[36]

Every facility is required to have detailed plans for preventing detainee self-harm and suicide. However, reports and inspections have repeatedly noted deficient responses to detainees at risk of self-harm.[37] This contributes to the alarming death rates in U.S. detention; from January 2017 to March 2020 (before the pandemic), there were twelve recorded deaths by suicide in U.S. detention facilities, with a spike in suicide after the onset of the pandemic.[38]

Solitary confinement is routinely used for detainees deemed at risk of suicide. One report noted that the "suicide watch program at the Hudson County Correctional Facility [...] may actually discourage people from seeking mental health care and may contribute to suicidal inclinations."[39] At the Orange County Correctional Facility, a detainee who attempted suicide did not receive any type of psychiatric evaluation and was placed in solitary confinement.[40] Two of the three detainee suicides that occurred at the Hudson facility between 2016 and 2018 took place in isolation cells, where suicidal inmates had been placed for suicide watch.[41]

Gender and care

In 2019, there were 163 U.S. detention facilities that held women. And yet, all too often, health care specifically for women is profoundly deficient.[42] Women in detention often do not receive routine gynecological care, such as pap smears and mammograms. ICE has a history of prohibiting prescribed contraceptive drugs to women in their custody, both for purposes of contraception as well as to manage chronic conditions.[43] Paradoxically, ICE has also been found to administer contraceptive drugs to detainees without their consent.[44] As recently as 2020, women in ICE custody have reported forced sterilization, as well as medical experimentation.[45]

Violation of detainees' rights to privacy, confidentiality, and informed consent can be especially acute in women's medical care. A 2009 Human Rights Watch report stated, "Security guards were sometimes inside exam rooms, invading privacy and encroaching on the patient-provider relationship. Some women feared retaliation or negative consequences to their immigration cases if they sought care." One interviewee quoted in the report said that security guards were present for all exam procedures, including pap smears.[46]

For pregnant detainees, substandard prenatal care is routine. Pregnant detainees may be shackled when transported outside the detention facility for examinations and to give birth. Mistreatment and denial of medical care has contributed to pregnancy loss. Nursing mothers who are detained and separated from infants are often "denied breast pumps in the facilities, resulting in fever, pain, mastitis, and the inability to continue breastfeeding upon release."[47]

Even maintaining basic gynecological hygiene is a common struggle in detention. A complaint repeated by female detainees throughout the detention system is that they are not supplied with feminine hygiene products or are made to make special requests that can be humiliating. A 2018 report explained, "Women at Elizabeth and Hudson [...] reported receiving an insufficient number of sanitary pads, leaving them no other choice but to purchase them at the commissary for high prices."[48]

Gender nonconformity is also a source of mistreatment, abuse, and medical neglect in U.S. immigration detention. Transgender detainees are often denied access to medical treatment such as hormone replacement therapy. They are regularly placed in isolation, and face harassment and humiliation.[49]

Finally, though it does not pertain specifically to the provision of medical care, it must be mentioned that sexual violence, abuse, and harassment occur in detention facilities all over the country, including at those in our study.[50]

Facility conditions

Even as many detention facilities fail to provide proper medical care, detention's actual physical environment can make detainees sick. Carceral facilities in the United States, including detention centers, are often located in sites that can contribute to poor health due to issues of contamination or pollution.[51] The Hudson County Correctional Facility is an example of this, located in an industrial area that experiences heavy pollution from the nearby freight train hub.[52] The Elizabeth Detention Facility is similarly located in an industrial area; the building itself is a repurposed warehouse retrofitted as a detention site.

Physical conditions at the facilities themselves can directly endanger detainees' health. The 2019 report about the DHS Office of Inspector General's visit to the Essex detention center stated: "we observed environmental conditions at the Essex Facility that pose serious health and safety risks for detainees, including leaking ceilings in detainee living areas, showers laced with mold and peeling paint, and dilapidated beds."[53] Pictures of shower stalls with mildew and mold were included. Such issues have been found at sites throughout the detention system.[54] Detainees at Elizabeth have lodged numerous complaints about worms and maggots in the shower area.[55] Investigations at Elizabeth (the repurposed warehouse) have documented poor ventilation, creating problems with dust contributing to allergies and asthma. The Bergen County Jail was cited in ICE inspection reports for unsanitary conditions, including water leaks.

Detainees are forced to live in conditions not conducive to maintaining good health. While detention facilities are supposed to provide access to outdoor recreational space to support both mental and physical health, the Elizabeth and Hudson County detention centers were notorious for failing to provide such space.[56] Inspections of the Essex facility repeatedly found that there were not enough showers for detainees. At the height of the COVID-19 pandemic, desperate detainees complained of overcrowding and dirty conditions.[57]

"COST CONTAINMENT" AND LITIGATION

Often detainees are not provided with products necessary for personal hygiene, such as sufficient quantities of soap and toothpaste.[58] Those at the Elizabeth CDF complained that they were issued obviously used razors, including with hair on them. To maintain their own health, detainees often must buy products from the facility commissary, a reality that we discuss in the next chapter.

Deaths in detention

Chronic, egregious medical neglect results in a shocking number of detainee deaths. Detainees have died at all the facilities in our study except the Buffalo center. In fact, as of 2021, "Hudson County Jail holds the record for deaths in custody—at least 17 deaths since 2013—most of them due to medical negligence and suicides."[59]

In recent years, there have been a considerable number of reports, congressional investigations, and public hearings on detainee deaths.[60] But unnecessary deaths in detention continue. Between 2018 and 2023—just a five-year period—50 people died in U.S. detention facilities. ICE reported nine deaths in (fiscal year) 2018, eight deaths in 2019, and 21 deaths in 2020—an alarming jump linked to the pandemic. Numbers have dropped somewhat since then—five in 2021, three in 2022, and four in 2023—lower numbers perhaps explained by the decrease in overall detention numbers during the pandemic.[61] Even these shocking numbers may be inaccurate. Evidence suggests that ICE under-reports and actively tries to conceal detainee deaths from public knowledge.[62]

Eight specific deaths in detention were examined in a 2016 independent report titled "Fatal Neglect: How ICE Ignores Deaths in Detention."[63] In all eight cases, facility staff, including medical staff, delayed in responding to detainee complaints, and, in some cases, ignored them. Staff consistently did not respond promptly or in line with standard medical practice in cases of severe emergencies (such as chest pain). A 2017 report examined 18 deaths in detention between 2012 and 2015. In 16 of the 18 deaths, evidence was found of substandard care. Medical staff ignored detainees' requests for medical attention, claimed detainees were faking symptoms, and delayed care for substantial periods until conditions became dire. This review included deaths in facilities run by private companies, ICE Health Services Corps, and county jails, showing that problems with care are system-wide.[64] The patterns are clear. Nearly all these deaths were preventable or attributable to negligent medical care.

Facilities and medical care providers throughout the U.S. detention system consistently fail to provide sufficient, appropriate, and timely care. This failure is not just in a few "bad apple" facilities; it is systemic. Our investigation shows that standard care in detention entails routine sickness and unnecessary pain for detainees. It also shows why: because private and public medical care providers are incentivized to weigh cost over quality of care.

COMPETITIVE CONTRACTING: LITIGATION, INFLUENCE, COST OVER CARE

As with food service, private companies play a huge role in the provision of medical care in U.S. detention facilities. They are contracted to operate in ICE-owned facilities, privately-owned facilities, and subcontracted by county jails that detain immigrants for ICE.[65]

While local and regional companies have vied for jails' medical contracts for decades, increasingly, they are being edged out by better-resourced national and international companies. Today, two companies are contracted to provide medical care for three of the county jails in our study: CFG Health Systems and Wellpath[66] (see Table 3.1).

The Essex County Correctional Facility's medical contract has been held by CFG Health Systems since 2006. The 2023–24 contract was worth $18.6 million, a one-year renewal of a contract awarded in 2021, worth $53 million for two years, with the possibility of two one-year renewal options. CFG (Center for Family Guidance) currently provides medical services to around 15 correctional facilities in New Jersey and New York. One independent website lists CFG's annual revenue as $140 million.[67]

The medical contracts for jails in both Hudson County, NJ, and Orange County, NY, are held by industry giant Wellpath. Wellpath was formed in 2018 by the self-described "global alternative investment firm" H.I.G. Capital through the merger of two correctional healthcare companies, Correct Care Solutions and Correctional

Table 3.1 Medical service providers for facilities in our study

	Bergen County Jail (NJ)	Essex County Correctional Facility (NJ)	Hudson County Correctional Facility (NJ)	Orange County Correctional Facility (NY)	Elizabeth Contract Detention Facility (NJ)	Buffalo Federal Detention Center (NY)
Medical service provider	County provides (multiple subcontracts)	CFG Health Systems	Wellpath	Wellpath	ICE Health Services Corps	ICE Health Services Corps
Contract value	Varied contracts	$18.6 million 2023–24	$13.5 million 2023–24	$7 million (2024–25)	*Facility run by CoreCivic, IHSC budget not available	*Facility run by Akima Global Services, IHSC budget not available

Medical Group Companies. With the merger, Wellpath became the largest provider of correctional medical care in the United States. At its formation, the company's owners said it was expected to generate around $1.5 billion annually.[68] The future of Wellpath, however, is currently uncertain; in November 2024, dealing with rising labor costs and multiple lawsuits, the company filed for bankruptcy.[69]

Hudson County's current contract with Wellpath was from a renewal in late 2023 for one year, worth $13.5 million.[70] Wellpath first won the Hudson contract in 2018 (as Correct Care Solutions, before the merger). From 2011 to 2018, CFG Health Systems had the Hudson contract. Prior to CFG, Correction Health Services had it.

Orange County's current contract with Wellpath is from a one-year renewal in January 2024, worth $7 million.[71] Wellpath (then CCS) was awarded the Orange contract in 2016. The contract was previously held by Quality Choice Health Care 2014 to 2016, and before then, Correctional Medical Care.

Medical care contracts for county jails are awarded through the same general process used for choosing food providers. First, a Request for Proposals (RFP) is issued; then competing bids are received and evaluated; and, finally, a recommendation is made to county leaders. Local and state guidelines are meant to ensure fair competition and impartial evaluation of bids, and to prevent undue influence from competitors.

Instead, however, the competitive bidding process is riddled with lawsuits, manipulation, political influence, and devaluation of care—many of the same issues found in carceral food services suppliers. The consequences in medical care are even more immediately dangerous for detainees.

Litigation

While some lawsuits may be expected in competitive industries, litigation has been weaponized within the correctional medical care industry. Tracing medical care at the county jails in our study over the last 25 years shows that litigation is a routine part of obtaining—and holding onto—medical contracts. The Hudson County contract was the subject of a long and contentious litigation process from 2008 to 2012.[72] Decisions about Orange County Correctional Facility's medical contract resulted in litigation two of the last three times it was open for bidding. *Every* time the Essex County contract has come open to bidding since 2007, the contracting decision has spurred lawsuits by a losing bidder.

When a contract is awarded to a company that did not submit the lowest bid, the winning company is often accused of undue influence. This strategy was how CFG Health Systems first acquired the Essex contract. When ECCF's medical contract came up for bid in 2006, Correctional Health Services (CHS) had held it for roughly 15 years. CHS and CFG Health Systems both submitted bids. CFG's bid was over $4 million *less* than CHS's bid, but county freeholders voted to stick with CHS. The bid evaluation committee noted substantial concerns with CFG's lack of experience related to required staffing and technical systems as reasons why CHS was chosen.[73] CFG then sued Essex County and CHS over the lost contract, alleging a rigged bidding process. After multiple appeals and over $500,000 spent by the county to defend its decision to award the contract to CHS, in 2008 a judge ordered Essex County to award the contract to CFG, explaining in his decision that awarding to a higher bidder suggested improper behavior on the part of county leaders.[74] Apparently, any choices deviating from the lowest bid look suspicious, leaving little room to factor in quality of care.

Influence

It is routine for carceral medical services companies to cultivate connections and grease the wheels of local decision-making, in the form of donations, personal relationships, and employment opportunities. A glaring example: in 2022, Wellpath's CEO pled guilty on multiple federal bribery charges for "pay-to-play" schemes related to prison medical contracts in Virginia.[75] Wellpath appears to employ similar strategies in our region of study. In 2020, New Jersey Democratic candidate for the U.S. House of Representatives Amy Kennedy was accused of taking thousands of dollars in campaign contributions from Wellpath, at the same time as her husband, Patrick Kennedy, was appointed to Wellpath's Board.[76] Kennedy lost, but, for companies like Wellpath, these attempts to cultivate political decision-makers appear to be simply part of doing business.

The medical contract histories for the Essex, Hudson, and Orange county facilities are littered with signs of attempted influence. Take the donation disclosure forms that companies submitting bids for the Essex County Correctional Facility's medical contract must fill out. The names of many county officials—including Joseph DiVincenzo, Essex County's long-time Executive—have appeared frequently on forms submitted by CFG, holder of the Essex jail medical contract since 2008, indicating that CFG has contributed to the political campaigns of elected county leaders for years.[77]

Accusations of improper influence were part of the four-year court battle over the Hudson County Correctional Facility's 2008 medical contract, between CHS and CFG. Court papers included revelations that the CHS president made a campaign contribution to a Hudson County freeholder, and that CHS's president had previously served as both a Hudson County administrator and jail warden.[78]

The Orange County Correctional Facility's medical contract was stripped from Correctional Medical Care (CMC) in 2014 and awarded to Quality Choice Correctional Health (QCCH), despite the latter submitting a higher bid. Bid evaluators explained that

CMC was excluded from consideration due to complaints at other jails it served.[79] CMC sued, alleging unfair influence behind the decision. The lawsuit cited a long-time friendship between one of QCCH's owners and the sheriff who ran the jail, and QCCH owners' attendance at county political fundraisers. Our point here is not to assess the validity of such claims, but to note their persistent occurrence in fights over the contracts.

It's also remarkable that rules ostensibly aimed at preventing corruption lead evaluators to value bureaucracy more than quality of care. State and county policies guiding the contracting process require counties to seek the "lowest responsible and responsive bidder." When evaluating bids for medical service contracts, the requirement for "responsible" bids does not mean that companies must be shown to act responsibly in the provision of medical care. Instead, it refers to bidders' success in accurately meeting the detailed bid criteria as laid out in the RFP, resulting in bid packets often hundreds of pages long.

Similarly, "responsive" does not mean that a provider must respond swiftly and effectively to inmates' medical needs. Instead, "responsive" refers to the bidder's ability to respond to the Request for Proposals within the requirements set by the county: meeting tight deadlines, submitting all required forms and documents according to strict guidelines, and responding to clarification requests. These bid guidelines also become fodder for legal challenges to contract decisions: the words "responsible" and "responsive" appear frequently in lawsuits accusing competing companies of not following appropriate procedures.

Devaluation of quality care

Political influence and favoritism notwithstanding, the competitive nature of medical services contracting means that providers are motivated to keep costs as low as possible; the lower the bid, in general, the more likely it is they will maintain or acquire contracts.[80] And the less money spent on medical care, the more money harnessed as revenue. Predictably, this constant drive to cut costs worsens care in prisons and detention centers. "For-profit companies and county governments receiving payments from ICE for holding immigrants in detention," warns one report, "have a finan-

"COST CONTAINMENT" AND LITIGATION

cial incentive to reduce costs related to both on-site and off-site care, with little risk of real penalties for medical care that does not meet the applicable detention standards."[81]

Wellpath epitomizes the problems resulting from a business model that requires cost-cutting in medical care. CNN's 2019 investigation into Correct Care Solutions (CCS, now Wellpath) found evidence that CCS's approach to medicine was driven by "cost containment," resulting in egregiously negligent care. "Across the country," laments CNN, "the same themes have been found: doctors and nurses have failed to diagnose and monitor life-threatening illnesses and chronic diseases. CCS employees have denied urgent emergency room transfers. They have failed to spot or treat serious psychiatric disorders and have allowed common infections and conditions to become fatal."

Former CCS employees admitted that the care they could provide was limited by company directives to keep costs down. Two nurses formerly employed by CCS even sued the company for wrongful termination, after they repeatedly raised concerns about medical care and unaddressed inmate medical requests. "CCS is about the mighty dollar," warned one nurse, "If they can cut costs [...] who cares who suffers in the process."[82]

Staffing—both quantity and quality—is another way contractors limit and cut costs. Counties' RFPs, and the bid proposals submitted in response, all lay out in great detail how facilities' medical services *should* be staffed, and this is one of the biggest areas of expense for companies. But as described earlier, detainees' care routinely suffers due to insufficient training for medical staff, not enough staff, and high turnover. For example, the 2019 CNN investigation of CCS found that the company "has repeatedly relied on inexperienced workers, offered minimal training and understaffed facilities."[83]

Even when county leaders try to change the company they contract with, they often cannot escape bad care—after all, negligence is now built into the business model. Market consolidation, tight competition, and a bidding process that weighs cost over quality lead to a lack of alternatives. An *Atlantic* investigative report into medical care at jails and prisons around the country found that "Just a handful of firms serve the nation's largest jails. A contractor deemed problematic can't always be replaced. And once jails go private, it's not necessarily easy to go back. With health care, lack of choice isn't just a market problem, but a factor in the quality of the care patients receive."[84]

For example, in 2013, a detainee died in a Westchester, New York jail, under the oversight of CCS. Consequently, county officials tried and failed to find a new contractor, because no other companies submitted bids that could fill the facility's needs.[85] In 2018, after a troubling series of deaths at the Hudson County Correctional Facility, county leaders stripped CFG Health Systems of their medical services contract. They awarded it to CCS—hardly a model for good care.[86]

Instead of making changes in the care they provide, these companies pay to litigate and hide evidence. In addition to fighting in court over lost contracts, carceral medical care companies regularly defend the level of care they provide against charges brought by local governments as well as inmates. Wellpath (formerly CCS) has been sued by detainees and inmates over care in facilities around the country.[87] The Private Equity Stakeholder Project report calculated that between 2008 and 2018, CCS was sued around 1,395 times in federal court,[88] for charges including negligence, inadequate care, denial of care, deliberate indifference, and cruel and unusual punishment. Many of these are further classified as civil rights violations and medical malpractice. Between 2014 and 2018, CCS faced lawsuits for over seventy deaths.[89]

Wellpath has tried to conceal its alarming litigation history. The company asks counties to which they submit bids to *not* release these histories to the public, claiming confidentiality, so our recent records requests to counties in our study excluded these pages. However, with some digging around, we found records for Klamath County, Oregon; they did not follow Wellpath's request regarding what to release to the public. From that bid, we obtained Wellpath's 2015–20 litigation history: ten pages listing over 600 cases filed against CCS and Wellpath. Wellpath (then CCS) has even been found to destroy evidence of negligent care in these cases.[90]

Clearly, the successful business model does not priortize the provision of quality medical service. Instead, success entails figuring out how to sell the company to county decision-makers, meet

"COST CONTAINMENT" AND LITIGATION

counties' bureaucratic requirements, and provide the minimum degree of care the company can get away with. Instead of paying to improve care, they pay to fight off lawsuits and influence decisions. After all, the customer to convince and satisfy is not the patients they are supposed to take care of. Instead, the customer—the county leaders who award the contract—measures success in dollars saved, not the quality of care provided.

THE ICE HEALTH SERVICE CORPS AND "PUBLIC" HEALTH

The ICE Health Service Corps, or IHSC, is a government-run agency that plays a substantial role in the delivery of medical care to detained immigrants. On its webpage, the IHSC declares that its "mission is to provide the safe delivery of high-quality health care to noncitizens in ICE custody."[91] But mounds of evidence document a consistent failure to meet this mission.

Though IHSC is a public, government agency, a marketized logic and private corporation involvement are central to its operation and provision of medical services. As with private medical care companies, a cost-cutting approach leads to delayed care, denial of care, and bad care. And IHSC's bureaucratic processes hamper and limit better care, rather than facilitate it.

The origins of IHSC can be traced back to 1891, when the national Public Health Service was tasked with medically examining and quarantining migrants at Ellis Island. In the decades following, a division within the Service continued to be involved in often intrusive and demeaning medical reviews of arriving immigrants. When the detention system began to take shape in the 1980s, the division took on the additional charge of providing medical care to detainees; it was eventually moved into the Department of Homeland Security and ICE, and renamed IHSC.[92]

Today, administering an annual budget (in 2024) of over $421 million,[93] the IHSC has two primary tasks. First, the IHSC provides direct medical care (including mental health and dental care) to detainees at 18 IHSC-staffed facilities. These include two of the facilities in our study, the Buffalo Federal Service Processing Center (run by Akima Global Services) and the Elizabeth

Detention Center (run by CoreCivic) (see Table 3.1). In 2024, IHSC provided care to approximately 138,000 people in these 18 facilities.

Even in the facilities where IHSC is directly responsible for detainee medical services, private contractors have a significant degree of responsibility in providing access to and delivering care. By IHSC's own estimate, over 50 percent of the agency's staff is contracted out to private companies, with the company STG International (STGi, by its self-chosen acronym) the main supplier.[94]

Additionally, as mentioned earlier, companies contracted for other aspects of facility operation often end up as gatekeepers to medical care. For example, in the Elizabeth Contract Detention Facility, while the contract between CoreCivic and ICE states that the IHSC is responsible for the "delivery" of healthcare services, it also tasks CoreCivic with supervising security and access to the health unit, as well as providing transport to outside medical facilities. This gives CoreCivic a lot of control over detainees' medical care. If a CoreCivic staff member doesn't pass on a detainee's request for medical care to the IHSC personnel, the detainee may not get in the door of the health unit. Or, if CoreCivic directs employees to decrease transportation expenses, then detainees may not be transported to care in a timely manner.

IHSC's second primary task is to "oversee" medical care in non-IHSC-run detention centers—that is, the other roughly 130 U.S. facilities that detain immigrants (in 2024, another nearly 190,000 detainees). Part of this oversight includes managing referrals for off-site care: any request for external medical services, including specialized or emergency treatment, requires approval and funding from IHSC.

IHSC often delays and balks at authorizing off-site care. IHSC goals of keeping costs down guide how requests for off-site treatment are decided. The agency has been criticized "for tracking cost savings from [Treatment Authorization Request] TAR denials."[95] There is evidence that IHSC sets yearly caps on medical expenses and delays care based on arbitrary limits.[96]

IHSC appears to discourage the approval of services for detainees who may be deported. Requests are routinely denied if deportation is thought to be imminent. But since deportation timelines are often hard to pin down, care may be ultimately denied for long periods of time.[97]

Indeed, IHSC has a reputation for not approving requests, regardless of patient need and medical staff recommendations. A 2018 Human Rights First report gave the specific example of a detainee who explained that "the facility doctor said that while his health condition made him a 'ticking time bomb,' ICE would not approve these additional recommended procedures." As one ICE officer quoted in the report said, "the decision to provide medical care is a 'cost-benefit analysis.'"[98]

Even reviewing requests for care is routinely delayed for excessive time periods. This may have to do with the lack of personnel allocated to the work of approving; a 2009 Human Rights Watch report noted that IHSC's predecessor (DIHS) "employed only three or four nurses to evaluate TAR submissions from around the country."[99]

Given this cost-over-general-care approach, IHSC has been the subject of repeated accusations and litigation around negligent care. For example, in July 2018, an IHSC employee filed a whistleblower complaint with the DHS Office of Inspector General, "rais[ing] serious claims regarding the care and oversight provided by IHSC at these facilities." Many lawsuits filed against the IHSC allege atrocious care: medical neglect, unnecessary surgeries, improper distribution of medications, and patient deaths.[100]

ISSUES THAT ADD UP TO THE INSTITUTIONALIZATION OF MEDICAL NEGLECT

In all the facilities in our study, whether medical care is government- or privately-run, we find strikingly little or no discernible differences when it comes to problems with medical care, which is just another node in the detention system through which value can be extracted, sucked out of the bodily needs of detained migrants. All players in the corrections medical care industry are governed by a logic of cost reduction, and processes that pave the way for the institutionalization of medical neglect.

Medical care companies understand that quality of care is not the most important factor when competing for jail contracts. As with the corrections food industry, medical care in prisons and detention facilities is a highly competitive industry, with fewer and fewer players amid high levels of consolidation. Detainees are commodified and turned into profit margins. Court decisions over lost contracts warn county officials that they must weigh cost over quality to avoid the appearance of improper influence. Still, all companies play a relentless game of favoritism with county decision-makers. The IHSC, the government-run agency integral to the provision of immigrant detainees' medical care, also operates under goals of minimizing costs and care provided.

However medical care is administered at detention facilities, detainees' lived experiences—and deaths—starkly demonstrate an ingrained culture of disbelief and dehumanization, and the normalization of detainee pain and illness. Their medical needs, and the care they require to stay alive, are exploited for financial and professional gain.

4

Starved for Profit: How Migrants Become Captive Consumers and Coerced Workers

An individual detained in Orange County, New York, in 2021 would need to work seven hours in the detention facility's coveted "volunteer" jobs program, just to be able to buy a single packet of ramen noodles. A four-ounce can of tuna fish, at $2.85, requires almost three full days of work. In Hudson County, New Jersey, in 2021, a pack of two Tylenol, at 40 cents, will eat up almost a half day of earnings, and a purchase of one pair of underwear requires 40 hours' work, or over one week's wages for detained migrants.

The depth of privation in detention means that working under such exploitative conditions is a coveted opportunity as, often, there is not enough work to satisfy demand. As one former detainee explained, "Many more people want jobs than there are jobs to have. There are only six to ten of each type of assignment. But people want the jobs when they don't have any money. They will work a couple of weeks just to be able to make a phone call."[1]

Why would detained migrants need to buy food items, toiletries, or clothing from a detention facility's commissary store? We've already touched on several reasons for this in Chapter 2; often detainees go hungry because the food quantities are insufficient and the quality abysmal. Inspection reports have also shown that in some cases, "ICE detainees [were] not provided socks and undergarments; those items must be purchased through the facility commissary," in violation of National Detention Standards.[2] The toiletries and personal care items provided, from soap to menstruation products, fall short of what most of us would consider reasonable to maintain health and dignity.

The lean budgets and other cost-saving mechanisms under which facilities operate mean that detained migrants are left needing to supplement meager provisions. And commissaries are the main—if not the only—mechanism to make up for such a shortfall. Worst of all is that, in essence, detention commissaries prey on the hunger, sickness, and other hardships these facilities seem to be *designed* to create.

Just as we've seen in Chapters 2 and 3 where we scrutinized contracts for food and medical services, detention and prison commissary contracts are highly coveted. In this chapter, we take a close look at the powerhouse of commissaries in the facilities that we investigate: Keefe Commissary Network. Tracing Keefe's gargantuan network not only identifies links with private equity firms, it also reveals another troubling beneficiary: local governments. So, while on the surface, commissary contracts are awarded to a single entity, myriad other actors are caught up with this system, making detention a valuable source of revenue for both the private sector *and* government entities. Understanding the array of entities at play in commissary contracts shows the enticing force of detention for communities, even where politicians and social groups are politically liberal or supportive of immigrant rights.

At the same time, detention's so-called "voluntary work programs" exploit detainee labor for a miniscule wage. While efforts to address these exploitative dynamics have grown, they frequently involve protracted legal battles that pit federal and state governments against one another and embroil corporations and advocacy groups in convoluted disputes.

By delving into the parasitic dynamics between detainee suffering, commissaries, and labor, we demonstrate how "immigration detention inc." actually *depends* on extracting from migrants. But since accumulating on migrants' backs drives detention, stalling or even halting these dynamics can perhaps start to unravel some of the dependencies on which stakeholders and policymakers rely.

DETENTION CONDITIONS THAT DRIVE DEMAND FOR HIGH-COST COMMISSARIES

"Multiple people noted that the only way to have enough to eat," revealed a 2012 independent report on detention at Hudson County, "is to buy extra food in the commissary and cook it on their own."[3] A 2019 DHS Inspector General's report on immigration detention at Essex jail said that: "Detainees [...] stated most of them now purchase their food through the commissary, which generally does not offer fresh meat and produce."[4]

Chronic hunger and deplorable day-to-day conditions drive migrant detainees to try to deal with the miseries of detention by turning to a facility's commissary. There, detainees can purchase a variety of items at inflated prices. A detainee places an order from a digital kiosk within a detention facility or they might use a paper and pencil format. Items are paid for by drawing on a detainee's commissary account. If the selected items are available, they are sent to the facility from a distribution center.

Beyond the inadequate food, several policies also appear designed to push detainees to buy food from the commissary. As stated in the detainee handbooks we reviewed, some facilities don't allow detainees to take food served to them to their cells to save for later. For most facilities, the *only* food allowed in dormitories is what can be purchased from the facility's commissary. Also, facilities typically do not offer snacks between meals. For example, as explained in Chapter 2, the policy written into Hudson's food contract states that three snacks a week *may* be provided to incentivize good behavior.

There can be unbearable gaps between meal times so detainees may need to supplement their calorie intake. The feeling among a lot of detainees, explains a New Jersey lawyer we interviewed, "is that that's done on purpose so you're forced to go to commissary and at commissary you're charged exorbitant prices."[5] Meal-time schedules also crop up as an issue elsewhere: a report on facilities in Texas notes that "in Texas's Jefferson County Jail, ICE requires the privately run jail to serve detained immigrants three meals per day, but, in a clear effort to keep attendance low and costs down, breakfast is served at 3:30 AM."[6] Our interviewees are not alone in pointing out how bad food and commissary purchases come together to create another way to profit from detainees.

Detainees turn to commissaries for more than just food. Detention facilities only provide minimal amounts of necessities for personal care—like toiletries—while health care is limited to basics at best. As a result, detainees frequently rely on commissaries to address health and personal care needs, even if in woefully inadequate ways.

Desperation pushes detainees to make commissary purchases. At the start of the coronavirus pandemic, a reporter noted that "In an effort to cut costs, for-profit detention centers ration out goods—like soap—with the expectation that detained people will buy more with money from their commissary accounts if they run out."[7] Around the same time, a report about the Hudson County Correctional Facility found "the facility [...] provided hand sanitizer for guards but not for detainees [... who] receive a single bar of soap for a week, both for showering and washing hands; if they want more, they must buy it from the prison commissary for $1.70."[8] In the same report, one migrant at the facility explained, "We started a hunger strike for them to give us toilet paper and soap—which is the most important—and hygiene supplies, like to clean our hands."

The goods detainees order from commissaries are *essential* to help alleviate hunger, cold, and ill health due to the conditions of their confinement. As one interviewee observed, "commissaries are a lifeline."[9]

THE HIGH COST OF RELYING ON COMMISSARIES

It is troubling to see exactly what kinds and quantities of items detainees buy from in-facility stores. Here, our public records requests provide important snapshots. Where we have received records of commissary sales—from Buffalo FDC and Orange County Correctional Facility, both in New York—there are striking patterns. Consistently, the top selling commissary items are ramen noodle beef or chicken soup, followed by beef and cheese sticks, and energy mix. Other popular items are hi-protein bars, peanut butter squeeze packs, and fish "steaks" in hot sauce.[10] These are not frivolous purchases; instead, detainees use commissaries to supplement the meager food and supplies provided.

Even more disturbing is the steep price that detainees pay for necessities. We compared prices for an assortment of basic items with the same items for sale in discount stores. Across almost every category, we found that commissary prices were between *four and seven times higher* than the same or similar products sold at Walmart. We also compared 2019 commissary prices at the Essex County facility with items sold at Target in 2019. Compared to prices outside detention, in the Essex County jail, a Hostess cupcake is 54 percent more expensive, at $0.57, compared to $0.37 per unit at Target. At the Bergen County facility, one AA battery costs $1.10, when a Target-brand AA battery costs $0.84 per unit in a package of 10—a 26 percent mark-up. The mark-up increases to 45 percent when compared with a 20-pack Target AA battery pack, which has a unit price of $0.65.

These mark-ups may be only cents per item. Still, they add up across multiple purchases—especially when these are for *necessities*—translating into revenue and real profits for commissary companies.

Such high commissary prices cannot be brushed off as an anomaly at a small number of facilities. Report after report highlights the high cost of commissary purchases, meaning that extortionate prices really are systemic. One report about lawsuits in several states, including California, Colorado, Texas, and Washington, showed that high-priced commissaries are commonplace. Similar to our price analysis, the investigation reviewed a copy of the "commissary price list [at the Adelanto facility in California] where detainees are charged $11.02 for a 4-ounce tube of Sensodyne toothpaste, which is available on Amazon.com for $5.20. Dove soap priced at $2.44 [costs] just over a dollar at Target. A 2.5-ounce tube of Effergrip denture cream that sells for $4.99 at Walmart is $7.12 at the commissary."[11]

Not only are the items for purchase overpriced, there are also costs associated with using commissary accounts. Every single deposit made into a commissary account incurs a fee. For instance, in Hudson County Correctional Facility, the 2021 fees were between $2.95 and $10.95 depending on the deposit amount and how deposits were made. Deposit fees add up, extracting money from detainees and their support networks even before they make a purchase. All-in-all, the costs associated with having to rely on commissaries for essentials add to the hardships and stress of being detained. These costs cascade beyond the facility and into the homes and communities of those impacted by detention.

It could be argued that, as businesses, there's a reasonable expectation for commissary providers to generate revenue for services they provide. However, the situation is more tangled than that, as other entities generate income from commissary contracts as well, in ways that spread a moral malaise and further cement an ethos of exploitation.

COMMISSION RATES AND COUNTY CONTRACTS

Scrutinizing commissaries lays bare the vicious cycle of unrelenting suffering that drives detainee reliance on in-facility stores. Significant dependencies are also produced at the scale of local governments; these become evident when we examine the contract bidding and evaluation process for commissary companies.

Commission rates are an important element of commissary contracts, and a key piece of the puzzle in understanding how "immigration detention inc." thrives, even in liberal states like New Jersey and New York. Basically, commissary Requests for Proposals (RFPs) stipulate that bids will not be considered unless they include a commission on sales for the facility operator. For instance, Hudson County's May 2021 RFP for a "full service commissary system for inmates" specifies that the contract will be awarded to the "highest responsible bidder," which here refers to "the fully responsible bidder who submits the highest percentage it is willing to pay the County on the Commissary Commission/ Service Fee and Electronic Deposit Commission."

The percentage size matters: at Essex County Correctional Facility, the memorandum of understanding for a two-year contract extension, from 2013 to 2015, with Keefe Commissary Network notes that the decision was "based on [the] highest percentage paid to Essex County [at] 48.2 percent." In fact, the commission rate is a key element in deciding which company is awarded a contract.

Hudson County records for the 2021 commissary bid evaluation indicate that "pricing of items and commissions" is worth 35 percent of the ranking. Other criteria listed are more formalities: "compliance with bid requirements" (35 percent), "organization and neatness of the proposal" (15 percent), and "references" (15 percent). What really matters when awarding commissary contracts is how much revenue the local government stands to gain.

We reviewed the commission rates for each of the four county jails in our investigation over a span of twenty years.[12] Currently, rates for the four jails are 15 percent (Essex County, NJ), 22 percent (Hudson County, NJ), 28 percent (Orange County, NY), and 30 percent (Bergen County, NJ). Rates on some previous contracts have been higher, for example, 42 percent (Hudson) and 48.2 percent (Essex). Keefe Commissary Network is the provider for all of them.

Despite these significant commission rates paid to county governments, goods are sold with such a massive mark-up that commissary operators still make a hefty profit. In 2019, the Private Equity Stakeholder Project noted that Keefe's 2012 financial statement "reported $375 million in total sales, with a net profit of $41 million. This equates to a 10.9 percent profit margin, much higher than most retailers—for example, three times that of Wal-Mart's 3 percent profit."[13] No matter the commission rate, detainees and their networks are fleeced, while commissaries provide a steady revenue stream from which private *and* public sectors benefit.

KEEFE, PRIVATE EQUITY, AND PROFITING FROM DETENTION

Keefe Commissary Network (KCN) is a significant player and a big winner when it comes to commissary contracts in New Jersey, New York, and the entire northeastern United States. Perhaps less obvious is that KCN is just one node in a tangled network of corporations, all of which gain from the privation and commodification of migrant detainees. To better understand this network, let's trace KCN's history and growth from a small independent company to member of a massive private equity firm.

Founded in 1975, the Keefe Supply Company pioneered the introduction of single-serve disposable food pouches to Florida prisons. Through the '90s and early 2000s, a number of affiliate companies—all involved in providing goods and services to the incarceration sector—were formed, under the umbrella name of Keefe Group. Keefe Commissary Network was established in 1993 to offer commissary services to prisons and detention centers. Advanced Tech Group (ATG) was set up in 1991 to provide software management systems, including for commissary funds and inmate financial transactions. Access Securepak, founded in 1997, provides an internal package delivery service, so families and friends can order and send items to inmates. Inmate Calling Solutions (ICS) was established in 2002, selling telecommunications products and related technology to carceral facilities. 2006 saw the founding of Access Corrections, a technical platform to enable and monitor financial transactions within facilities. After 2004, Keefe Group engaged in a series of acquisitions and mergers through which it gained an ever tighter grip on both the economy and financialization of prisons and detention.

Keefe Group's growth as a network of companies expanded its market and, by extension, control of the "consumer discretionary sector" in prison and detention, as described by Bloomberg financial news and information company. In 2016, Keefe Group merged with food service and commissary provider Trinity Services Group (profiled in Chapter 2), the subject of numerous complaints about the quality of food detainees receive. These two Groups, plus a company called Courtesy Products, became TKC Holdings, based in St. Louis, Missouri. At the time of the merger, one report estimated that the companies would take in "more than half of the total $1.6 billion commissary market."[14] TKC, the same report notes, "is clearly the largest commissary company that has ever existed."[15]

The carceral corporate network doesn't end there. TKC Holdings is part of a portfolio of investments controlled by the private equity firm H.I.G. Capital, which also owns the corrections healthcare company Wellpath (described in Chapter 3), so this global financial investment company has a stake in practically every dimension of detention infrastructure. "H.I.G. has one of the most unusual side hustles of any private equity firm" notes journalist Tim Requarth,

"Over the decade, it has quietly helped consolidate correctional phone, food, commissary, and health-care companies into behemoths that dominate their markets and, according to critics, drive prices up for families while lowering quality."[16]

H.I.G. Capital was founded in 1993, with U.S. headquarters in Miami. The firm has investments in over four hundred companies in the U.S., Europe, Latin America, and the Middle East. According to its website, H.I.G. Capital is a "leading global alternative investment firm with $67 billion of equity capital under management," whose primary goal is to manage investments in order to optimize value and return profit for investors; to do so, H.I.G. looks to "consistently drive attractive returns for our investors."[17]

Private equity firms play an increasing role in the U.S. and global economy. A 2023 report notes that private equity companies have made up more than one-third of merger and acquisition activity in the U.S. recently, with deals valued at more than $1 trillion in the year 2022.[18] These firms link investors—who may be individuals with significant wealth, or institutions, including entities such as pension funds, banks, and insurance companies—with opportunities to invest. They use different strategies to generate returns, including leveraging debt or introducing changes to how a company operates or is governed. Typically, the life cycle for investment and return on a given portfolio is ten years. So, a company may be managed quite aggressively, in investment terms, for a period of three to seven years, after which the portfolio is sold off to reap benefits for its investors.

Although private equity firms generate high returns and are understood to contribute to economic growth, they are problematic for several reasons. Precisely because they are investments, the focus is on generating value and profit, *not* on the possible consequences for employees or the services that companies provide. Media reports highlight mixed impacts.[19] Where tangible products are involved, management by private equity professionals can bring increases in productivity, more product offerings, and geographic expansion. But where services are connected to "social interests"—care homes or detention facilities, for example—the available evidence suggests fewer improvements.[20]

Private equity firms are known to take advantage of a host of tax breaks and tax avoidance mechanisms to benefit investors and fund managers, which result in lost revenue for the federal government.[21] One estimate suggests that every year, the United States loses $75 billion from investors in partnerships failing to report their income accurately.[22] Another report concludes that private equity firms "can lead to reduced public revenue, widening income inequality, and short term investment strategies."[23] Private equity firms are complex and amorphous entities, involving multiple layers of partnerships and potentially thousands of direct and indirect partners or investors. This makes monitoring them and their compliance with tax and other regulations exceedingly challenging. Private equity firms are also bolstered by a substantial political lobby protecting their interests.[24]

When it comes to detention, several characteristics of private equity firms—their complex structures, impenetrability, tendency to avert accountability, and lobbying influence—mean that H.I.G can avoid scrutiny of how they have exacerbated detainees' degradation and exploitation.[25]

Corporations and investment firms influence detainees' and inmates' experiences in jails and detention centers in messy, murky ways. Consider New York's Orange County Correctional Facility. In Orange County, Keefe Commissary Network is the commissary provider. Though Aramark currently has the food service contract, Trinity Services Group had it until 2022.[26] Keefe and Trinity are companies within TKC Holdings, which, in turn, is owned and managed by H.I.G. Capital. This corporation soup helps to hide the fact that *these companies are related.*

By not providing adequate food, Trinity saved on its bottom line, but also helped to boost revenue for Keefe, as well as medical service provider Wellpath. One could even say that they are vertically integrated: lobbying for laws to incarcerate more migrants, who are sickened and starved by one entity within the corporation, and then, when they seek to buy food or medicine, are ripped off by another. Ultimately, this manufactured dependency benefits none other than H.I.G. and its army of invisible investors.[27]

CAPTIVE CONSUMERS, EXPLOITABLE LABOR, AND "VOLUNTARY" WORK PROGRAMS

Ill-provisioned detained migrants are driven to use commissaries, in a cycle that produces willing, and, at times, desperate, "captive consumers,"[28] who need access to money in detention. Some detainees have their own money, which is placed into that person's commissary account. Some have family and friends who can send money to their accounts (with a transaction fee, of course). Without these funds, or when they run out, detainees may be in dire need of opportunities to earn more. Enter detention facilities' "voluntary work programs." If commissaries are a lifeline, voluntary work programs offer a sick kind of life support system.

Most facilities offer work "opportunities" to detainees. The 2013 Essex County jail Detainee Handbook notes that "All individuals who are detained at the Essex County Correctional Facility are eligible on a voluntary basis for available ICE Detainee worker openings." It goes on to characterize participating in voluntary work programs as a privilege: "Work is a privilege that may be rescinded for not reporting for work, appearing in an unsanitary condition, or performing unsatisfactorily." For this "privilege," detained migrants earn $1.00 per day. A small fraction of jobs such as barbering are considered "special work details," which can pay up to $3.00 per day. Nonetheless, on the whole, a detained migrant working eight hours is paid on average roughly just *12 cents per hour.*

How can this be legal? It's because this rate of pay was set when voluntary work programs (VWPs) originated in 1950. Adjusted for inflation, $1.00 a day in 1950 was equivalent to a rate of pay of $13.00 a day in 2024. Despite numerous challenges in the courts under the Fair Labor Standards Act (for example, in 1990), the $1.00-per-day wage has remained unchanged in most detention facilities since its introduction.[29] Still, there are a few facilities where detainees and advocates have fought extended legal battles that have resulted in changes to work programs; we examine some of these lawsuits below.

Despite the absurd rate of compensation, many detainees feel compelled to participate. As one interviewee pointed out "what can you even do with one dollar! [...] But there, there, when you are in need, when you do not have money for a water, then one dollar is useful."[30] Migrants are also incentivized to work in detention with offers of extra food; for instance, our review of Hudson County records shows that individuals who labor in the facility's kitchen may receive double meals.

Jobs available for detained migrants include working in housing units doing cleaning and maintenance of dorms and common areas; laundry; kitchen work doing meal preparation, cleaning, and runner roles; and law library and barbershop assistants. Typically, shifts are eight hours per day, with morning (a.m.) and afternoon/evening (p.m.) shifts. In principle, individuals are allowed to work a total of 40 hours or five days per week.

Detained migrants are required to sign agreements that stipulate punctuality, dress code and appearance, and satisfactory work performance. These expectations are also reinforced in detainee handbooks, where detainees are made aware that refusing to complete an assigned task as part of the VWP represents a disciplinary violation. The consequences for violations may include expulsion from the program as well as "loss of privileges" such as recreation time or access to TV for up to five days, through to "disciplinary segregation" (otherwise known as solitary confinement).

As you can imagine, this work is often difficult, taxing, and tedious. A former detainee in a facility in Essex County, NJ explained, "those that work have to work very hard. For cleaning, start at 7 a.m. For kitchen, start at 6 a.m.—they help cook, then clean in kitchen and in eating area, finish breakfast at about 10 a.m., then at 11:30 have to come back for lunch, repeat, then have to work again for dinner."[31]

Inspection reports by DHS's own Office of Inspector General (OIG) call out how working conditions exploit migrants. For example, a 2023 inspection of a Virginia detention facility "determined that eight kitchen volunteers worked hours that exceeded the 40-hour work week limit. One detainee worked more than 65 hours in one week and as long as 14 hours in a single day. Another detainee averaged 56 hours of work per week during a six-week period (until the detainee left the facility)."[32] Detainees also expressed concerns that "recreation time was canceled because it was scheduled at the same time as [the] kitchen shift." The report noted that areas of the facility, such as the kitchen, were understaffed, and as a result "the facility sometimes required detainees to work more hours than the prescribed maximum, in violation of the standards."

ICE's response to this report illustrates how the agency perceives detained migrants to be an expandable and exploitable labor pool. ICE rejected the OIG report's recommendation for additional assessment to ensure that facility needs can be met without detainees working more than eight hours per day or 40 hours per week. In their response, ICE stated that the facility makes every effort to ensure compliance within the parameters set out in detention standards but "due to the limited number of cleared volunteers the facility may experience a temporary shortage [… and] this may necessitate longer shifts."[33] ICE also identified newly implemented measures to expand the category of detained migrants so that those classified as "non-violent, medium-high detainees" are now allowed to do kitchen work, speeding up processes for "clearing" volunteer kitchen workers, and "identifying potential volunteer kitchen workers during intake" in order to expedite clearance processes. The OIG's analysis of the ICE response notes that "ICE openly disregards" standards related to the VWP, which "is designed to provide detainees opportunities to work and earn money while confined, not to augment facility staffing shortages."[34] But the OIG could do nothing further to force ICE's compliance.

We see that detained migrants are not only deprived within the detention system, but simultaneously commodified and exploited as consumers and as workers. In other words, a pernicious cycle operates, reaping benefits from detaining and depriving migrants and then using those migrants to keep facilities going—even while saving on costs, generating revenue, and, ultimately, turning a profit—all at migrants' expense.

SAVING ON LABOR COSTS

Earlier we saw figures on some of the revenue that detention generates for county governments, and additional benefits accrue from commissary contracts. Through voluntary work programs, contractors, including local governments, save massively on labor costs associated with running detention facilities. Although specific details about detention facility staffing and wages are often redacted from publicly available documents, we can piece together different sources of information to develop a picture of labor cost savings from work programs. The contract between ICE and Core Civic for operation of the Elizabeth detention facility was originally put in place in 2005, and has been continuously extended. The contract and every extension include a lengthy list that details Labor Law Wage Determination policy (wage determination under the Service Contract Act) and lists pay rates for different jobs.

In 2018, which was the most recent contract we were able to access, the lowest wage is $9.49 per hour for a dishwasher, while a detention officer's hourly wage is listed as $34.40 per hour. When we consider the $1.00-per-day wages that detained migrants receive alongside these mandated wage rates, a jarring irony is apparent. While contract requirements ensure that labor regulations are adhered to for non-detained staff, detained migrants are routinely excluded from the very same regulatory framework.

Taking this a step further shows—even more starkly—the injustice that migrant detainees endure. While numbers for wages paid out to detainees are almost entirely redacted in the Elizabeth facility's contracts, one number left visible is the monthly costs associated with payments to detained migrants. That figure is $1,500 per month (it's noteworthy that this amount has remained the same since the 2005 contract was signed). If we break this figure down to what it would equate to in terms of detention officer hourly rate (aligning with federal Labor Law), $1,500 would pay for less than one week—just 23 hours—of a detention officer's salary. And yet, it pays the *entirety of monthly wages for an undisclosed number of detained migrants* employed in Elizabeth's VWP.

One human rights organization employee we interviewed estimated that at one facility in New Jersey, the savings on labor represent about $5–6 million per year.[35] And the bulk of the paltry wages that detainees receive go back to contractors through commissary sales.[36] In other words, the $1,500 on that contract represent much more than just savings on payroll costs. Detention work programs also ensure that detained migrants are able to access the commissary—where they pay dearly for essential items.

Contractors that increase profits through cheap detainee labor smooth over the inherent injustice operating here, claiming that allegations of exploitation are "completely false." In the words of one GEO Group spokesperson, "the labor program is strictly voluntary and wage rates are federally mandated."[37]

PUSHING BACK AGAINST THE CYCLE OF EXPLOITATION

From what this chapter has shown so far—a cycle where every need becomes an opportunity for commodification, detention conditions produce a vulnerable labor force, and corporations, private equity firms, and local governments stand to gain—it certainly appears that extraction and exploitation are unshakably entrenched in the detention system.

It is remarkable, then, how many challenges—and some successes—have taken place in the last few years. A groundswell of advocacy and action has denounced the iniquity of detention work programs and called for justice for detainees, who themselves have protested their conditions broadly, and demonstrated against $1.00-a-day wages with hunger strikes.[38]

In addition, lawsuits across the U.S. have exposed the system's injustices, as well as how contractors try to "work" the legal system to their advantage. Importantly, digging into the arguments in these lawsuits demonstrates both opportunities and obstacles in breaking the extractive logic of commissaries and labor, as well as in immigrant detention more generally.

Voluntary work programs and labor laws

In the last decade alone, at least eight lawsuits about detainee labor have been brought against private contractors operating detention facilities.[39] The first, in 2014, was brought against GEO Group, and by individuals who were being held at Colorado's Aurora Detention facility. Then, in 2018, a lawsuit was filed against CoreCivic centered on work programs at the Stewart Detention Center in rural Georgia. Next, lawsuits modeled on the Aurora case were filed regarding two facilities in Texas: the Laredo Detention Center and T. Don Hutto Residential Center, again against CoreCivic.[40] In late 2017 and in 2018, lawsuits were initiated at two California facilities: Adelanto in the Mojave Desert, which is run by GEO Group, and Otay Mesa, near San Diego, run by CoreCivic. In a 2020 lawsuit, individuals detained at the Buffalo detention center filed against facility operator Akima Global Services.

To date, lawsuits against detention providers have been based on three issues: 1) the provider violated the Trafficking Victims Protection Act (TVPA), legislation that protects against forced, fraudulent, or coerced labor; 2) the provider violated state minimum wage laws, and 3) the provider has gained "unjust enrichment," which relates to profit at another's expense without fair compensation. Not every lawsuit claims all three issues; however, each case accuses private entities running detention facilities of unjust enrichment, which highlights the cruel and corrupt logic underpinning voluntary work programs.

The 2014 Aurora, Colorado case was the first lawsuit of this kind. Nine named individuals along with "others similarly situated" brought a class action complaint against GEO Group.[41] Specifically, their claim was based on both unpaid labor and labor at just $1 per day. Both kinds of work were performed in the facility's "volunteer work program"; and yet, as the lawsuit noted, the facility's own handbook stated that detainees would be punished with solitary confinement if they didn't participate in what the detainees called "mandatory housekeeping crews."[42] The lawsuit argued that GEO Group violated the Trafficking Victims Protection Act (TVPA) and that GEO Group was "unjustly enriched" as a result of the program. A subsequent motion allowed the case to go forward as a civil class action lawsuit, involving up to 60,000 members.[43]

The Aurora lawsuit has been going back and forth in Colorado courts for several years, with GEO Group repeatedly contesting aspects of the case, including its status as a class action suit and whether or not a jury trial is warranted.[44] GEO Group's critique of the class action aspect is revealing. The company noted that to certify the case as a class action lawsuit "poses a potentially catastrophic risk to GEO's ability to honor its contracts with the federal government."[45] This statement could be read as a veiled threat, such that bringing the case forward would leave the federal government high and dry with its massive population of migrant detainees. But it *also* makes clear that, without VWPs, running detention facilities simply would not be viable for companies like GEO Group.

Arguably, one of the most successful suits to date was initiated in 2017 by the Washington State Attorney General's Office. This suit also targeted GEO Group in its operation of the Northwest ICE Processing Center (NWIPC), the fourth largest in the country.[46] The suit argued that GEO Group violated Washington State's minimum wage laws, as "civil detainees […] essentially run the facility."[47] A first trial resulted in a deadlocked jury in 2021. But at a second trial, the jury sided with the Attorney General's Office—that GEO Group violated Washington's minimum wage laws—and, like the case at the Aurora facility, GEO Group was "unjustly enriched" in connection with the facility's work program. Consequently, GEO Group was ordered to back pay detainees $17.3 million, along with a $5.9 million award to the state.[48] Subsequently, GEO Group suspended the facility's work program.[49]

Predictably, the corporation appealed the decision to the Ninth U.S. Circuit Court of Appeals, which then sought the opinion of the State Supreme Court. In December 2023, the Washington Supreme Court issued their unanimous opinion and rejected GEO Group's contention that, like the facilities owned or run by state, county, or municipal authorities, GEO Group is *also* exempt from following State minimum wage regulations.[50] Deciding against the corporation, the Washington Supreme Court noted that NWIPC is a private facility, even though it operates under a federal contract.[51] The court's written opinion noted, "If the legislature intended to also exclude persons detained in private institutions, it would have done so explicitly."[52]

GEO Group claimed the ruling would cost them $3.4 million, yet their annual profits at NWIPC are between $18.6 and $23.5 million.[53] Following the State Supreme Court's opinion, GEO Group appealed. Subsequently, the work program at the facility was terminated. Complaints mounted about deteriorating food and hygiene conditions, and the company repeatedly blocked access to the facility by state inspectors.[54] On January 16, 2025 the Ninth U.S. Circuit Court of Appeals affirmed the earlier judgement by the Washington Supreme Court, which means GEO

Group is required to pay all workers, including detained migrants who participate in the VWP, at least Washington State's minimum wage.[55] Predictably, GEO Group responded stating "The company strongly disagrees with the court's decision and intends to pursue all available avenues of appeal."[56]

Another ongoing lawsuit argues violation of labor rights in New York State. At the Buffalo Service Processing Center, operated by Akima Global Services (AGS), two formerly detained individuals, represented by a legal aid and advocacy group, filed a complaint similar to the case filed by the Washington State Attorney General's Office.[57] The case states that AGS is in violation of a number of sections of New York Labor Law, including minimum wage, provision of contract information, and weekly pay stubs.[58] In the Buffalo facility, moreover, the measly $1.00-a-day payment was only given as commissary credits and not as a cash deposit, binding detained migrants' labor even further into this abusive dynamic. One plaintiff in the case noted that "she and others provided 'basically free' labor [... that] is bordering on slavery."[59]

These cases "turn their [i.e. contracted providers'] profits upside down" notes Andrew Free, an attorney who was involved with several detention labor lawsuits: "It would be a money-losing enterprise if they had to pay the people to operate this facility under the current contract."[60] In short, when possibilities for exploitation are removed, the system becomes unsustainable. We see that targeting such work programs—and corporate profit more broadly—not only has the potential to end corporate involvement in detention but could also open the door to ending detention entirely.

Contractor work-arounds and state and federal responses

Worryingly, it is apparent that contractors are adapting their legal defense of labor programs, presumably on the basis of earlier lawsuits, and attempting to cherry-pick regulations and legal frameworks.

In the Washington State case against GEO Group, for instance, the State Supreme Court ruled that private contractors are not exempt from minimum wage labor regulations in the same way as state prisons, local jails, and other government-run sites of confinement. Subsequently, in the case against AGS about detainee wages in the Buffalo facility, the contractor identified a workaround: arguing that the site where the Buffalo detention center is located, from a legal perspective, can be considered an "enclave." The "enclave clause," which is set out in the U.S. Constitution, gives the federal government legislative authority over "all places purchased by the consent of the legislature of the state in which the same shall be, for the erection of Forts, Magazines, Arsenals, Dock-Yards, and other needful Buildings."[61] AGS is claiming that the Buffalo facility is part of an enclave, therefore the private provider operating within is subject to federal regulations, but exempt from any state laws that may be inconsistent with "federal purposes."[62] On these grounds, AGS is claiming to be exempt from New York State minimum wage regulations.

Such an argument is noteworthy, as it pits state and federal governments against each other. Moreover, it exposes how much power private detention corporations assume they have, and, indeed, have been granted at all levels.

Similar kinds of legal battles are becoming more common across various campaigns to end immigration detention. For example, after Governor Phil Murphy signed into law the 2021 state ban on detention contracts in New Jersey, CoreCivic, the federally contracted provider at the Elizabeth detention facility, filed a lawsuit against the New Jersey State government. In that suit, remarkably, the federal Department of Justice (under the Biden administration) submitted a statement *supporting* CoreCivic. In the District Court ruling on the matter—which ultimately enabled CoreCivic to renew its Elizabeth contract with ICE—Judge Robert Kirsch sided with the company, noting that "states passing similar laws would 'result in nothing short of chaos.'"[63]

Likewise, California's ban on private immigration detention centers, signed into law in 2019, was struck down in September 2022.[64] This occurred because GEO Group and the first Trump and later Biden administrations challenged the ban.[65] In their appeal, GEO Group argued that it stood to lose "an average of $250 million a year in revenue if its facilities had been forced to close."[66] The Ninth Circuit Court's ruling observed "ICE has decided to rely almost exclusively on privately owned and operated facilities in California."⁶⁷ By banning private contractors, the court decided, the state government would interfere with the federal government and "California cannot exert this level of control over the federal government's detention operations."⁶⁸

Such legal developments demonstrate that any effort to institute change—whether to improve conditions or to ban migrant detention—involves protracted legal battles and many setbacks. In this context, it's important to acknowledge smaller steps towards justice.

In this vein, in 2023, California passed legislation aimed at reducing unfairness and price gouging by prison commissary providers. The BASIC Act sets a limit of 35 percent on mark-ups on items for sale at commissaries until 2028 and, after that, the California Department of Corrections will set commissary prices. This law follows legislation introduced in 2019 that eliminated commissary mark-ups in San Francisco jails.⁶⁹ Recently, the state governments of Nevada and Massachusetts instituted caps on price mark-ups on hygiene and other items sold at commissaries.⁷⁰ Developments like these work toward reeling in contractors like Keefe, alongside efforts to make detention's big players, like CoreCivic and GEO Group, more accountable.

Considering the consequences for advocacy and activism

Detention contractors view detained migrants as captive consumers *and* as extremely cheap laborers. Without this arrangement, the revenue, profit, and power that contractors—as well as different government entities—gain from detention simply would not be possible. Because of this, contractors aggressively fight efforts not only to end detention but also efforts to improve conditions for detainees. As we've shown, contractors contest initiatives ranging from instituting more reasonable prices in commissary stores to campaigns for a fair wage and better labor conditions. They employ tactics like pitting state and federal governments against each other, and stretching obscure definitions in existing law. In effect, contractors attempt to wield government and legal structures for their own gain.

Given the ferocity and flexibility of the private sector's strategies to defend its bottom line, advocacy and activism campaigns must not only target for-profit private contractors. Outreach efforts also need to, for instance, force transparency about how the federal government expands the warehousing of detainees through private contracts. Publicity campaigns could do more to spread information about how detainees are forced into slave-like labor arrangements. Advocates should increase public awareness of how local governments cash in on detainee suffering, via commission rates from commissary contracts. Recent successes with detention labor lawsuits and legislative changes that limit commissary mark-ups show the importance of holding local, state, and federal government agencies to account, as well as the need for lobbying efforts within state legislative bodies.

It *is* possible to break these cycles of utter exploitation. To achieve changes, we must follow the money, unraveling the knots of economic dependence at the heart of "immigration detention inc." We return to these and other strategies for dismantling detention in more detail in Chapter 6.

5

The Accountability Industry: Rubber-stamping Bad Care

Previous chapters have shown the remarkable deprivation forced onto detainees, and the extraordinary lengths that officials, facility operators, and businesspeople go to hide that violence. Even when detainees do manage to lodge complaints about their treatment through legally required systems of redress, their complaints are often dismissed or ignored.

Consider the Hudson County, New Jersey detention facility. During a 2011 inspection by ICE's Office of Detention Oversight (ODO), three detainees complained of being denied medical treatment. In response, ODO reviewed the detainees' medical records, but did not gather their own evidence. The inspection report simply parroted the medical records, stating that one detainee rejected medical treatment, while the other two received treatment that was documented in their medical records. Similarly, a 2017 inspection report of the Hudson facility noted that "One detainee reported she has a tumor on top of brain, gets headaches with dizziness and the nurse only tells her to keep still and lie down." In the "Action Taken" paragraph that followed, the report succinctly explained that a review of the detainee's medical record and interview with the medical director showed that the detainee's complaint was unwarranted, and that her medical care was being handled appropriately.

Other examples abound, from detention centers all over the country, of inspectors flatly rejecting the statements of detainees, instead accepting—as unquestionably valid—the documents compiled by those doing the detaining. The blanket acceptance of existing records as corroboration for officials' narratives over detainees' is nonsensical and dangerous, given the history of poor record-keeping and falsification of records throughout the detention system. Even when called in to perform their duty of inspection, ICE personnel simply rubber-stamp their approval.

This chapter digs into how the systems meant to provide oversight and protect detainees—minimum detention standards, inspections, grievance procedures, and facility accreditations—supply only illusions of accountability, while masking poor care and institutionalizing migrant exploitation.

NATIONAL DETENTION STANDARDS

All detention facilities are supposed to adhere (or, at least, *appear* to adhere) to some version of the National Detention Standards (NDS). These are government-defined guidelines regarding many aspects of detention management and operation, including—among other things—safety, security, detainee rights, food provision, and medical care. They are woefully inadequate.

As noted in earlier chapters, the minimal conditions that the NDS require are shameful: they insist on minimum amounts of daily calories below what is healthy, response times that are far longer than needed for almost any medical emergency, and a wage of $1 per day that would be disgraceful on its own, let alone the fact that, in the "Voluntary Work Program," such labor is functionally mandated. Moreover, the basis for many of the detention standards were standards written and used earlier by the American Correctional Association (ACA), again showing the indistinguishable line between U.S. immigration detention and incarceration industries. Given all this, the NDS are a sham that authorize injustice.

And yet, even if these cruel standards *were* strictly followed, the conditions of forced confinement would be more humane and bearable than they generally are in many detention facilities. Because, as with the ACA standards in prisons, there is often a wide gulf between standards on paper, and how they are implemented in reality.

This is why we find it significant when detention standards are *not* met, showing that facilities (and ICE in general) do not have the will or ability to follow even such bare bones guidelines. These mixed feelings about detention standards mean that we sometimes disparage them and at other times complain that they are not being followed. In other words, while detention standards are insufficient and weak, at least they provide some type of guardrails. Yet even these are regularly broken.

The NDS have evolved since they were first defined. The first version, known as the National Detention Standards, was released in 2000. In 2008, they were renamed the Performance-Based National Detention Standards (PBNDS), and revised to be more detailed, specific, and rights-focused. The PBNDS were revised again in 2011, with some additions in 2016, to become the most rigorous set of written standards yet.

But the mere existence of the PBNDS did not mean that all contracted facilities had to follow them. While newly-contracted facilities did have to agree to this more rigorous set of standards, facilities with pre-existing contracts were not forced to adopt them. The American Immigration Council noted that "DHS' only justification for continuing to use the NDS 2000 when extending its contract with Laredo Processing Center [in Texas] in 2018 was that the facility would charge more per detained individual under the stronger standards."[1] Clearly, price was more important than better, more tolerable conditions and care.

Then, in 2019, during the first administration of President Donald Trump, ICE issued "updated" standards; once again these were referred to as the National Detention Standards. The ICE website explained the 2019 NDS as "streamlined" to "eliminate or greatly reduce a number of prior standards based on ICE's experience with local law enforcement partners and the understanding that existing local practices appropriately cover some of these requirements."[2] In other words, the 2019 NDS are supposed to be less cumbersome for detention operators, and, consequently, make it easier for ICE to find new detention facilities.

The 2019 NDS are significantly less detailed than the 2011 PBNDS. For example, the 2019 food guidelines are just 10 pages long, down from 24 pages in the 2011 PBNDS. The medical guidelines are just 12 pages instead of 25. These changes therefore indicate a substantial reduction in ICE's scrutiny of detention facilities. The new NDS don't just "streamline" the previous standards. In fact, they significantly weaken them.[3]

A 2018 report from the National Immigrant Justice Center found that just 65 percent of ICE adult facilities adhere to *any* version of the NDS.[4] The remaining 35 percent are facilities that follow another set of standards; these include the ACA accreditation guidelines, Department of Justice standards for prisons, standards devised by ICE's predecessor the Immigration and Naturalization Service, or even just, as the report explained, "the vaguely worded 'minimum service standards,' 'local standards,' or [...] 'COR Detention Standards' which refer to the Contracting Officer Representative and pertain to enforcement of the technical aspects of a facility's contract rather than conditions inside the jail."

Possibly one of the biggest problems with detention standards—whatever version a particular facility is supposed to use—is how they are manipulated, together with ICE facility inspections and the trussed-up complaint system, to make it *appear* as though the detention system consistently follows fair and compassionate guidelines.

ICE INSPECTIONS

For many years, ICE has conducted periodic inspections of its detention facilities, supposedly assessing how individual facilities follow National Detention Standards.[5] Routinely, these inspections yield reports finding that facilities meet nearly all standards. Thereafter, the ICE reports are cited as evidence of appropriate care and conditions, providing the appearance that the nation's detention network is a well-administered and organized system deserving of additional funding.

But, as discussed extensively in previous chapters, it is clear that, in reality, "passing" ratings in ICE inspection reports often translate to poor and sometimes abusive care, unsafe conditions, routine sickness and unnecessary pain, denial of rights, and profiting off detainees. We contend that inspections are also part of the money-making machine that ensures detention's entrenchment. ICE's repeated failure to address any standards violations that *are* identified shows the agency is not committed to real quality assurance or improving detention conditions.

Two inspectors, one problem

As part of its detention oversight, ICE has administered two primary types of inspections to assess compliance with National Detention Standards.[6] One type has been done by the ICE Enforcement and Removal Operations' (ERO) Office of Custody Management, contracting with a private company to inspect facilities that detain immigrants for more than 72 hours. From 2007 to 2022, that contracted company was the Nakamoto Group.[7] The second type of inspection is through ICE's Office of Professional Responsibility—a unit within ICE distinct from the ERO—which has an Office of Detention Oversight (ODO). ODO employs its own lead inspectors, and contracts with the company Creative Corrections to provide additional inspectors.

The ODO inspections were originally meant to do more thorough inspections on a smaller number of standards. Until 2018, ODO inspections of any given facility occurred approximately every three years. Then, in 2018, the Department of Homeland Security released a report by its Office of the Inspector General (OIG), tellingly titled "ICE's Inspections and Monitoring of Detention Facilities Do Not Lead to Sustained Compliance or Systemic Improvements."[8] Simultaneously, Congressional hearings found many problems with the ERO inspections conducted by Nakamoto. And so, in 2019, Congress allocated $6.9 million to ODO to improve its inspections program by investigating each facility twice per year beginning in 2021.[9] It appears that ERO—and Nakamoto—have not done any inspections since 2022.[10]

We have reviewed dozens of ICE inspection reports (both ERO and ODO) for the six facilities in our study.[11] Typically, facilities sail through these inspections, usually passing with "acceptable," "adequate," or "meets standard" ratings in every category.[12] Occasionally, an inspection report identifies a small number of issues; yet even these are often noted in the report as already having been addressed. This pattern is consistent with all facilities in the detention system.

However, as discussed in previous chapters, nearly all other assessments of facility conditions and detainee experiences starkly contrast with the picture presented in ICE inspection reports (whether ERO's or ODO's). "Inspections are designed to facilitate passing ratings for facilities," explains a 2015 independent report, "not identify or address violations."[13] When inspected by ICE, facilities almost never fail. This blanket approval is extended to facilities and companies no matter what the conditions or what has occurred there, including detainee deaths.[14]

A number of governmental and nongovernmental entities have been probing and criticizing ICE's inspections for years. One source of scrutiny is the DHS OIG, which has conducted unannounced inspections of facilities, although infrequently. The surprise inspections of two facilities in our study (Essex and Elizabeth) document remarkably different conditions than those indicated in ICE inspection reports, even when conducted within weeks of each other.

In 2017, ICE's ERO inspected the Essex County Jail, reporting that all medical care "Meets Standard," and giving a nearly glowing summary of perfect compliance. Yet soon after that positive report, the OIG conducted an unannounced inspection that found multiple egregious violations, in all areas of facility conditions, care, and safety; some of these were detailed in Chapters 2 and 3.[15] The OIG has also published critical reports documenting problems with ICE inspections and oversight more generally, system-wide.[16]

Additionally, the Government Accountability Office (which conducts investigations for the U.S. Congress) has recently focused on ICE inspections, with reports conveying alarm in 2021, 2022, and 2023.[17] The Office of Senator Elizabeth Warren also conducted its own investigations of detention inspections.[18] In 2019, 2020, and 2022, a series of Congressional hearings were held on detention standards and inspections by the House of Representatives' Committee on Homeland Security.[19] Serious misrepresentations in ICE inspections reports have also been uncovered by nongovernmental organizations (NGOs), such as the American Civil Liberties Union, Detention Watch Network, and National Immigrant Justice Center.[20]

These investigations identified the ERO inspections as particularly poor, as noted above. A 2018 report by the DHS Inspector General quotes ICE employees who "described Nakamoto inspections as being 'very, very, very difficult to fail.'"[21] Indeed, the Nakamoto Group likely understood that the ERO wanted facilities to pass; Nakamoto took over ICE inspections after the previous inspections company, MGT of America, Inc., failed a detention facility. At that time, ICE essentially voided the MGT inspection, stripped MGT of the contract, and awarded it to Nakamoto.

All this gave Nakamoto a clear message: "Failure was not an option."[22] Predictably, Nakamoto listened. There is substantial evidence that the ERO inspections done by Nakamoto were not thorough or serious, and that they attempted to review too many standards in too short of a time.[23] In our review of inspection reports of the facilities in our study, we found instances of cutting and pasting identical text from report to report, with facility names not changed, and whole descriptive passages copied from one report to another.

One primary reason behind the ERO inspections' superficial nature is that they were impossibly broad in scope. As explained by the OIG:

> Under its Statement of Work (SOW) with ICE, Nakamoto must determine compliance with all 39 to 42 applicable detention standards by examining more than 650 elements of the standards at more than 100 facilities a year. Typically, three to five inspectors have only 3 days to complete the inspection, interview 85 to 100 detainees, brief facility staff, and begin writing their inspection report for ICE.[24]

This means that Nakamoto inspectors were not only under pressure to complete their inspections and reports in a very short time, but were also under pressure to cut corners.

A particularly grim indication of the more extreme "rubber-stamp" approach of ERO inspectors, as compared to ODO inspectors, is evident in an NGO account comparing these agencies' reports after detainee deaths. The NGO account examined the causes of the 56 deaths in detention that happened between January

2010 and May 2012, with in-depth examination of eight. Remarkably, in seven of these eight cases, when ODO noted issues with the medical care that may have contributed to the deaths, "ICE ERO inspectors gave facilities passing ratings prior to and following deaths related to egregiously substandard medical care."[25] For example, the account evaluated ICE reports assessing a 2011 death in the Elizabeth facility, and found that ERO and ODO reports drew "mutually inconsistent conclusions about the quality of care at Elizabeth."[26] ERO's assessment, just three weeks after the death, indicated no problems with medical standards at the facility. The ODO report, conducted three months later, found 22 violations. Other accounts exist of facilities passing ERO inspections with flying colors, even if closely before or after a detainee death.[27]

Given that ODO inspections are generally more accurate and comparatively less of an automatic pass than those done by ERO/Nakamoto, making the ODO the primary inspection agency, and essentially firing Nakamoto, was a positive step. But only a small one. A 2023 assessment by the National Immigrant Justice Center found that the shift to ODO has still failed to solve many of the existing problems with inspections.[28]

The persistent failure of the inspection system

ICE's inspection system is riddled with fundamental flaws that cannot be fixed by simply switching agencies. For example, ODO inspections are announced in advance,[29] so facilities have time to make things look good for the inspectors.[30] NGO reports include accounts of detainees who said that the food they were served on inspection days was vastly different from what they were served normally.

Facilities have also simply eliminated evidence of substandard care. Medical care company Wellpath employees, interviewed by a CNN team in 2019, described medical requests that were hidden or shredded.[31] Some detainees have experienced retaliation—such as being locked up in solitary confinement—for telling journalists and inspectors about conditions in their facility.[32] Such retribution undoubtedly makes many detainees reluctant to speak truthfully.

Others weren't even given that choice. Before inspections, certain detainees were removed from view, such as those with obviously improperly treated medical problems, and those who frequently complained about medical care.³³ One report told of detainees being drugged against their will during facility inspections and locked in areas not visited by inspectors, preventing them from being asked about or providing visual evidence of conditions and treatment.³⁴

Clearly, most ICE inspections are superficial at best. But this negligence was on full display in 2020, when, for roughly the first year of the COVID-19 pandemic, ICE inspections went remote. Inspectors, instead of physically entering facilities, reviewed documents prepared by facility managers, asked questions of managers, and spoke to a small number of detainees by video conference or phone. As might be imagined, these remote inspection reports show that the inspectors found very little wrong at every facility—at the exact same time as independent organizations and journalists were publishing detailed accounts of alarming conditions, widespread infection, and record numbers of deaths. In fact, the New Jersey jails in our study were national hotspots for the virus.³⁵

Also, as noted earlier, in 2019 the revised National Detention Standards significantly weakened requirements for facilities. Those that have adopted the 2019 NDS (including Orange County Correctional Facility in our study) are now being evaluated according to less stringent and more vague standards.

In the best of times, inspection reports have little impact. "ICE does not adequately follow up on identified deficiencies," warned a 2018 DHS Office of Inspector General report on both ERO and ODO inspections, "or systematically hold facilities accountable for correcting deficiencies."³⁶ An online tracking system for reports was created in 2019, but a 2021 Government Accountability Office (GAO) report noted that data was entered inconsistently across the system, and that information was incomplete.³⁷ Additionally, the tracking tool was not used to analyze information gathered, such as identifying patterns in problems or repeat offender facilities. A follow-up GAO report in January 2023 noted some improvements since the 2021 report, but still found that "ICE does not analyze its inspections findings to identify trends in noncompliance, which makes it difficult for ICE to focus resources on the areas needing improvement."³⁸ As a result, even though ODO reports may contain more accurate information than previous ERO/Nakamoto reports, this will not lead to positive changes if no one reads them and follows up.[39]

ICE's structure and organization further hinder quality control. Driven by the aim of meeting agency performance goals, ICE is disincentivized to admit and address issues.[40] The 2021 GAO report also explained that ICE oversight management had been changed in 2010 to shift detention facility oversight to field offices, in a way that created conflicting responsibilities for leaders: that is, they were responsible for both running the facility and assessing its performance. Many facility managers also reported that they didn't have sufficient time and resources to carry out their oversight functions, and they feared retaliation and being overruled by others when trying to take corrective action.[41]

Fundamentally, ICE appears to have little interest in using available enforcement mechanisms to improve facility conditions. It is rare that ICE fines facilities for violations (as it has the power to do), and rarer still that facilities are stripped of ICE contracts—no matter how egregious, numerous, or repeated the violations.[42] ICE even issues waivers that give facilities permission to *not* meet certain standards. This example was given in the 2019 Congressional hearing: "from October 2015 to June 2018, ICE only issued two financial penalties and granted 65 waivers, 63 of which of those [*sic*] waivers had no end date."[43]

The inconsequential nature of ICE inspections was especially evident during the first Trump administration's aggressive expansion of detention capacity; as an ACLU report explains, under Trump, ICE "opened immigration detention centers at facilities where federal contracts had been terminated in prior administrations due in part to poor conditions of confinement."[44] Then, under the Biden administration, ICE kept facilities open despite continued abuses, inspections finding multiple violations, and recommendations by the DHS Inspector General to close them.[45]

Silencing detainee complaints

The routine burying of detainee complaints is yet another indication of how ICE's "oversight" system is largely smoke and mirrors. Technically, there are numerous ways that detainees and allies can lodge complaints. Concerns can be called in to hotlines, mailed, faxed, or submitted online. Complaints can be made to entities in the DHS as well as specifically within ICE, such as the ICE Detention Reporting and Information Line, ICE Office of Professional Responsibility, DHS Office of Inspector General, and DHS Civil Rights and Civil Liberties office. And in 2020, a new Office of the Immigration Detention Ombudsman was formed to provide an independent office for reviewing complaints.[46] Also, according to every version of the National Detention Standards, all detention facilities should have an on-site grievance procedure in place through which detainees can submit complaints. Finally, facility inspections are supposed to entail interviews with detainees that would give them the opportunity to report problems.

Still, despite all these potential mechanisms for filing complaints, real opportunities for detainees to lodge open and accurate complaints that receive appropriate responses are curbed. Non-ICE reports detail how, at facilities throughout the detention system, detainees are not given information about how to file a grievance, grievances are not addressed, or detainees may fear retaliation for filing one. Investigations show facilities routinely fail to record, review, and analyze filed complaints in a way that would allow ICE to identify recurring problems or particularly problematic facilities.

The handling of detainee complaints during ICE facility inspections further shows how complaints are silenced. Inspectors are supposed to interview a variety of detainees about the conditions at each facility, in a confidential setting. But a review by the DHS OIG noted that inspectors' "interviews" with detainees are mainly group conversations in common areas, where facility employees can listen in.[47] Outside investigations also found that the "interviews" are usually only conducted in English, and that inspection reports often misrepresented their findings, by writing something different than what a detainee told them in the facility's favor.[48]

ACCREDITATIONS FOR SALE

Accreditation is meant to offer evaluation and certification of meeting recognized standards of excellence by a neutral, independent body. Facilities, companies providing services to the facilities, government officials, and lawmakers routinely trumpet such accreditations as proof that conditions in detention centers are adequate. The facilities in our study—Elizabeth Detention Center, Buffalo Federal Detention Facility, Orange County (NY) Correctional Facility, Bergen County (NJ) Jail, Essex County (NJ) Correctional Facility, and Hudson County (NJ) Correctional Facility—are currently accredited by the American Correctional Association (ACA), and all but one by the National Commission on Correctional Health Care (NCCHC).

It's common for facilities to receive glowing accreditation scores of "100% on mandatory standards," at the same time as other measures reveal them to be rife with poor conditions, including appalling violations regarding health and safety. Indeed, as far as we have found, *no facilities in the entire detention system* have *ever* failed an accreditation renewal.

For example, the Essex County jail was accredited by both the ACA and the NCCHC in June 2018, but just one month later, the surprise inspection by the DHS OIG found shocking violations of standards related to food, health care, and safety.[49] Similarly, the Essex, Elizabeth, and Hudson facilities all held active accreditations by ACA and NCCHC in February 2018, when researchers for Human Rights First visited them and compiled a report detailing abysmal conditions.[50]

The real reasons for accreditation

If it's not part of a sincere, effective process to ensure quality, then why are detention facilities accredited? There are several reasons. Most basically, both the U.S. federal Bureau of Prisons and all fifty states *mandate* ACA accreditation as a condition of contracting with private prison companies.[51] This means that any state and county jails (that are part of the criminal justice system) contracted by ICE already have ACA accreditation. ICE doesn't technically require ACA accreditation but does strongly recommend it. ICE's National Detention Standards *did* require contracted facilities to be accredited by the NCCHC until the 2019 revisions.[52]

Facilities that detain immigrants are typically accredited by more than one agency, with the ACA and the NCCHC being the primary ones. Then, facilities run by state and county law enforcement agencies can also claim accreditation by the national Commission on Accreditation for Law Enforcement Agencies, Inc. (CALEA), the National Sheriff's Association (NSA), as well as their state's sheriff and corrections associations. Service providers contracted by these facilities must agree to meet the requirements of agencies accrediting a particular facility. For example, Requests for Proposals for medical care at the Orange County Correctional Facility state that the healthcare provider must meet the standards of the American Correctional Association, the National Commission on Correctional Health Care, the State Sheriff's Association, the National Detention Standards, and the State Commission of Corrections.

Here, we focus on the ACA and the NCCHC, because they accredit nearly all ICE detention centers, regardless of ownership and specific contracting arrangements. We draw on these agencies' own websites, as well as some independent investigations into jail and detention accreditations. One particularly illuminating report on the ACA accreditation process was compiled by the Office of Senator Elizabeth Warren in 2020.

Besides being mandated, accreditation offers a convenient appearance of excellence. Accreditation agencies all proclaim lofty goals of ensuring better care and conditions in correctional facilities. On their websites, these agencies pitch themselves as benevolent guides, with a mission to improve the corrections industry in general. The ACA's stated goals include promoting diversity, professional development, developing standards and accrediting facilities, conducting research, and promoting ethics in corrections professions.[53] The NCCHC's website declares that its "mission is to improve the quality of health care in jails, prisons, and juvenile facilities."[54]

Carceral facilities and subcontractors, for their part, wave accreditations around, like a feather in their cap, as proof of excellence. For example, in Wellpath's bid proposal for the Orange County Correctional Facility, the company claims it "has never failed to achieve accreditation, nor lost accreditation at any site where we provide services," and that "we carry the distinction of counting 20 Triple Crown sites among our clients, including Orange County,

New York." The bid text explains, "The National Sheriffs' Association (NSA) presents its prestigious Triple Crown Award to correctional facilities that achieve accreditation by the NCCHC, ACA, and CALEA."⁵⁵

Additionally, accreditation adds a layer of protection against charges of inappropriate care. Accrediting agencies aren't subtle about this perk. On its website, as one of the "Benefits of Accreditation," the ACA lists "Defense against lawsuits," and elaborates "Accredited agencies have a stronger defense against litigation through documentation and the demonstration of a 'good faith' effort to improve conditions of confinement."⁵⁶ Rather than improving care, these agencies emphasize that one of the most important reasons for accreditation is avoiding lawsuits.

For that avoidance, and keeping up appearances, accrediting agencies charge hefty fees. The ACA charges between $8,000 and $20,000 to accredit one facility, depending on facility size and number of auditors used (this is good for three years, after which the facility must pay for re-accreditation).⁵⁷ The NCCHC charges a $400 initial application fee, but we haven't been able to determine a price range for accreditation from publicly available information. According to their website, CALEA's fee to accredit a facility of 200–999 full-time employees is over $16,000 for the initial accreditation, and then $5,000 annually to renew.⁵⁸

It is on these fees that accrediting agencies depend for their survival. For example, the Warren investigation found that nearly half of ACA's revenue comes from accreditation fees.⁵⁹ According to a 2014 report on the ACA, "The organization thus has a financial incentive to provide as many accreditations as possible."⁶⁰

"Impossible" to fail

These accreditation processes—like the ICE inspections—are designed to be passed. ACA and NCCHC audits are pre-scheduled. For example, the ACA allows facilities to schedule their own audits, and then gives them three months to prepare. Agencies also provide facilities with multiple tools to ensure they will pass. The ACA will even conduct an initial, "practice" audit, to make sure the facility is prepared for the inspection.⁶¹

Evaluations are based on the materials assembled and presented by facility employees, who can choose what information to present. The ACA's accreditation process is essentially a review of policies on paper, *not* a review of actual practices and conditions.[62] Inspectors do not check to make sure that information provided is accurate; instead, they are interested in forms being filled out correctly and files being complete. Facilities are also given opportunities to rectify any problems found, and sometimes the agencies simply ignore problematic inspection findings and go ahead and accredit facilities. Accreditations may be maintained for a period of years with the submission of yearly written reports attesting to adherence to standards. These reports, written by facility employees, are not verified by the accrediting agency.

Reporting on the NCCHC, for example, found that the NCCHC looks at a facility's *infrastructure* to provide adequate care, not whether it really provides that care.[63] Similarly, the Orange County Sheriff posted a video online of the 2019 ACA audit, in which the ACA audit team briefly summarized their findings. All three auditors were effusive in their praise, emphasizing that the staff had all been nice to them, their files were well organized, the facility was clean, and staff morale was high. While one auditor briefly mentioned talking to inmates, it was clear that inmate experience was not a substantial focus.

As might be expected, if a facility pays the required fees, it obtains accreditation. The ACA's process is merely another "rubber stamp," according to the Warren report, which contends that "It is almost impossible for a facility to fail an ACA audit." The Warren report also states that "Neither the ACA nor the private prison companies Senator Warren's office contacted could provide a single, recent example of a prison or detention facility that had been denied accreditation – even when the facility had a public record of safety, health, or security violations."[64] Even facilities with grossly inadequate care still obtain accreditation, and confirmed reports of bad care do not lead to a loss of ACA accreditation.[65]

Additionally, falsified documents have been used to achieve ACA and NCCHC accreditation: at a 2008 California county hearing about a new proposed Corrections Corporation of America (now

CoreCivic) facility, a former employee testified "I was the person who doctored the ACA accreditation reports for this company."[66]

Many facilities that had recently obtained ACA and/or NCCHC accreditation, as documented by a 2016 *Prison Legal News* report, were found to have severe instances of violence or horrible conditions.[67] Detainee deaths at accredited facilities point to the uselessness of ACA and NCCHC accreditation. Even when facilities have lost wrongful death lawsuits, they maintain their accreditations.[68]

Mired in conflicts of interest

Accreditation processes are riddled with serious conflicts of interest.[69] For example, the ACA and the NCCHC set their own standards, with no input or oversight by outside entities, including the government. What's more, the same people who run prisons—sheriffs, other law enforcement personnel, prison company managers—contribute to the writing of standards, meaning that they set the standards for their own evaluation. Like the accreditation process itself, membership in accreditation agencies hinges on paying dues, not on maintaining excellent facilities. Take the case of Emre Umar, the current president of Correctional Medical Care (CMC), a medical services company that previously held the contract at the Orange County Correctional Facility. Though CMC was stripped of several facility contracts and sued by New York State in 2014 due to negligent care, according to his personal website, Umar remains a member of both ACA and NCCHC.

Leadership of these accrediting agencies is a revolving door of member companies' upper-level management. The ACA's board and committees are populated by current and former executives of the three major private prison companies, including CoreCivic which runs the Elizabeth Contract Detention Facility.[70] In bidding documents submitted to Orange County for the 2020 contract, Wellpath even explicitly claims—as a point of pride—a "Unique Accreditation Perspective," explaining that many of Wellpath's top management have previously held positions in NCCHC and ACA, and play a role in standards development, on-site accreditation surveys, and training surveyors.

These tight relationships filter all the way down to the inspection teams. As a *Prison Legal News* report summed up, "The ACA's executive and accreditation staff are primarily composed of current and former corrections officials, who accredit facilities run by other corrections officials – an inherent conflict of interest."[71] NCCHC inspection teams can even include members of the staff of the facility being inspected. To top it all off, there is little transparency in the accreditation process, and no oversight from government or other entities.[72]

The Warren report flags another fundamental issue with ACA accreditations:

> The ACA has two primary and conflicting functions: accreditor and trade association. As an accreditor, the ACA is responsible for providing private prisons and detention facilities with a key stamp of approval that is often required by their contracts with federal, state, and local governments. At the same time, the ACA serves as the primary lobbying group for private prisons—acting as "the voice for corrections"—and relies on the fees paid by the corrections facilities it accredits for a large chunk of its revenue.[73]

So, it is highly unlikely a facility would not be accredited—after all, they're all in this together, with the same goal of maximizing profit.

Carceral facilities, and the companies subcontracted to run them, have other ways to transfer money to accreditation agencies. They purchase agencies' materials to prepare for accreditation, pay fees for individual certifications and memberships, and, in the case of private companies, make financial "gifts" to accrediting agencies.[74] According to the NCCHC website, in May 2021, CFG Health Systems made a "generous gift" to the NCCHC Foundation (the "philanthropic and charitable arm" of the NCCHC).[75] CFG Health is one of several companies listed as a "Platinum" donor, which means the company gives the NCCHC an annual gift of at least $25,000. The other companies also listed as Platinum-level donors are all companies in the thick of the carceral health industry, such as Centurion Health and YesCare. Such gifts could be interpreted as attempts to influence decision-making when it comes to accreditations.

Conferences are another major source for accreditation agencies' finances. While roughly half of the ACA's annual income comes from accreditations fees and payments, one-quarter comes from conferences hosted by the agency.[76] Registration fees aren't cheap: for the summer 2024 conference, individual registration started at $240 for correctional field practitioners, and $800 for private company representatives.[77] And since facility representatives are required to attend an ACA conference as part of the accreditation process, some of these conference fees are essentially required.[78]

There are many other opportunities for accrediting agencies to collect revenue through conferences. For exhibitor tables in the conference exhibit hall at their fall 2024 conference, the NCCHC charged $2,500 for a standard table, or $3,000 for a prime table. Depending on location, the ACA sold booth space at their annual conference for $1,995 to $3,295. Agencies also charge for conference program advertising. To be in the NCCHC's fall 2024 conference program, companies paid $1,650 for standard placement, and $2,175 for premium placements.[79]

Private companies may also funnel money into conferences by sponsoring events, prizes, and materials. The ACA, for example, sells "sponsorship opportunities" at conferences, such as sponsoring a "General Session Keynote Speaker" for $25,000, conference app for $17,500, "Health Care Networking Reception" for $16,000, and placement on lanyards/badge holders for $6,000. Companies can also buy placement on items like hotel room key cards for $6,000, charging stations for $6,000, and exhibit hall floor maps for $1,000. Companies listed as major sponsors on the ACA's August 2023 conference website are all deeply involved in carceral industries, including Centurion, Keefe Group, Wellpath, Wexford Health, Aramark, CoreCivic, YesCare, CorrectRX Pharmacy Services, and GEO Group, among others.

Beyond conferences, accreditation agencies provide valuable marketplaces, and a venue for carceral companies to reach potential customers. These agencies aren't just selling accreditation and resources: they also sell access to their constituent lists. A graphic in the online NCCHC's 2024 Marketing and Resource Guide makes this very clear: "Your Product + Our Constituents = Success," with a promise to reach the $13 billion prison healthcare market.

The NCCHC promotes their sales team as ready to put together "packages" that companies can purchase to increase their visibility in the prison healthcare market. For example, they sell ads in their digital e-newsletter "CorrectCare Extra," which is "emailed to 30,000+ correctional health professionals every other week." Banner ads, the slightly cheaper option, start at $1,000 for appearance in one issue, and go up to $13,000 for appearance in all 26 yearly issues. Ads in the biannual CorrectCare magazine, which "is distributed for free in print (circulation 7,000) and digital (more than 20,000) formats to Certified Correctional Health Professionals, NCCHC-accredited facilities, members of the Academy of Correctional Health Professionals, and other qualified recipients," are between $1,200 and $5,050.

The NCCHC also "rents" their mailing lists, either physical addresses or email addresses, by whole lists or by segments according to job titles or work settings. The agency sells ads and other ways to promote company messages in their "peer-reviewed, scientific journal" *Journal of Correctional Health Care* (such as providing "Educational supplements" and "Expert roundtables"). Finally, they sell placement in their online NCCHC Buyers Guide, which "connects correctional health professionals with the suppliers they need, promoting products and services relevant to correctional health care." Options include $150 for "Priority Placement", the $200 Keyword Search Package, and $7,500 for "Catfish (floats at the bottom of the guide)."

The ACA has an even more extensive "Marketing Kit," which breaks down its marketing opportunities into Electronic Advertising, Sponsorships, Print Advertising, and Exhibits. The Marketing Kit sells, for example, advertising in *Corrections Today*, its online magazine published every two months. Prices range from $1,000 for a one-time, quarter-page black-and-white ad, to $4,400 for a one-time, full-page color ad.[80]

For sure, marketing like this is nothing unusual. Our point is that these accrediting agencies are far from benevolent nonprofits. Instead, they have monetized every possible aspect of their services and functions, even while allegedly ensuring the health and safety of hundreds of thousands of detained migrants and inmates.

As with inspections and bogus complaint systems, accreditations serve as tools for ICE, facilities, and private companies to claim that they are doing their due diligence. Facility operators and prison company managers regularly state that other inspection processes aren't necessary because they are ACA-accredited. They defend themselves in lawsuits and dispute complaints by pointing to their accreditations, and wield accreditation to access ICE contracts and hide abuses.[81] In reality, accreditation processes are awash with conflicts of interest, and they are more about looking good than being good.

Concealing detention's many injustices

National Detention Standards, ICE facility inspections, and accreditation by external organizations operate under the guise of providing accountability and quality care, while actually doing the opposite. Worse, this concocted detention oversight system creates a semblance of supervision that heads off any real investigation and improvement in detention facilities.

The agencies and companies involved in creating the appearance of oversight comprise yet another industry eager to latch onto the web of dependencies spinning out from the nearly $3.5 billion annual immigration detention budget. Like the food, medical, and commissary sectors, the detention oversight industry benefits from detention not despite bad food and care, price gouging, detainee complaints, and death, but, rather, *because* of those evils. The money made by detention industries is a direct reflection of how detainees are capitalized on. Instead of revealing the systemic exploitation of detainees, inspections and accountability processes profit from it, and the public does not see the scale and depth of dehumanization and injustice that "immigration detention inc." allows.

6

Breaking Unjust Detention Dependencies

On Long Island, in New York State to the east of New York City, there are currently no ICE detention facilities. And yet, even there, at least twelve businesses contract with ICE at present. Most of these contracts are valued at under $100,000, for goods and services as diverse as office supplies, dental services, security services, uniforms, linens, hygiene products, and charter flights. There doesn't need to be nearby detention facilities for businesses to be financially entangled with immigration enforcement. Across the country, hundreds of these smaller businesses now count on ICE detention money.[1]

Similarly, thousands of larger national corporations now profit from incarceration and detention. There are, of course, the well-known prison operators and service providers—among them, CoreCivic, GEO Group, Aramark, Trinity Services, Keefe Group, and Wellpath—that we have discussed in this book. But there are also corporate giants that are not typically associated with incarceration: Amazon, Microsoft, and Northrop Grumman provide data and information systems. Stanley Black & Decker and VF Corp. supply carceral facilities with equipment. Investment companies such as Bank of America, Fidelity, J.P. Morgan, Vanguard, and Wells Fargo are also drawn to carceral industries. Altogether, some 4,100 major national corporations' revenue and profits are somehow connected to ICE detaining migrants.[2]

WEBS OF DEPENDENCE: PRIVATE COMPANIES

In previous chapters, we focused on primary contractors in the immigration detention industry—companies as well as county governments that contract directly with ICE, and businesses that subcontract to deliver key services in detention facilities: food, medical, and commissary. Of course, there are also other major services and subcontractors that this book does not investigate, including communication, money transfers, inmate package delivery, security, and transportation.[3]

This chapter highlights how keeping a captive population alive—and (appearing to) meet the bare minimum of standards set by the accountability industry—requires a plethora of additional companies. Given its persistent stability and growth, the incarceration and immigration detention industry attracts interest from many businesses that might not seem obviously connected to it.

Prison and detention food services alone entail relationships with a huge range of companies. In a report about the food services industry, market analysis company IBISWorld details all the providers that comprise the supply chain for this industry. The list includes "first tier suppliers" like Beef and Pork Wholesaling, Grocery Wholesaling, Egg and Poultry Wholesaling, Dairy Wholesaling, Fish and Seafood Wholesaling, Restaurant and Hotel Equipment Wholesaling, Frozen Food Wholesaling, and Fruit and Vegetable Wholesaling. "Second tier suppliers," whose involvement is more indirect but nonetheless significant, are listed as: Major Household Appliance Manufacturing, Frozen Food Production, Dairy Product Production, Meat, Beef and Poultry Processing, Seafood Preparation, Bread Production, and Snack Food Production.[4] Thinking about all the companies, big and small, that are included in this industry supply chain illuminates how the business of feeding immigrant detainees financially entwines so many different enterprises.

Medical care also relies on outside vendors for many services and products. Indeed, health care within detention facilities is simply "a microcosm of the health care system at large," according to a 2024 Marketing and Resource Guide put together by the agency that accredits carceral medical care providers, the National Commission on Correctional Health Care (NCCHC). This same NCCHC's marketing guide lists the products that detention facilities seek:

[...] dental care and supplies, dialysis services, education and training, electronic health records, health care management, health care staffing, infection control products, information technology services, medical devices and equipment, medical supplies, mental health services, optometry services, pharmaceuticals, pharmacy services, safety equipment, substance use disorder treatment and services, suicide prevention.[5]

Clearly, providing medical care in prisons and jails offers opportunities to many different types of companies.

Likewise, commissary companies depend on a wide network of relationships to acquire the items to sell to inmates. For example, Keefe Group (with Keefe Commissary and Keefe Supply Company) proclaims on its website that they "offer more than 10,000 name-brand and private-label products" through its national network of prison stores. Keefe also boasts about its nationwide distribution network of 20 facilities. The sale, movement, and storage of commissary products, as well as related employment opportunities, are spread out around the country.[6]

Yet even these services are only the beginning. Any business has standard operating needs and materials, such as office supplies and equipment, communication infrastructure (phones, internet), technology support, facility repair and maintenance, cleaning, insurance, and employee benefits administration. Any residential facilities have relationships to businesses that supply things like laundry products, equipment, and maintenance; transportation vehicles and maintenance; linens and uniforms. Thus, financial ties spin out far beyond the obvious day-to-day demands of detention.

Thousands of companies, then, of all sizes and types, depend for some portion of their income on supplying, staffing, or maintaining facilities that detain migrants. Whenever a county or private company contracts with ICE, or a company subcontracts to provide services in a detention facility, more and more relationships of economic interdependence are created. In short, "immigration detention inc." absorbs and extends its reach as ever-more entities and people become directly or indirectly invested in detaining migrants and sustaining a detained population.

Indeed, many corporations are *literally* invested in detaining migrants. Detention money feeds national and international corporations and investment groups, which see carceral industries as a growth opportunity. Consider the portfolio of H.I.G. Capital, a global private equity investment firm. As discussed in Chapter 4, in 2016, H.I.G. Capital formed TKC Holdings, by adding leading prison commissary supplier Keefe Group to its already-existing collection of carceral industries, which included Trinity Services Group and Courtesy Products.[7] A considerable amount of consolidation takes place as smaller companies are gobbled up by bigger companies. Of the six facilities in our study, Keefe currently has the commissary contracts for five of them; Trinity has the commissary contract for the Buffalo facility. H.I.G. Capital also owns correctional medical services company Wellpath,[8] which is contracted for medical services at two facilities in our study.

For global corporations looking for new markets, incarceration and detention seem like sure bets. Take, for example, Aramark, one of the biggest providers of food in U.S. prisons and detention centers, including two of the sites in our study.[9] Aramark now *also* provides food for asylum seekers in residential centers in Ireland.[10] In addition to food, Aramark offers an array of services, such as facilities management, uniform service, and custodial services. The corporation already operates far beyond the United States, including in Canada, Mexico, Argentina, Chile, Belgium, Czech Republic, Germany, Spain, the U.K., Ireland, China, Japan, and Korea. Like many global corporations, Aramark is positioned to become more involved in detention operations around the world, as opportunities arise.

WEBS OF DEPENDENCE:
LOCAL GOVERNMENTS AND COMMUNITIES

In Hudson County in 2018, when anti-detention activists sought to end the county's contract with ICE, the head of the county board, Anthony Vainieri, warned that if the jail ended its ICE contract a hundred corrections officers would be out of work. "We're going to be hurting our own staff," said Vainieri, "and we're going to be hurting our own county families. That's the bottom line."[11]

At local and regional levels, even marginal economic ties with ICE can take on great significance. County government leaders, like Vainieri, may view detention as a financial lifeline for struggling local economies. It's common for politicians to claim that detention facilities are needed in a region's economy to keep businesses afloat or to support individuals' livelihoods.

It's also important to note that despite state-level bans on detention, as instituted by New Jersey in 2021, local communities continue to be involved with detention and view it as a potential business opportunity. This reality is apparent in recent developments in New Jersey, where ICE officials are considering proposals to, again, expand the state's detention capacity. Documents obtained by the ACLU show several facilities on the table as options that would be run for the federal government by GEO Group and Core Civic. These facilities would increase New Jersey's detention capacity by 1,500 people, raising total state capacity to 2,500. As of early January 2025, similar facility expansion possibilities were under consideration in 15 states.[12] Detention plainly has enduring appeal as a source of revenue.

Indeed, ICE contracts *can* be a significant contributor to county revenue. For the three New Jersey county jails in our study, before COVID-19, ICE detainees made up around half of their total inmates. At that time, Bergen's ICE contract contributed more than 15 percent of the Sheriff's office 2018 budget.[13] Money from detention also goes into general county coffers. In 2019, ICE money was about 5 percent of Essex County's total revenue,[14] meaning that detention funds were used to pay for general county expenses. As stated in the Introduction of this book, this issue was highlighted in an account of a 2018 meeting in Essex County when a community activist posed the following question to an elected official, "If I take my kids to the zoo, am I supporting—are we visiting something that was built using money from $117 per night per detainee?" In response, the county leader noted that ICE money "is certainly part of" what pays for Essex County Parks, including the zoo.[15]

Local dependence on detention can also be expressed in terms of cost to residents. For example, Hudson County estimated that its ICE contract saved residents $11 million in tax payments in 2018.[16] Additionally, ICE contracts can provide stability in the face of changing jail populations. In 2017, New Jersey enacted bail reform laws that led to an immediate drop in county jail inmates. Taking in more ICE detainees was one strategy for filling facility space and making up for the resulting lost revenue.

Detention's economic rewards are enticing, especially for cash-strapped local governments, so the end of detention in one state can present an opportunity for another state. In 2021, a new ICE detention center opened in Clearfield County, Pennsylvania, using the facilities that had been part of a federal prison that closed earlier that year. The Moshannon Valley Processing Center's capacity for nearly 1,900 detainees is significantly more than the York County Prison in Pennsylvania, which ended its ICE contract in 2021. This means that Clearfield County's new facility leaves plenty of room for detainees from other states, including neighboring New Jersey. The new ICE facility, run by GEO Group, was celebrated in Clearfield as an economic boon, hailed as providing jobs and much-needed tax revenue to the hard-hit county.[17] Same justifications, different state.

All these contracting webs not only pull in more companies, government agencies, and people into relationships of financial dependence, but also make it difficult to hold anyone accountable. Different players can claim that responsibility for problems—poor detention conditions, rights violations, cost bloat—lies elsewhere in the web.[18]

Financial entwinement feeds the ever-expanding system. Detention capacity does not just grow to fill demand; instead, *more capacity leads to more people being detained*. This is the larger consequence of contracting with ICE. "The likelihood of immigration arrest increases with ICE detention capacity," according to a 2022 report from a coalition of organizations, pointedly titled "If You Build It, ICE Will Fill It: The Link Between Detention Capacity and ICE Arrests." The report goes on to note that "Immigrants are more likely to be arrested and detained by ICE in counties with more detention beds."[19] So economic gain from detention—even aspirations of gain—shapes immigration policing and how many people are detained.

The economic appeal, as well as economic dependency on detention, shape public attitudes toward it, making detention morally acceptable. After all, no one wants to see their neighbors lose their job, watch local businesses suffer, or give up municipal amenities like parks and zoos or community services like garbage collection. Our point here is that while it might be tempting to depict everyone involved in "immigration detention inc." in a malicious light, doing so fails to recognize the deeply-entrenched political and economic pull that detention has on communities across the U.S.

As we've shown throughout this book, revenue-making and profit-seeking opportunities continuously draw more and more stakeholders into the orbit of detention industries. Every stakeholder, whether directly or indirectly, winds up with a vested interest in maintaining—and even expanding—carceral industries. So ICE, working through myriad contracts and subcontracts, makes the incarceration of migrants appear to be a logical, rational choice that happens to benefit individuals, communities, and beyond. The social endorsement that results makes it harder to envision a world without detention.

LOBBYING AND REVOLVING DOORS

Those involved in the detention industry do not simply respond to existing needs. In fact, they play a pivotal role in determining capacity and making sure it is filled—by actively influencing policy. For decades, corporations have invested heavily in lobbying to shape proposed laws around immigration enforcement and how politicians vote on them. From local to federal levels, lobbyists have focused on solidifying and increasing detention infrastructure.

Corporate money has propelled the explosive growth of immigration detention in the last twenty years.[20] One very popular policy among prison corporations is the immigration detention "bed quota" (discussed in Chapter 1), which *requires* ICE to finance a particular number of detention spots per year. This policy, pushed by carceral company lobbyists, has played a central role in increasing immigration detention.[21] One report noted that "CCA had 25 lobbyists in Congress when the detention quota was passed in 2009."[22] Both CoreCivic (formerly CCA) and GEO Group have poured a lot of money into lobbying politicians who support the bed quota;[23] between 2006 and 2015, CCA invested $8.7 million and GEO Group $1.3 million in this effort.[24]

Corporate money continues to flow to politicians who support policies bringing more business to private detention operators. When major prison corporations (like CoreCivic, GEO Group, and Management and Training Corporation) make campaign donations to U.S. Congress members, they typically do so after members have voted in favor of legislation that would increase immigration detention numbers.[25] One study also found that the donations tended to be more generous for politicians who faced greater political risk by sponsoring such legislation.[26]

The leading Congressional recipients of GEO Group and Core-Civic political contributions in the 2022 midterm election cycle were all Republicans and vocal supporters of tougher immigration enforcement and border security. Republican Senator Marco Rubio (now U.S. Secretary of State) received a whopping $62,000, Senator Jerry Moran $27,000, and House Representative (then Minority Leader) Kevin McCarthy $21,765. Representative Chuck Fleishmann, who got $12,500, used his position as a member of the Congressional Homeland Security committee to push to expand detention capacity. Before the 2022 midterm elections, GEO Group and CoreCivic also gave money to gubernatorial candidates who advocate for tough immigration enforcement policies. For example, $25,000 went to Governor Brian Kemp of Georgia, site of CoreCivic's Stewart Detention Center, the biggest ICE detention facility in the country, and GEO Group's Folkston Processing Center, which was planning to significantly increase capacity.[27]

While Republican lawmakers receive the lion's share of lobbying money, private companies target politicians of both political parties, again revealing how detention is popular across party lines. For example, while New Jersey Senator Cory Booker has publicly spoken out against ICE, for years he largely remained silent about ICE detention contracts in his state, even attending fundraisers hosted by some of the powerbrokers behind New Jersey detention jail contracts.[28] As evident in records of campaign contributions to county leaders, favoritism has long played a role in contracting decisions in the Democrat-led New Jersey county facilities in our study.[29]

It is not just big prison companies that use cash to influence policies and decisions around immigration detention. Lobbying and campaign contributions are part of routine operations for other stakeholders profiled in this book. Chapter 3 recounted the case of New Jersey Democratic candidate Amy Kennedy's acceptance of campaign contributions from medical company Wellpath in her bid for a House of Representatives seat. Chapter 4 noted H.I.G. Capital's lobbying efforts to sway political decisions. Companies that depend on and benefit from detention invest in maintaining and even deepening those financial ties.

In some states, efforts to influence contracting decisions have descended to outright corruption. One notable scandal came to light in Mississippi in 2014, where Commissioner of the Mississippi Department of Corrections (and former American Correctional Association president) Christopher Epps was charged with taking over $1.4 million from consultants linked to GEO Group, Management Training Corporation (MTC), Global Tel*Link, and Keefe Commissary Network, in return for funneling about $800 million of lucrative Department of Corrections contracts to those companies.[30]

Additionally, as mentioned briefly in Chapter 1, ethics watchdogs highlight the concerning practice of individuals shifting back and forth from jobs in the private sector, which profits from detention, and roles in the public sector, where detention policies are shaped and implemented:[31] a 2016 report found that "seventy percent of CCA and GEO lobbyists have previously worked on the Hill."[32] In Chapter 5, we discussed the "revolving door" of personnel between organizations that accredit carceral facilities and private companies that are paid to provide services in the same facilities.

Politicians who shape key immigration laws often employ consultants who have also worked for private prison companies. For example, as a Florida senator, Marco Rubio hired a number of individuals previously employed by GEO Group.[33] In addition to those involved in politics, it is also common for officials in the Federal Bureau of Prisons and the Department of Homeland Security, and ICE specifically, to obtain jobs with private prison companies after they leave their government positions.[34] Several recent high-profile examples include officials who were in charge of contracting *and* overseeing the companies that hire them.[35] One notable case, mentioned in Chapter 1, is former DHS Secretary and Chief of Staff during the first Trump administration, General John Kelly, who just four months after leaving the DHS joined the Board of Directors of Caliburn International, one of the private companies that ICE (which is housed within DHS) contracted to detain unaccompanied minors, a practice that increased during Kelly's time there. Basically, Kelly supervised policies that separated families and put "kids in cages" in appalling, abusive conditions, and then went on the payroll of one of the companies that cashed in.[36]

What we have here is a sticky, knotted mass of companies, agencies, local governments, communities, and individuals that have all come to gain from or to rely on detention money. These dependencies are the bricks in the foundation of the United States' immense detention system *and* the engines that drive new policies resulting in even more detention. Financial incentives link with other logics we discussed in Chapter 1: race-based ideas of national identity, changing demographics and xenophobia, painting immigrants as threats to national security and the economy, the U.S. demand for cheap labor, and the popular—and yet faulty—idea of deterrence. These economics and logics have worked together for decades, and they continue to work, to expand the detention system.

BREAKING THE WEBS DEPENDING ON DETENTION

It is daunting to even begin to think about how to dismantle this massive, complicated system of intertwined ideologies and political and economic dependencies. We suggest that any approach should employ the idea of the web: aiming to pick apart the tangle of relationships strand by strand. Since economic incentives are central to the detention system, as we've shown in this book, unraveling those strands is vital to successful anti-detention efforts.

Fighting for rights and against abuses in detention facilities

Important initiatives are already in play led by immigrant advocacy and human rights organizations that have been working against the detention system for years. Numerous groups, from local to international, gather and publish information about detention that is critically important in anti-detention efforts. Law school clinics and non-profit organizations that offer reduced cost or pro bono legal services to migrants make a huge difference in immigration proceedings.

In New Jersey and New York, an impressive range of groups provide various forms of support and advocacy. These include community and faith-based organizations that aid detainees and their families through visitation programs, assistance after release, coordinating actions to fight deportation, and providing funds for commissary purchases. Many of these organizations also coordinate public demonstrations protesting and calling attention to detention.[37]

While many groups have been working tirelessly for years (and some for decades), there was a surge in anti-detention activism and advocacy after President Donald Trump was first elected in 2016. Trump's open hostility to immigrants—and public embrace of policies like family separation, broader denial of asylum seekers, and his calls to "build the wall"—spurred previously uninvolved people into action.

In New Jersey, in the Democratic-leaning counties of Bergen, Essex, and Hudson, some activists broadened their goals to include ending detention in their area. Activists in Essex and Hudson counties called for their local governments to terminate detention contracts with ICE, using tactics such as rallying in front of county government buildings and detention centers, interrupting county leaders' meetings, holding hunger strikes, and publishing opinion pieces in local news venues. Anti-detention activists in Hudson County won a short-lived victory in October 2018 when county leaders voted to end their ICE contract by 2020. But, in 2020, the county reversed this decision, renewing the contract for ten more years.[38] In Essex County, the Board of Commissioners moved to end ICE detention at the Essex County Correctional Facility by August 2021.

Simultaneously, a coalition of local and national activists and organizations was working for the larger goal of banning detention in New Jersey altogether. In so doing, they followed California's lead. As detailed in Chapter 4, California passed a law prohibiting local governments from entering into new detention contracts with ICE in 2017 with a subsequent law banning private companies enacted in 2019. In August 2021, after years of protest and campaigns to influence local, state, and national officials, New Jersey became the fifth state to enact a law to limit or end detention in the state. However, just before the bill was signed into law, GEO Group and ICE snuck in a contract renewal for the privately-run Elizabeth Detention Center. Consequently, some ICE detainees continued to be held in New Jersey. GEO Group then sued the state of New Jersey to keep the facility permanently open, as will be discussed below.

New York State has also seen protests for the closure of facilities and calls for a state detention ban. In July 2019, when a nationwide coalition coordinated vigils for the end of immigration detention around the country, residents of nearly fifty towns and cities in New York participated.[39] In 2021, the Dignity Not Detention bill was proposed in the New York State legislature. While many organizations and legislators expressed support, the bill never got out of committee.

Activists around New York continue to call for the end of detention in the state, but without success. One reason might be New York's different political landscape. The two facilities in New York State used by ICE for long-term detention—the Orange County Correctional Facility in Goshen and the Buffalo Federal Processing Center in Batavia—are in considerably more politically conservative areas compared to Bergen, Essex, and Hudson counties of New Jersey.

Immigrant detainees themselves have also taken action to fight against detention, at times at considerable risk to themselves. Individual acts of protest might involve communicating—in person or via phone, email, or social media—with journalists, lawyers, facility visitors, or organizations, all of whom can share information about what goes on inside facilities with a wider audience. As might be imagined, many released detainees may be fearful of possible negative impacts on their immigration cases. Yet some do speak out to journalists, in local government hearings and meetings, and at public events.

For detained migrants, one powerful tool is the use of hunger strikes. By refusing to eat for extended periods, detainees seek to bring about better conditions and draw public attention to the injustice of detention.[40] Hunger strike demands have included more food, better medical care, visitation rights, more clothing, better COVID safety, an end to facility transfers, wages higher than $1 per day for in-facility labor, safer work conditions, turning the lights off at night, and release from detention.

While it is extremely difficult to get information from ICE about hunger strikes in detention facilities, there is evidence that they occur with alarming frequency. The national organization Freedom for Immigrants compiled documentation of hunger strikes by at least 1,600 people in 20 facilities from 2015 to 2020.[41] Moreover, there was a notable increase in hunger strikes during the first Trump administration.[42] Accounts of local hunger strikes in detention centers appear every few months around the country.

Detainees at all six facilities in our study have used hunger strikes, with a surge in strikes during the COVID-19 pandemic. Beginning in late March 2020 and continuing into 2021, groups of detainees at all four New Jersey facilities active at that time—Bergen, Elizabeth, Essex, and Hudson—went on hunger strikes to demand hygiene products critical to preventing the spread of the virus, like hand sanitizer, soap, and more cleaning supplies, as well as better medical care and an end to round-the-clock lockdowns. Some strikes were coordinated with advocates who protested outside the facilities, or with detainees in the Buffalo facility.[43] In 2022 and 2023, detainees at both the Orange County Correctional Facility and the Buffalo facility engaged in hunger strikes to protest abysmal conditions, racist abuse, and out-of-state transfers.[44]

ICE appears to recognize the inevitability of hunger strikes (given the conditions of detention), since how to handle such strikes is included in all versions of the National Detention Standards guidelines. Facility and ICE officials respond to hunger strikes by force-feeding participants, transferring them to other facilities, throwing them in solitary confinement, confiscating and destroying personal belongings, and harassment. Alongside communications with advocates outside, hunger strikes can be very effective for attracting public attention and putting pressure on officials to make at least some changes. Organizations and individuals fighting for justice rose to the challenges that the first Trump administration presented, continued their work in the Biden administration, and will oppose and confront whatever is unleashed in Trump's second term. Regardless of the party in power, and the degree of open hostility toward immigrants, activists recognize that the detention system will remain a malignant core of the U.S. approach to immigration until the addiction to detention money is cured.

State detention bans

Another anti-detention strategy has been to try to pass state legislation forcing the closure of existing detention facilities and preventing the opening of new ones. There are two kinds of state-level detention "bans": a ban on Intergovernmental Service Agreements (IGSAs) and a private prison ban. An IGSA ban forbids local governments from contracting with ICE (or other federal agencies) to detain immigrants; a private prison ban, meanwhile, forbids the operation of private facilities for immigrant detention.[45]

California was the first state to enact an IGSA ban in 2017, and then the first state to attempt a private detention ban in 2019. IGSA bans have been passed in Washington (2019), Illinois (2021), Maryland (2021), Oregon (2021), New Jersey (2021), and Colorado (2023). IGSA bans were proposed but did not pass in Wisconsin (2020), New York (2021), and New Mexico (2023). Private detention bans have been either included in IGSA ban laws or passed separately in California (2019), Illinois (2019), Maryland (2021), Washington (2021), Oregon (2021), and New Jersey (2021).

Despite their increase in number, anti-detention state laws have had mixed results.[46] In states that passed IGSA bans, detention has largely been phased out in jails owned by state and local governments. But attempts to end detention in *private* facilities have failed, as private companies and the federal government have worked together to get around state laws. In California, just days before the ban on new private detention agreements was set to take effect in 2019, GEO Group, CoreCivic, and MTC signed new 15-year contracts with ICE that added private detention capacity, more than compensating for the end of detention in county government jails. Then the Trump administration—in a case continued by the Biden administration—teamed up with GEO Group to sue California, on the grounds that the state law interfered with the federal right to control immigration. This case was won by ICE and GEO Group in July 2023, with repercussions for bans on private detention in other states.[47]

In New Jersey, the Bergen, Essex, and Hudson county facilities stopped detaining immigrants for ICE after the 2021 law went into effect. But CoreCivic took advantage of a few weeks in between the law's passage and when the governor signed it to extend their Elizabeth contract with ICE by two years.[48] Then, just before the existing Elizabeth contract would have expired in August 2023, CoreCivic and ICE, backed by the Biden administration, sued New Jersey, repeating that detention bans would undermine federal authority to enforce immigration laws. A federal judge decided in CoreCivic and ICE's favor.[49] And now, as explained earlier, ICE is entertaining new proposals from private contractors to expand detention capacity in New Jersey.

The 2023 rulings in California and New Jersey—combined with the collaboration of the federal government and private corporations—suggests that some of this anti-detention activism has backfired. Working at local and state levels to force county jails to stop detaining immigrants has, paradoxically, led to more immigration detention in *private* facilities, instead of a decrease in detention overall. Even Biden's push to end private company involvement in criminal justice system incarceration means that there are more private facilities available—and private companies eager—for increased involvement in detention. Additionally, in states that don't have bans, new local governments are now entering into IGSAs with ICE to detain immigrants.

This points to another unintended consequence: out-of-state transfers of detainees. In all states where detention in county facilities was banned, detainees were not released as activists demanded. Instead, they were transferred to detention facilities in other states. After California's 2017 law, ICE transferred detainees from county jails to locations in Washington, California, and Hawaii.[50] As New Jersey county jails phased out detention, detainees were sent to the Orange County Correctional Facility and Buffalo Federal Processing Center in New York, and also farther away to Georgia, Massachusetts, and Nevada.[51] Now, immigrants taken into ICE custody in New Jersey and downstate New York are often sent to the Moshannon Valley facility in Pennsylvania run by GEO Group, in addition to sending them to the New York centers.[52] After Maryland's ban passed, immigrants detained there have been sent to Moshannon Valley, as well as to facilities much farther away in, for example, Georgia and Louisiana.[53]

It is clear that ICE does not respond to state bans by releasing detainees. John Sandweg, former acting director of ICE under the Obama administration, said about the New Jersey law:

> Unfortunately, when you say "Hey I don't want any detention facilities in New Jersey," what the inadvertent consequence of that could be is that it forces the agency to take people who are priority for detention, or who meet the public safety criteria and you end up moving them far from their support groups or family members, so there could be some negative consequences around that.[54]

Instead, ICE figures out where to transfer detainees, taking into consideration bed-space cost and where beds are available. These calculations may mean that states who charge the least—and may also give the worst care—are more than ready to receive transferred detainees. It's a race to the bottom for the detainees, then, who might be shuttled far away from their support networks, and into even worse conditions.

These transfers don't just take detainees far away from family and friends. They also hurt their chance of fighting deportation, since they are pulled away from legal representation. The states with the political will to pass anti-detention laws typically also provide more access to legal services to detained immigrants, compared to states where they may be transferred. For example, detainees in the three New Jersey county facilities were represented by lawyers in several organizations in New York City and eastern New Jersey that provide pro bono immigration legal services. In response to anti-detention activism, in 2018 the state of New Jersey began budgeting to offer legal services to detained immigrants.[55] Before county detention ended in New Jersey, Essex and Hudson county governments had also begun to allocate funds to cover legal representation for detainees.[56]

The reality of these responses to detention bans—far-away transfers instead of release, and loss of legal representation—has led to some unexpected alliances. In New Jersey, those who spoke publicly against the proposed ban included county elected officials, sheriffs, legal organizations representing immigrants, and some organizations of family members and supporters of detainees. For example, amid activist efforts to end detention in Hudson County in 2018, local elected official Anthony Vainieri said, "They'd be shipped to Montana or Texas where they're not gonna care about the inmates from the area because they're not gonna have the families outside ringing the doorbell saying, 'Hey my son's in there, my father's in there, my mother's in there, help her.'"[57]

Given Vainieri's other defenses of the county's ICE contract (quoted above), it's tempting to dismiss this logic as a bald attempt to defend county coffers. Yet Vainieri's statement chimes with sentiments expressed by some advocates who noted: "We care about the plight of individuals incarcerated, and we believe if the facilities are closed in New Jersey, then ICE will transfer individuals to remote locations where there is no access to advocates holding ICE and facilities accountable to the conditions. These individuals will suffer more without support."[58]

Without doubt, local and state efforts to close detention facilities can be a powerful statement. Yet, they are not the ultimate step, as this can be like trying to stop a leak in a dam. As long as some states allow jails to contract with ICE and private detention facilities continue to exist, detention won't decrease or end; it will just move elsewhere—often to the detriment of detainees.

THE DECEPTIVE APPEAL OF "ALTERNATIVES TO DETENTION"

In discussions about reducing ICE's use of detention, a seemingly benign option often appears. "Alternatives to Detention" (ATD) refer to various forms of monitoring of immigrants by ICE, primarily electronic. For those combating detention, however, increased monitoring is *not* the answer. While ATD programs may seem like a good way to keep people out of detention facilities, in practice they facilitate the entrapment of more and more migrants within the webs of financial dependence in immigration enforcement.

The new focus on digital monitoring and surveillance is part of a broader trend in all carceral systems.[59] ICE's ATD program, also known as the Intensive Supervision Appearance Program (ISAP), first began in 2005, with the electronic monitoring of 1,339 people.[60] With a $28 million budget in 2006,[61] the program grew gradually until 2019, when it started growing exponentially. ATD programs expanded rapidly during the Biden administration, framed as filling Biden's promises for a "more humane immigration system" (as stated in 2022 budget), with Biden asking for $527 million for fiscal year 2023 to digitally monitor 200,000 immigrants.[62] A supplemental funding request Biden submitted to Congress in October 2023 asked for a whopping $1.29 *billion* for ATD in 2024, to massively increase the program.[63]

Participation in ISAP involves various forms of surveillance, including office visits, home visits, and monitoring using technology. People in ISAP may be required to visit program offices for scheduled appointments, and to allow visits to their home at any time. Enrollees may be required to phone in at designated times, when their call is checked by voice recognition technology. Some are outfitted with electronic ankle shackles for GPS tracking 24 hours a day, 7 days a week. And there are new technologies being developed for ICE surveillance, such as devices, like wristbands and head gear, that collect biometric data.[64]

Currently the most widely used technology is a phone application called SmartLINK. Users are required to download the SmartLINK app to their smartphone, which means, for starters, that they must have and maintain a smartphone. Next, enrollees must "consent" to all the permissions the app requires, upload documents and other personal information to the app, take photos of themselves checked by facial recognition technology, and do video check-ins. The app records GPS coordinates of the enrollee's device, allowing constant location monitoring. Program officers are also allowed to collect other information from enrollees' phones through the app, such as phone network information and IP addresses.[65]

There are a lot of problems with ISAP practices and with the technology used in this program. Home visits can include invasive searches, in ways that impact not just ISAP enrollees but their entire household. Ankle shackles frequently cause pain or discomfort, often being too tight or chafing. About 20 percent of wearers report being shocked by their ankle device. The shackles must be recharged, and some do not hold a charge as they are supposed to, so wearers must spend significant chunks of time by an outlet. The SmartLINK app is reportedly clunky to use; it can glitch at crucial times and the facial recognition feature can malfunction. Such glitches prevent people from submitting required locator information and selfies, or attending required meetings; yet these technical errors have major repercussions for their immigration standing and cases. False alarms caused by device malfunction are not infrequent.[66]

Whether using the latest SmartLINK or older monitoring technologies, ISAP participants also describe negative psychological effects, "including anxiety, depression, sleep disruptions, and social isolation."[67] ISAP enrollees report that the program requirements make it difficult for them to leave their home, find employment, and participate in family and community activities.

These practices and technologies also threaten the privacy and safety of everyone in enrollees' families, homes, and communities, and digital monitoring of immigrants entails all the same privacy and data security issues all digital users face, but the stakes are much higher.

Importantly, ATD programs provide yet another opportunity for money-making, another sticky strand in the web of detention dependencies. The very same companies that already profit from immigration detention profit off ATD. BI, Inc. (Behavioral Interventions) is the primary provider of ATD schemes for ICE. BI, headquartered in Boulder, Colorado, was originally founded in 1978 to electronically monitor cattle.[68] In 2011, BI was purchased by none other than GEO Group.[69]

Given their market share, GEO Group was in prime position to hear the growing calls for "alternatives to detention," and to know that such calls threatened one of their primary products: detention facilities. Incorporating BI into GEO Group was a strategic move. The 2011 acquisition set the stage for more fast-paced growth and expansion of "immigration detention inc." through digital monitoring. In 2020, ICE signed a five-year contract with BI, Inc. for $2.2 billion.[70] The number of people ICE was digitally monitoring tripled from 2021 to 2022.[71] GEO Group's revenue stream is diversified, expanded, and secure.

Indeed, in 2022, income from BI's activities made up over 20 percent of GEO Group's revenue.[72] A 2022 estimate found that BI does the monitoring for over 75 percent of ICE's ATD programs.[73] Every single day, according to a 2022 *Guardian* investigation, BI receives from ICE $4–5 per ankle monitor, and 25 cents per person using the SmartLINK app.[74] The sheer number of people enrolled in ISAP means these dollars and cents add up to substantial sums for the companies involved.

These figures do not translate into better circumstances for immigrants. As part of their ICE contract, BI provides case managers to monitor and supposedly "support" ISAP enrollees. But the 2022 *Guardian* investigation found that case managers were severely overtasked, making it impossible for them to appropriately manage their cases or provide any real support to people in the program. A 2022 U.S. Government Accountability Office report found that ICE does little to monitor compliance and quality of ATD contractors.[75]

Through digital monitoring, ICE has vastly expanded its capacity for surveillance of immigrants, families, and communities. As of December 2024, there were 185,707 families and individuals in ICE ATD programs.[76]

The explosion in detention "alternatives" has not meant a corresponding reduction in detention. Instead, the detention infrastructure remains intact. Indeed, as we've discussed, after a COVID-era drop in detainee numbers, the numbers are back up to previous levels. ISAP has also facilitated the extension of ICE surveillance into more places around the country, away from the border. For example, from 2021 to 2022, there was a 91 percent increase in electronic monitoring in the Newark (New Jersey) ICE field office, and a 120 percent increase in the New York field office.[77]

In August 2023, ICE proposed a massive expansion in the ICE ISAP program to include nearly all the 5.7 million people with a pending immigration case.[78] *Jacobin* magazine detailed a November 2023 GEO Group meeting in which investors were nearly giddy about the possibilities. One investor asked the CEO about the possibility of such an expansion: "I mean, we're talking five million people that could potentially be monitored [...] That business, which has 50 percent margins, could be substantially higher next year if this comes through, is that correct?"[79]

So, ATD programs are not really an "alternative" to detention. Instead, they are "digital prisons" that vastly expand ICE's capacity to monitor more immigrants, while increasing private companies' profits.[80] Meanwhile, the detention infrastructure remains intact and poised to expand.

WHAT NOW?

The United States' immigration detention system is set up to make money off captive people. It relies and thrives on the poor treatment of criminalized, racialized immigrants. There is no doubt or question that advocates will and should continue to push for humane treatment of detained people as well as accountability in detention centers. Yet, as is well known in activist communities, a focus on alleviating abuses and curbing the violation of rights is not enough.

The research we've detailed in this book leads us to conclude that the detention system is irredeemable, and the long-term goal must be to dismantle the system entirely. We align with ideas and movements that understand the interconnected nature of injustices that detention depends upon, that denying the rights of migrants is linked with the struggles of marginalized and racialized groups elsewhere and everywhere.[81] We support local- and state-level anti-detention strategies, which are important and transformative. We also firmly believe that it is essential to simultaneously focus on identifying the various, interlaced strands of the "immigration detention inc." dependency web. Disentangling and shredding the many strands is necessary to achieve an end to detention. With this goal in mind, we conclude with suggestions, a roadmap of sorts, aimed at exposing, disrupting, and disabling key stakeholders' influence and activities in the U.S. detention system.

Increase public awareness

Access to information about detention and the money behind it is crucial. So much about the detention system is hidden from public view. *Who makes money? How is that money grounded in daily injustices? How does detention spin out webs of economic dependence that local governments are caught up in and cashing in on?* While some may not be bothered, many members of the general public will be alarmed at how U.S. immigration policy is not driven by "safety" or "laws," but instead, often, by brazen profiteering. Raising such awareness is a primary goal of this book.

Increasing awareness also involves sharing knowledge and tools to access the hidden information about who is involved and how money is made in connection with the detention industry. It is necessary to teach more people how to file public information requests, tactics to push back when requests are stalled, denied, or riddled with redactions, and how to decode and piece together disparate information sources. It's also important to train others in safely circulating details and insights that deep reading of contracts and other documents can provide.

Increasing public knowledge must also entail advocating for, making, and enforcing more laws around transparency and accountability. Public access to information must be expanded: to contracts and costs, to conditions inside detention, to relationships between detention stakeholders and policymakers.[82] People need to be able to follow the money to be able to see who is benefiting and who to hold to account.

Don't appropriate more money!

The money allocated for detention has continuously, and at times exponentially, increased since the 1980s. Often negotiated as part of packages to "get tough" on immigration and border enforcement, bigger budgets result in more permanent detention infrastructure, and more individuals, communities, and companies becoming more reliant on detention as a source of revenue. Some individuals and groups have found it viable and effective to work alongside elected officials to break the spiral of ever-growing funding. We recognize such close advocacy work as pulling at one of the dependency strands and thus as complementary to more radical efforts to dismantle relationships sustaining the detention system.[83] Without more money being made available, dependent companies will need to find alternative ways to make money.

Stop leapfrogging from state to state

As long as there are state agencies and private companies that ICE can work with to detain migrants, the system can continue to thrive and even expand. Recall the ICE response to the detention ban in states like New Jersey: instead of detaining fewer people, many detainees were transferred out of state, to places far from family and legal support. The likelihood of this reality made for some unusual bedfellows: in some cases, lawyers and family members felt compelled to advocate for the continuation of detention in New Jersey, at variance with anti-detention activists. The percentage of detainees held in privately-run facilities is at an all-time high, and ICE is scouting for more business with for-profit corporations that are accountable to shareholders, not voters.

To be clear, pursuing actions to enact state-level bans—"beacons for the anti-detention movement"[84]—are worthwhile. Despite setbacks, there's been a flourishing of state bills to end detention in recent years. Now it's necessary to build support across state lines, as the long-term strategy must be to end detention at the *national* level, not just state by liberal-leaning state. Otherwise, there will always be another state where ICE can transfer detainees, or another private operator anxious to fill space.

Activists and policymakers working to change laws and practices at the local and state level must think about how to incorporate provisions for *releasing* instead of transferring detainees. We must build coalitions and design strategies to prevent detention from being geographically relocated according to political will, with maps of detention that resemble political party maps.

Make detention not worth it

It's very clear that disincentivizing detention as a profit-making venture is a critical strategy. How can we do this when profit is *the* key driver, and when the second Trump administration is crowded with billionaires, business sharks, schemers, and ideologues?[85] Our research points to some potential weak seams where profit-seeking and revenue incentives can be held in check. If involvement in the detention system is less profitable, fewer companies will be enthusiastic about participating in it.

Reducing economic incentives includes strategies such as real enforcement of existing guidelines and contract terms. Insisting on improving detention conditions for detainees, and enforcing standards and guidelines as hard rules, inevitably means higher costs for detention providers. By reworking the system that exists to hold exploitation in check, it's feasible to chip away at detention's appeal and the returns it yields. Another strategy is to end detainee labor for $1–3 per day; paying even the federal minimum wage to detainees—or making companies hire from the general population—will dramatically increase costs for detention operators.

Legal experts must persist in mounting legal challenges to labor exploitation, and doggedly thwart companies' crafty strategies to get around labor rights. Laws like California's 2023 BASIC Act, which limits how much commissary companies can gouge their prices, can be passed in other states and at the federal level. Picking away at the potential for profit margins renders detention itself less lucrative and therefore less attractive as a business proposition.

Refuse to do business with detention players

Other powerful strategies include petitions, boycotts, and divestment from entities that make money from detention. Individuals can refuse to invest in companies, funds, and investment groups involved in detention provision.

Even more impactful is when companies and governments pull investments from, or otherwise refuse to do business with, detention stakeholders. There have been important initiatives to divest from major prison companies, like CoreCivic and GEO Group. For example, New York State divested its state pension funds from these two companies, and many major banks refused to do business with them.[86] Amid public anger over reports that immigrant children were being detained in particularly horrific conditions in makeshift detention camps during the first Trump administration, Bank of America, JPMorgan Chase, Wells Fargo, Barclays, U.S. Bank and others exited relationships with some of the companies operating detention centers and prisons.[87] Around this time, Wayfair employees in Boston walked off the job to protest Wayfair's business with detention operators, demanding the company cut ties and write a code of conduct that would prevent future involvement.[88]

As the second Trump administration takes shape, with plans already in motion to exponentially expand the use of detention, it's important to be reminded that actions such as these make important public statements that can and do force involved companies to enact changes. At the least, such actions create interference that makes it more difficult and less profitable to participate in detention and incarceration.

For maximum impact, this strategy of divesting must target the *entire* web of detention dependencies. Not just those companies operating directly in detention facilities, but any entities that make money off supporting immigration detention must face public and political pressure to cease involvement. If it becomes more costly than profitable to be in the detention business, they will stop. A sustained, large-scale divestment campaign could eventually bring about the end of the detention system.

This approach also entails targeting the image and credibility of detention players at the local level: identifying and bringing public attention to local companies and investors that contract with ICE or county and state facilities that provide detention capacity and services. In New Jersey, when the Elizabeth Detention Center remained open after other centers had closed, local anti-detention activists drew public attention to the company that owns the property on which the Elizabeth facility is located. After intense negative publicity, the Elberon Development Group announced that it wanted to cut ties with GEO Group and end the use of the property for detention.[89]

This victory was short-lived, because of GEO Group's successful lawsuit against the state. But it highlights the need for and the potential of targeting detention players at local and at broader levels. Continuing to change the terms of the game forces companies to spend time, political capital, and funds to continue their operations, all of which can decrease the appetite for expanding detention.

A global campaign

Efforts to dismantle the detention system in the United States must not result in building detention systems elsewhere. To try to deter migrants and halt journeys to the United States, the U.S. already pays Mexico and other governments in Central America and the Caribbean to detain migrants. The absence of safeguards to protect migrants in these places means that outsourcing detention brings even worse detention experiences.

The goal must be to dismantle "immigration detention inc." dependency webs everywhere, and not to push them elsewhere. U.S. laws and policies around detention must include explicit provisions to decrease detention overall, in ways that will not allow detention systems to relocate.

Action is also needed to develop, support, and expand *international* coalitions that do all these things, so that immigration enforcement activities can't simply balloon and relocate to far-flung places where migrants are all but abandoned. There are some existing organizations that do research and compile information about detention around the world, like the International Detention Coalition and Global Detention Project. Some international human rights organizations draw attention to the global spread of immigration detention, like Human Rights Watch and Amnesty International. Within the United Nations, there are several agencies that gather information and administer programs intended to support detainees.

But there are surprisingly few initiatives that bring together advocates and activists working against detention from the United States and other countries. A big issue is lack of resources. Most activists are working within the parameters of nonprofit organizations, which struggle to find sufficient funding for their own national operations and staff, much less funding to fuel an international initiative. Be it through government allocations or private donors, anti-detention organizations need money and resources to dismantle national detention webs and also to stop detention dependencies from spinning off additional international strands.

Build other opportunities and possibilities

Finally, we need to think creatively and concretely about futures without "immigration detention inc." This means creating alternative economic and social opportunities. Instead of laws and policies that facilitate making money from detaining people, we need laws and policies that make money from *not* detaining people.

A Detention Watch Network report aiming to create a path to a post-detention United States urges funding to help communities develop sources of revenue that do not involve detention or incarceration in any way. Anti-detention economic and social development foregrounds justice.[90] It includes grants for technical assistance, business planning, and skills training that are part of the active transformation of communities and society more broadly. Community leaders need to work with economic advisors and community members to craft realistic and localized plans that draw on regional strengths.[91] These types of initiatives could be paid for by re-allocating the billions of dollars that currently prop up the detention system.

Breaking detention dependencies, then, means not merely up-ending the political, economic, and social conditions that sustain these systems, it also means imagining and realizing more just communities everywhere.

Afterword: Chaos and Cruelty in the First Month of the Second Trump Administration

At almost the exact moment that we finished writing this book, in January 2025, Donald Trump was inaugurated as U.S. President for a second time. The second Trump administration kicked off by launching an offensive against migrants that is chaotic, damaging, and inhumane. We decided to write this Afterword one month into "Trump 2.0" to take stock of the new administration's actions related to immigration so far, with a focus on the role of and implications for the detention dependencies we have detailed in preceding chapters, and to keep in view the long game of pushing back against and bringing an end to "immigration detention inc."

Immigration was a core issue of the 2024 presidential campaign, even though the number of border crossings between Mexico and the U.S. had dropped more than 60 percent since May 2024 and, in January 2025, numbers were 50 percent lower than in January 2021, the end of Trump's first stint as president.[1] The 2024 campaign rhetoric was a repeat of long-established patterns where immigrants are politically useful scapegoats for economic woes, frustration with government ineffectiveness, and fears of a changing racial hierarchy and national identity.

On the campaign trail in 2024, both Trump and Biden expressed—albeit with different levels of vitriol and aggression—the goal of reducing immigration. For both candidates, increasing detention was a central mechanism for achieving this goal, and a clear sign, once again, that incarcerating immigrants is a popular bipartisan strategy. The election results showed, however, that Trump's hyperbole—calling all immigrants "invaders" and "criminals," and blaming all manner of social and economic problems on immigrants—especially resonated with voters.

Right away, Trump's new administration moved to make good on the "mass deportation plan" that was front and center of his campaign. The slew of executive orders relating to immigration that were issued starting on day one "signal to immigrant communities that they are under attack [while they also set out] a blueprint for future actions."[2] The speed and quantity of the new administration's initial actions are also intended to overwhelm. So, one month into Trump's second presidency, migrant communities, advocates, activists, and concerned individuals are in the midst of a confused, chaotic, and cruel onslaught of changing rules and shifting practices, as well as wildly spinning rumors.

In broad terms, Trump's directives expand "the enforcement dragnet,"[3] cast any unauthorized migration as an "invasion," enroll the military in immigration and border policing, thwart and punish organizations and state and local governments working with migrants, and radically alter future possibilities for migration to the U.S. except in highly restricted cases—meaning by migrants who are elite, wealthy, white, and well-connected. By declaring immigration and border control a national security emergency, the new administration has been able to immediately draw on resources from multiple government agencies not usually involved in immigration policing, as well as call on the military to assist with its plans.

Among the specific actions taken so far by the second Trump administration are attempting to end birthright citizenship; requiring government registration of all immigrants; revoking prohibitions on ICE agents entering sensitive locations such as schools, hospitals, and churches; setting arrest quotas for all ICE field offices; expanding the use of expedited removal; threatening to prosecute any individuals, agencies, and other organizations that refuse to cooperate with ICE; using military planes to transport deportees; and promising to impose tariffs against countries who refuse to accept deportees. Trump also signed the Laken Riley Act into law, which (among other provisions) vastly expands the number of immigrants subject to mandatory detention.

Trump officials have stated goals of deporting up to 20 million immigrants. Most estimates suggest that there are around 11.7 million undocumented immigrants currently in the U.S.[4] The new administration has also made it clear that they are going after those who have various kinds of temporary legal status. For example, Trump immediately cancelled status granted to asylum seekers during the Biden administration through humanitarian parole and use of ICE's CBP One app,[5] totaling about 1.5 million people. With the stroke of a pen, vulnerable migrants who followed legal channels and sought entry to the U.S. "the right way" suddenly became "illegal," and were lumped together with Trump's distorted idea that all immigrants are "criminals."

The new administration quickly proclaimed sharp increases in arrests. In Trump's first week in office, the agency reported an average of 787 arrests a day; in reality, this is less than 4 percent higher than the average of 759 arrests per day in 2024.[6] ICE has also begun deporting migrants on military flights, frequently with a spectacle of media coverage, to destinations including Brazil, Colombia, Ecuador, Guatemala, Honduras, India, and Venezuela. Even while early analysis indicates that "the hype does not in fact reflect what actually has occurred on the ground,"[7] the highly publicized optics—of chained migrants being loaded single-file onto military planes—convey a sense of "promises delivered" to the general public and invoke fear and distress within migrant communities.

The Trump administration is also aggressively pursuing more partnerships between ICE and local governments for their immigration crackdown. This contributes to a checkerboard of immigration policing activities. For example, the New York State Attorney General has directed county governments to not facilitate ICE arrests. But some counties have disregarded directives; for instance, the County Executive of conservative Nassau County on Long Island (east of New York City) has ordered county police to partner with ICE in their operations.[8] While it is difficult to sort fact from rumor, uncertainty is rife; arguably, this is intended. The intensity and speed of the new administration's orders are combined with unpredictability and a lack of transparency that, altogether, cause turmoil and amp up the enforcement system's inhumanity.

IMPLICATIONS FOR "IMMIGRATION DETENTION INC."

Vastly increasing detention capacity is central to the new administration's deportation goals. It is likely that such extensive capacity expansion will entail heavy use of private operators, inadequate facilities, insufficient care, poorly trained personnel, abuse of detainees' human rights, and weak oversight.

ICE documents available so far indicate plans to expand detention "beds" to around 100,000, more than doubling existing detention capacity. This would include the construction of new capacity for over 50,000, with four, massive 10,000-bed detention facilities, plus 14 smaller facilities. These would most likely be contracted to private prison companies. Additionally, Trump administration officials have indicated they will also seek more space in existing state and county jails, and to house migrants on military bases.[9]

The second Trump administration is clearly willing to be brutish in their efforts to supersize the detention system. In early February, officials began using federal prisons to hold detained immigrants. While numbers were not being released, this move was alarming, given the already poor state of the federal prison system, marked by abuse, staff shortages, and violence. The first Trump administration had also used the federal prison system to detain immigrants, resulting in numerous lawsuits regarding their treatment.[10] In addition, the administration has floated the possibility of using huge tents—called "soft-sided facilities"—to rapidly expand capacity,[11] and is reported to be discussing the possibility of using shipping containers to house detainees.[12] Even more disturbing is the news that the administration is currently preparing Requests for Proposals inviting bids by private prison companies to restart family detention.[13]

What's more, the administration has moved quickly with plans to detain migrants on military bases. So far, a base in Colorado is making space available to serve as a temporary holding facility for migration. The biggest move yet is the plan to use the Guantánamo Bay military base in Cuba to detain up to 30,000 migrants, with an estimated price tag roughly five times what it costs to detain a migrant in the continental United States.[14]

The United States housed thousands of migrants interdicted at sea in Guantánamo in the 1970s, '80s, and '90s, some in permanent structures, but most in tent camps.[15] In recent years, small numbers of interdicted migrants, an average of 20 per day, have

AFTERWORD

been housed in one designated area. In September 2024, the International Refugee Assistance Project released a report detailing the abysmal conditions and routine mistreatment experienced by migrants detained there.[16]

The permanent structures for housing migrants that are currently in existence on Guantánamo (including those condemned by observers) have a capacity of roughly 220, if you count facilities used for military detention of suspected terrorists. Trump has sent several hundred military troops to the island to set up hundreds of tents for incoming migrants. The base is in a tropical location, where tents are inadequate protection from the elements. So far more than 175 individuals have been moved from the U.S. to the Guantánamo base, and subsequently, and quite suddenly, deported to Venezuela.[17] Almost one third of those detained were believed to be without any serious criminal conviction, which gives the lie to the current administration's claim that they are targeting "high-threat" migrants. Lawyers and advocates warn that detainees sent to Guantánamo are effectively placed in a "legal black hole," with little access to lawyers and removed from mechanisms for accountability.[18]

Lowering (the already low) detention standards is central to the Trump administration's plans to quickly expand capacity. Tom Homan, designated Trump's "border czar," announced that ICE will relax detention standards to encourage more state and county jails to contract out bed space to detain immigrants. Homan promised that ICE will accept less rigorous state-level standards in lieu of the National Detention Standards (NDS) and decrease the number of federal inspections.[19] As we have discussed throughout this book, the NDS and ICE inspections are already inadequate and do not deter abysmal and unjust detention conditions. Further weakening these minimal guardrails will only exacerbate existing problems, likely with even more deadly consequences.

Also deeply troubling are the immediate actions taken under the new administration to cut off all outside access to detention facilities. Funding was suspended for organizations contracted to ensure detainees' legal rights are not violated. Groups that routinely provided Know Your Rights information to detainees were suddenly denied access to facilities.[20] Detainees have also reported that detention-center personnel have removed posted information for detainees regarding their legal rights and how to access legal counsel. Advocates point out that without minimal information about rights and legal resources, detainees' deportation is almost certain.

Finally, the risk of further expanding the U.S. immigration system outside of U.S. borders has become even more real. In early February, El Salvador's President Nayib Bukele offered to jail, at a "relatively low" fee, both U.S. citizen prisoners and immigrant detainees in El Salvador's huge, notoriously violent prison built to contain gang members.[21] While it is still unknown if this offer will be accepted—and how the clear legal barriers to such a move could be circumvented—Secretary of State Marco Rubio called the offer "very generous." A deal has been made with Panama to use Panamanian territory as a staging point for U.S. deportation operations; several hundred migrants, including children, have already been flown there, and are currently being held captive in hotels and a remote jungle camp.[22] Agreements have also now been signed between the U.S. and Costa Rica, as well as between the U.S. and Guatemala.[23]

The Trump administration's willingness to outsource detention outside its borders shows a profound disrespect for national and international laws and migrants' human rights. At the same time, it's important to acknowledge that this is not new. Previous administrations, beginning with that of President George W. Bush, have supplied Mexico and to a lesser extent Guatemala with funds and resources to detain U.S.-bound migrants.[24]

Outsourcing detention in exchange for substantial sums of money and other resources is also a familiar playbook internationally. Australia's "Pacific Solution" policy is infamous, where migrant arrivals were not permitted to set foot in Australia and summarily sent to languish on remote, independent, sovereign territories in the Pacific Islands. More recently, under the U.K.'s previous Conservative government, a deal was struck with the Rwandan government to send migrants who crossed the English Channel, arriving to the U.K. via "small boats," to Rwanda where they were to be detained in facilities funded by the U.K. government until being granted asylum in Rwanda (not in the U.K.) or deported.[25]

We mention these already existing deals and international outsourcing agreements for two reasons: first, to note that massive amounts of money and resources are exchanged and revenue generated with these arrangements, and second, to flag prospects for building international networks that expand possibilities for a global campaign pushing back against the avaricious power of "immigration detention inc."

PRIVATE COMPANIES CONTINUE TO DRIVE DETENTION

The rapid, explosive growth of the detention system under Donald Trump will depend on heavy use of private companies—and they have banked on it. The CEOs of both GEO Group and CoreCivic gave significant donations to Trump's campaign, and the CEO of CoreCivic also donated to his inaugural committee. Stock prices of both companies have almost doubled since the election.[26] In fact, soon after Trump's win, the GEO Group executive chairman stated, "This is to us an unprecedented opportunity."[27] Other statements from prison industry leaders expressed barely contained excitement at the prospects for cashing in on detaining migrants.

As this book has detailed, the economic benefits of more detention are not merely limited to prison corporations. Other kinds of businesses are poised to profit—those that provide food, medical care, commissary items, transportation, communication, to name the most obvious. And remember, all of those companies spin out additional webs in their supply chains and day-to-day operations. County and state governments also stand to scoop up more federal money. Local, state, and federal government agencies may be compelled to participate in detention in ways that become integral to their routine operations. Employees of all these entities could find their livelihoods increasingly tied to detaining immigrants.

The second Trump administration also exemplifies the "revolving door" between government agencies involved in detention and private prison corporations. Just before the November election, a top ICE official took a job with GEO Group. Soon after, as reported by the Project on Government Oversight, "GEO Group announced it was investing $70 million to bolster its ability to support the agency."²⁸ And the connections between top Trump officials and companies who will benefit from the promised "crackdown" are thick. For example, Pam Bondi, Trump's Attorney General, previously worked as a lobbyist for GEO Group.²⁹ As mentioned in Chapter 6, Trump's new Secretary of State, Marco Rubio, has long had a relationship with GEO Group, receiving tens of thousands of dollars in campaign contributions over the years.³⁰

SORTING FACT FROM FICTION IN THE FRENZY TO EXPAND DETENTION AND DEPORTATION

At the same time as we express profound concern and alarm at the new administration's actions, a cautious position is necessary when assessing what is really happening. It's not yet possible to sort bluster and performance from actual policy changes and begin to assess lasting impacts.

Trump and his allies have shown themselves capable of masterfully manipulating both media coverage and public perception. For example, in the weeks immediately following Trump's 2025 inauguration, rumors of ICE raids taking place all over the country ripped through social media. It appears that ICE manipulated Google algorithms to fuel these rumors. Google searches for ICE raids and arrests returned a long list of ICE press releases that seemed to show massive new ICE activity everywhere. But when astute observers looked more closely, they realized that ICE had marked old press releases, from as far back as 15 years ago, as updated, which bumped them higher in Google's search results.³¹

When it comes to immigration detention, publicly reported ICE detention numbers do show an increase in the total detained population between the end of December 2024 and February 9, 2025: from 39,150 to 41,169.³² However, looking at the weekly breakdown (for February 1–8, 2025), a TRAC report shows that, on average, 724 individuals were newly detained in this period. Comparing this with the 2024 average—759 ICE arrests per day throughout 2024—the new administration's arrest and detention numbers are, in fact, considerably lower than in the last year of the Biden administration. As the TRAC report notes, this is "despite assigning personnel from other agencies to immigration enforcement."[33] Reports note that ICE released some detained migrants after the detention system ran out of space.[34] ICE data also show that the agency is increasingly targeting immigrants without criminal records, contrary to the agency's press releases and social media posts.[35]

Critically, it is unclear if the massive operations the Trump administration is pushing are feasible, on multiple levels. While exact funding sources are hard to trace, the Trump administration's flurry of initial actions is likely being paid for with already-appropriated funds, moving existing personnel and funds around, and short-term military deployments. But the promised "mass deportation" will require repeated large appropriations by Congress, including money to permanently increase detention.

The proposed rapid growth of the detention system in particular will require mind-boggling sums of money. In fiscal year 2024, $3.4 billion dollars was budgeted for 41,500 detention beds. Estimates suggest that increasing detention capacity by 110,000 beds (a provision of the Laken Riley Act passed after Trump took office) would cost at least $26.9 billion.[36]

The Trump administration is pushing Congress to quickly appropriate hundreds of billions of dollars to fund their broad agenda, with a big chunk of that designated for immigration and border enforcement. While the Republican-led Congress has promised to act quickly, the slim majorities in both houses, as well as competing agendas among Republicans, have slowed passage of a funding package.[37] Although Trump is likely to have some immediate victories in appropriations, sustaining the level of funding required may be difficult to wrangle.

There are other potential roadblocks for long-term implementation of Trump's plan. In the near future, duties and functions typically performed by the government agencies and personnel shifted around to augment Trump's anti-immigrant agenda will eventually need to be reinstated. State and local agencies contributing their own money and personnel need to be compensated, or they will not be able to perform routine functions for their constituents. For example, while Texas Governor Greg Abbott has offered empty Texas jail space for immigration detention, he has also asked the federal government to reimburse his state $11 billion for immigration enforcement actions Texas took on their own initiative during the Biden administration.[38] The outcome of Abbott's new request is still unknown, but it does indicate that even states and local governments most enthusiastic about their participation in Trump's anti-immigration campaign will reach their own financial limits. And sheriffs across the country warn that the assistance they can provide is limited by already-existing problems with lack of funds and staff.[39]

Additionally, legal challenges to the new Trump administration's cacophony of actions are piling up. Various combinations of local and state government agencies and offices, independent organizations, and individuals have already filed dozens of lawsuits pertaining to anti-immigration initiatives. Just a small sampling includes pending litigation against Trump's executive orders attempting to end birthright citizenship; allow immigration enforcement in sensitive locations; suspend the U.S. refugee admissions program and refuse all asylum claims; freeze federal funds allocated to organizations assisting noncitizens; order federal employees of agencies outside DHS to apprehend migrants; extend mandatory detention to more categories of migrants; deport migrants to and detain them in third-party countries; and revoke multiple categories of already-granted legal status. Legal experts are confident that many of the current administration's actions are illegal and will eventually be overturned. While these legal challenges may take months, if not years, to wind their way through the courts, several have resulted in immediate halts to policy implementation.[40]

In the longer term, other factors may also come into play. The involvement of state and local law enforcement agents in immigration policing has previously been shown to reduce trust in local authorities and contribute to an increase in crime at the local level. Such concerns are among the issues driving officials in New Jersey to condemn ICE's forcefulness, and call for swift implementation of legislation to supplement and bolster existing directives that limit cooperation by state and local police departments with federal immigration enforcement efforts.[41] Economists predict that large-scale detention and deportation will have profound economic consequences for the broader public. The lack of cheap immigrant labor could lead to significant price increases in foods and services, and real shortages in people to perform vital tasks. Despite anti-immigrant myths, immigrants contribute in essential ways to the economy not just with their labor, but also by paying taxes, contributing to Social Security, and as consumers. Voters who supported Trump may shift their thinking if their communities are torn apart and local economies become depressed.

FIGHTING AND ENDING "IMMIGRATION DETENTION INC."

Amid the chaos and fear, we need to remember that the current anti-immigrant juggernaut—and the detention apparatus that is central to it—did not originate with Donald Trump. Far from it: anti-immigrant ideology has been constructed over decades, and both Republicans and Democrats have contributed to its entrenchment and growth.

Racist ideas of American identity have always been key propellants.[42] The Trump administration's roots in white supremacy and the egregious yet increasingly blatant notion that true citizenship is only for "white" Christians permeate wide-ranging policy actions so far, including Trump's plans for mass deportation.[43] The skyrocketing fear and a sense of isolation and non-belonging among immigrants, both authorized and unauthorized, is wholly intentional on the part of the Trump administration; it does the work of sorting "real Americans" from those deemed—by the MAGA faithful—to be unassimilable "aliens."

But it's important to recognize how these actions are also propelled by economic interests, as we have argued throughout this book. These interests range from employers desiring cheap, flexible labor all the way through to entities and industries that profit liberally from immigration enforcement. These groups lobby and support politicians calling for more detention and deportation. They write the laws put forward by elected officials. They own the tech that spins and spews propaganda and disinformation. And now, in the second Trump administration, more explicitly than many could have imagined, self-interested capitalists, billionaires, and tech oligarchs are pulling all the strings.

We reiterate and amplify calls for solidarity and transformative justice in the face of the current regime. In doing so, we stand on the shoulders of generations of people: those who are or have been detained, others who are concerned advocates, activists, scholars, and community members—many of whom have informed and illuminated the issues we've discussed here—and emphasize, again, the necessity of dismantling "immigration detention inc." We recognize that such a demand might come across as merely aspirational given the detention system's entrenchment, and given the uncertainties and vulnerabilities of the current moment.

And so, we close by emphatically orienting toward practical actions to combat "immigration detention inc.," which we outlined in Chapter 6. Expose, expose, expose those who benefit from immigrant detention. Call, write, show up at elected officials' offices to protest laws and policies that result in detention and to voice opposition to funding detention. Find out who gives campaign contributions to your elected representatives. Speak out and demonstrate against local law enforcement participation with ICE, including the provision of local space for detention. Fight misinformation and manufactured narratives about immigrants. Share accurate information about the cruelty and profiteering driving detention. Demand the right to visit and assist detained migrants. Contest the transfer of detainees away from family and legal support. Fight efforts to lower standards for detention, and call for regular, frequent, earnest inspections of facilities. Support efforts to require minimum wage for detainee labor. Demand transparency and accountability about detention contracting decisions and provisions. Boycott companies with links to detention contracts. Refuse to invest in businesses profiting from the mass deportation initiative. Invest in strategies for alternative development initiatives at local to global levels.

These tasks remain as important today as they were one month ago, or one year ago, or whether Democrats or Republicans hold power. It is only with a sustained focus and the accumulation of small-scale—as well as networked and expansive—probing and persistent scrutiny, alongside practical demands and actions to dismantle economic drivers and dependencies that we can, collectively, shatter "immigration detention inc."

Notes

All URLs were last accessed in January 2025.

Introduction: Immigration Detention Inc.'s Deep Dependencies

1. Katz, M. (2018, August 16). Should New Jersey Democratic officials keep jailing immigrants for ICE? *WNYC*. www.wnyc.org/story/should-new-jersey-democratic-officials-keep-jailing-immigrants-ice
2. O'Dea, C. (2019, April 25). Protestors demand Essex County end contract to house ICE detainees. *NJSpotlight*. www.njspotlight.com/2019/04/19-04-24-protestors-demand-essex-county-end-lucrative-contract-to-house-ice-detainees/
3. Guerguerian, A. (2021, April 21). Cold as ICE: North Jersey counties rake in millions from the Feds while holding immigrant detainees in subhuman conditions. *The Indypendent*. https://indypendent.org/2021/04/corruptandinbed/
4. Katz, M. (2021, April 28). New Jersey County ends lucrative and controversial jailing of ICE detainees. *WNYC/Gothamist*. https://gothamist.com/news/new-jersey-county-ends-lucrative-and-controversial-jailing-ice-detainees
5. National Immigration Forum. (2021). *Fact sheet: Immigration detention in the United States*. https://immigrationforum.org/wp-content/uploads/2021/01/Immigration-Detention-Factsheet_FINAL.pdf
6. Saadi, A., De Trinidad Young, M.-E., Patler, C., Estrada, J. L., & Venters, H. (2020). Understanding US immigration detention. *Health and Human Rights*, 22(1), 187–197. PMCID: PMC7348446.
7. In Chapter 3, we break down the figures on migrant deaths in detention; we also note under-reporting as a persistent issue.
8. Marlow, M. A., Luna-Gierke, R. E., Griffin, P. M., & Vieira, A. R. (2017). Foodborne disease outbreaks in correctional institutions-United States, 1998–2014. *American Journal of Public Health*, 107(7), 1150–1156. doi.org/10.2105/AJPH.2017.303816
9. Cho, E. (2023, August 7). Unchecked growth: Private prison corporations and immigration detention, three years into the Biden administration. *ACLU News and Commentary*. www.aclu.org/news/immigrants-rights/unchecked-growth-private-prison-corporations-and-immigration-detention-three-years-into-the-biden-administration
10. We refer to profit as gains linked to capital.
11. Global Detention Project. (2024, April). *Annual report*. www.globaldetentionproject.org/annual-report-important-victories-amidst-inexorable-expansion (p. 6).

12. Baker, J. (2019, October). HIG Capital's prison food and commissary store racket. *Private Equity Stakeholder Project.* https://pestakeholder.org/reports/report-hig-capitals-prison-food-and-commissary-store-racket/
13. Hiemstra, N., & Conlon, D. (2016). Captive consumers and coerced labourers: Intimate economies and the expanding US detention regime. In D. Conlon & N. Hiemstra (eds.), *Intimate economies of immigration detention: Critical perspectives* (pp. 123–163). Routledge.

Chapter 1 Probing U.S. Detention's Unhealthy Growth

1. Transactional Records Access Clearinghouse (TRAC). (2025). *Immigration detention quick facts.* https://tracreports.org/immigration/quickfacts/detention.html
2. Immigration and Customs Enforcement (ICE). (2023). *ICE annual report: Fiscal year 2023.* U.S. Department of Homeland Security (p. 18).
3. Siskin, A. (2004, April 28). *Immigration-related detention: Current legislative issues.* Congressional Research Service Report for Congress, The Library of Congress; Loyo, R. & Corrado, C. (2010, April). *Locked up but not forgotten: Opening access to family & community in the immigration detention system.* New York University School of Law Immigrant Rights Clinic, American Friends Service Committee, New Jersey Advocates for Immigrant Detainees. https://afsc.org/sites/default/files/documents/LockedUpExSummFINAL.pdf
4. ICE. (2023). *ICE budget overview fiscal year 2024 congressional justification.* Department of Homeland Security (p. 5).
5. Detention Watch Network (DWN). (2016). *A toxic relationship: Private prisons and U.S. immigration detention.* www.detentionwatchnetwork.org/sites/default/files/reports/A%20Toxic%20Relationship_DWN.pdf (p. 11).
6. Cho, E. (2023, August 7). *Unchecked growth: Private prison corporations and immigration detention, three years into the Biden administration.* American Civil Liberties Union (ACLU). www.aclu.org/news/immigrants-rights/unchecked-growth-private-prison-corporations-and-immigration-detention-three-years-into-the-biden-administration
7. *Open Secrets Annual Lobbying Database.* (2024). Client Profile: CoreCivic, Inc. 2023. www.opensecrets.org/federal-lobbying/clients/summary?cycle=2023&id=D000021940&year=2016; Client Profile 2023: GEO Group. www.opensecrets.org/federal-lobbying/clients/summary?cycle=2023&id=D000022003
8. Morín, J., Torres, R., & Collingwood, L. (2021). Cosponsoring and cashing in: US House members' support for punitive immigration policy and financial payoffs from the private prison industry. *Business and Politics, 23*(4), 492–509. doi:10.1017/bap.2021.6
9. Hiemstra, N. (2019). *Detain and deport: The chaotic U.S. immigration enforcement regime.* University of Georgia Press.

10. There are numerous accounts that provide a more thorough history of immigrant detention in the U.S. than we undertake here. Among these are: Dow, M. (2004). *American gulag: Inside U.S. immigration prisons*. University of California Press; Golash-Boza, T. (2012). *Immigration nation: Raids, detentions, and deportations in post-9/11 America*. Paradigm Publishers; Ryo, E., & Peacock, I. (2018). A national study of immigration detention in the United States. *Southern California Law Review, 92*(1), 1–68; Loyd, J. M., & Mountz, A. (2018). *Boats, borders, and bases: Race, the Cold War, and the rise of migration detention in the United States*. University of California Press; Hernández, C. C. G. (2019). *Migrating to prison: America's obsession with locking up immigrants*. The New Press; Kassie, E. (2019, September 24). Detained: How the United States created the largest immigration detention system in the world. *The Marshall Project*. www.themarshallproject.org/2019/09/24/detained.
11. Hiemstra, *Detain and deport*.
12. Hernández, D. M. (2016). Surrogates and subcontractors: Flexibility and obscurity in U.S. immigrant detention. In N. Elia, D. M. Hernández, J. Kim, S. L. Redmond, D. Rodríguez, & S. E. See (eds.), *Critical ethnic studies: A reader* (pp. 303–325). Duke University Press.
13. Welch, M. (2002). *Detained: Immigration laws and the expanding I.N.S. jail complex*. Temple University Press; Dow, *American gulag*; Hernández, D. M. (2008). Pursuant to deportation: Latinos and immigrant detention. *Latino Studies, 6*, 35–63, https://doi.org/10.1057/lst.2008.2; Doty, R. L., & Wheatley, E. S. (2013). Private detention and the immigration industrial complex. *International Political Sociology, 7*, 426–443, https://doi.org/10.1111/ips.12032; Hiemstra, *Detain and deport*.
14. While initially the category was limited to a narrow set of serious crimes (murder, drug and weapons trafficking), subsequent legislation has significantly expanded it to include even minor crimes such as using a false ID and shoplifting; Tosh, S. (2023). *The immigration law death penalty: Aggravated felonies, deportation, and legal resistance*. NYU Press.
15. Kahn, R. S. (1996). *Other people's blood: U.S. immigration prisons in the Reagan decade*. Westview Press.
16. Martin, L. (2012). "Catch and remove": Detention, deterrence, and discipline in US noncitizen family detention practice. *Geopolitics, 17*(2), 312–334, https://doi.org/10.1080/14650045.2011.554463; Hiemstra, *Detain and deport*.
17. Figure 1.1 data was extracted from multiple sources: ICE Yearly reports, DHS yearly Budgets in Brief, DHS yearly Budget Justifications, and TRAC.
18. American Friends Service Committee (AFSC). (2015, December). *The role of for-profit prison corporations in shaping U.S. immigrant detention and deportation policies*. https://afsc.org/sites/default/files/documents/BedQuotaWhitePaper.pdf; Detention Watch Network (DWN) and Center for Constitutional Rights (CCR). (2015). *Banking on detention: Local lockup*

quotas & the immigrant dragnet; https://ccrjustice.org/home/get-involved/tools-resources/publications/report-banking-detention. DWN & CCR. (2016). *Banking on detention: 2016 update.* https://ccrjustice.org/home/get-involved/tools-resources/publications/report-banking-detention

19. United States Government Accountability Office (GAO). (2021, January). *Immigration detention: Actions needed to improve planning, documentation, and oversight of detention facility contracts.* GAO-21-149. www.gao.gov/assets/gao-21-149.pdf; Cho, E., Tidwell Cullen, T., & Long, C. (2020, April 30). *Justice free zones: U.S. immigration detention under the Trump administration.* ACLU, Human Rights Watch, National Immigrant Justice Center. www.aclu.org/report/justice-free-zones-us-immigration-detention-under-trump-administration.
20. Hooks, G. & Libal, B. (2020, December). Hotbeds of infection: How ICE detention contributed to the spread of COVID-19 in the United States, Detention Watch Network. www.detentionwatchnetwork.org/sites/default/files/reports/DWN_Hotbeds%20of%20Infection_2020_FOR%20WEB.pdf; New York Lawyers for the Public Interest (NYLPI). (2020, April). *Still detained and denied: The health crisis in immigration detention continues.* www.nylpi.org/resource/still-detained-and-denied-the-health-crisis-in-immigration-detention-continues/; Tosh, S. R., Berg, U. D., & Leon, K. S. (2021). Migrant detention and COVID-19: Pandemic responses in four New Jersey detention centers. *Journal on Migration and Human Security,* 9(1), 49–62, https://doi.org/10.1177/23315024211003855
21. Cho, Unchecked growth.
22. While campaigning, Biden promised to end private prisons, and anti-detention activists hoped this promise extended to immigration detention. However, not only did the detention population quickly rebound under the Biden administration, but the use of private prison corporations for detention intensified.
23. Cho, Unchecked growth.
24. TRAC, *Immigration detention quick facts.*
25. Difilippo, D. (2024, November 22). Feds look to add immigration jails in New Jersey. *New Jersey Monitor.* https://newjerseymonitor.com/2024/11/22/feds-look-to-add-immigration-jails-in-new-jersey/; ACLU (2024, November 22). ACLU FOIA litigation reveals new information regarding ICE plans to expand immigration detention in New Jersey. *ACLU Press Release.* www.aclu.org/press-releases/aclu-foia-litigation-reveals-new-information-regarding-ices-plans-to-expand-immigration-detention-in-new-jersey
26. Department of Homeland Security, U.S. ICE. (2024). *Multi-state detention facility support – Request for information.* https://sam.gov/opp/ca0a3904f27d49039f75509932de0d3b/view; DWN (2024, September 18). ICE continues to eye immigration detention expansion, now on the West Coast, flying in the face of community values and state legislation. *DWN Press Release.* www.detentionwatchnetwork.org/pressroom/releases/2024/ice-continues-eye-immigration-detention-expansion-now-west-

coast-flying-face; Valenzuela, V. (2024, November 20). "Cruelty is built into the system": ICE set to open new immigration detention center in New Jersey. *Documented*. https://documentedny.com/2024/11/20/ice-detention-new-jersey-deportation-trump/
27. Rahman, B. (2024, December 13). Donald Trump considers detention camps for immigrants: "Whatever it takes". *Newsweek*. www.newsweek.com/donald-trump-detention-camps-immigration-2000271
28. Hetzner, C. (2024, November 7). Trump's election win sends private prisons stock soaring as investors anticipate crackdown on migration. *Fortune*. https://fortune.com/2024/11/07/president-donald-trump-election-immigration-border-detention-ice-geo-group-corecivic/
29. U.S. Department of Justice Archive. (n.d.). *Budget trend data 1975–2003: Immigration and Naturalization Service*. www.justice.gov/archive/jmd/1975_2002/2002/html/page104-108.htm
30. Kennedy, K. (2020, November). Correctional facilities in the US, US industry (NAICS) report 56121. IBISWorld. IBISWorld.com; Executive Order No. *14006*. Reforming our incarceration system to eliminate the use of privately operated criminal detention facilities. DCPD 202100088. www.govinfo.gov/content/pkg/DCPD-202100088/pdf/DCPD-202100088.pdf
31. Figure 1.2 information source is DHS yearly budgets, which are posted online at www.dhs.gov/dhs-budget
32. Cho, Unchecked growth.
33. AFSC, *The role of for-profit prison corporations*; DWN, *A toxic relationship*; Warren, E. (2020, January 17). Warren leads colleagues investigating the revolving door between federal agencies and the private detention industry. Office of Senator Elizabeth Warren. www.warren.senate.gov/oversight/reports/warren-leads-colleagues-investigating-the-revolving-door-between-federal-agencies-and-the-private-detention-industry.
34. The United States funds detention centers in several countries en route to the United States, including Mexico, Guatemala, and Honduras, in an effort to prevent migrants from reaching the U.S. border; Hiemstra, N. (2019). Pushing the US-Mexico border south: United States' immigration policing throughout the Americas. *International Journal of Migration and Border Studies*, 5(1/2), 44–63. doi:10.1504/IJMBS.2019.099681; Vogt, W. (2018). *Lives in transit: violence and intimacy on the migrant journey*. University of California Press.
35. The number of facilities reported by ICE was 150 in 2023: ICE, *U.S. ICE budget overview fiscal year 2024*. However, the number of active detention facilities in the United States has been as high as around 250 during the Obama and first Trump administrations, further demonstrating the cobbled-together nature of the system. Indeed, 40 new facilities were opened during the first Trump administration: U.S. GAO. *Immigration detention*. GAO-21-149; ACLU, Human Rights Watch, National Immigrant Justice Center. *Justice free zones*.
36. Maps for Figures 1.3 and 1.4 were made by Cassandra Skolnick.

37. DWN & CCR, *Banking on detention;* U.S. GAO, *Immigration detention.* There are additional facility arrangements involved in immigration detention, particularly for temporary, short-term detention, that we do not discuss here.
38. Data on guaranteed minimums, average length of stay, if the facility holds men and women obtained from: ICE. (2024). *ICE detention statistics.* www.ice.gov/detain/detention-management; TRAC. (2024). *Detention facilities average daily population.* https://tracreports.org/immigration/detentionstats/facilities.html; DWN & CCR, *Banking on detention* and Freedom for Immigrants. (2022). *Mapping U.S. immigration detention.* www.freedomforimmigrants.org/map.
39. The 2023 contract value was $28.5 million. *USASpending.gov.* (2024, June 3). Akima Global Services, Batavia. www.usaspending.gov/search/
40. It is interesting that Akima Global Services markets its Native Alaskan heritage, claiming on their website: "For 10,000 years, the people of the NANA region successfully fought for survival in one of the harshest environments on earth. When faced with the challenges that modernization, globalization, and changes in climate brought, they continued that success, forming enterprises that would help them thrive in the modern world." It is worth additional discussion that immigration detention is among the enterprises that allows a native company to "thrive in the modern world." www.akima.com/our-heritage/
41. We obtained information regarding current subcontracting through ICE Office of Detention Oversight (ODO) inspection reports, posted online as mandated by law, and facility contracts obtained through public information requests.
42. TRAC. (2025). *Detention facilities average daily population.* https://tracreports.org/immigration/detentionstats/facilities.html; Kaulessar, R. (2023, August 29). Federal judge rules NJ law cannot ban prison company from operating last ICE facility. *NorthJersey.com.* www.northjersey.com/story/news/new-jersey/2023/08/29/ice-detention-center-nj-continue-federal-ruling-corecivic/70711496007/
43. Perez-Pena, R. (1995, June 19). Illegal aliens overrun a jail in New Jersey. *New York Times.* www.nytimes.com/1995/06/19/us/illegal-aliens-overrun-a-jail-in-new-jersey.html; Stout, D. (1995, June 19). Detention jail called worse than prison. *New York Times.* www.nytimes.com/1995/06/19/nyregion/detention-jail-called-worse-than-prison.html
44. Goshko, J. M. (1995, July 21). INS blames riot on mismanagement by contractor at New Jersey detention site. *Washington Post.* www.washingtonpost.com/archive/politics/1995/07/22/ins-blames-riot-on-mismanagement-by-contractor-at-new-jersey-detention-site/a7be00d6-e029-4f32-840a-0fa2cbad8d72/. It is noteworthy that while that contract cancellation was the end of Esmor's operations at the Elizabeth Detention Center, it certainly wasn't the end of its involvement in

government confinement. Esmor soon changed its name to the Correctional Services Corporation and specialized in juvenile detention, again facing charges of abuse in other facilities it operated. Then, Correctional Services Corporation was bought by prison operator giant GEO Group in 2005; *Prison Legal News*. (2006, January 15). GEO Group buys out Correctional Services Corporation. www.prisonlegalnews.org/news/2006/jan/15/geo-group-buys-out-correctional-services-corporation/

45. Alvarado, M. (2021, May 3). Landlord of private ICE detention center in Elizabeth files suit to terminate lease. *NorthJersey.com*. www.northjersey.com/story/news/new-jersey/2021/05/03/landlord-ice-detention-center-elizabeth-nj-sues-terminate-lease/4929230001/; DWN, AFSC Immigrant Rights Program Newark, First Friends of NY & NJ, Pax Christi New Jersey, and New Jersey Alliance for Immigrant Justice. (2023). *Anthology of abuse: End three decades of abuse at the Elizabeth detention center*. www.detentionwatchnetwork.org/pressroom/reports

46. Mather, S. (2023, September 8). Biden administration fights to keep private immigration jails open, despite promises. *Immigration Impact*. https://immigrationimpact.com/2023/09/08/biden-keeps-private-immigration-jails-open-despite-promises/

47. Freeman S., & Major, L. (2012, March). *Immigration incarceration: The expansion and failed reform of immigration detention in Essex County, NJ*. New York University School of Law Immigrant Rights Clinic in cooperation with New Jersey Advocate for Immigrant Detainees. www.law.nyu.edu/sites/default/files/upload_documents/Immigration%20Incarceration.pdf

48. US Marshalls Service (USMS). (2002). *USMS capital funding agreement-Hudson County NJ*. National Immigrant Justice Center's Transparency and Human Rights Project. www.documentcloud.org/documents/4374266-USMS-Capital-Funding-Agreement-2002-Hudson

49. Curcio, L., Joshi, A., Mackler, C., & Mandel, M. (2013, November). *Expose and close: Hudson County Jail, New Jersey*. Detention Watch Network. www.detentionwatchnetwork.org/sites/default/files/reports/DWN%20Expose%20and%20Close%20Hudson%20County.pdf

50. McKenna, C. (2022, August 3). ICE moved 65 detained immigrants from Orange County Jail to Mississippi and Buffalo. *Times Herald-Record*. www.recordonline.com/story/news/local/2022/08/03/ice-moves-detained-immigrants-orange-county-correctional-facility-to-mississippi-buffalo/65389710007/

51. Parra, D. (2023, April 5). Hunger-striking detainees sue over conditions at NY's Orange County Jail. *City Limits*. https://citylimits.org/2023/04/05/hunger-striking-ice-detainees-sue-over-conditions-at-nys-orange-county-jail/

52. TRAC, *Detention facilities average daily population*.

53. National Immigration Forum. (2021). *Fact sheet: Immigration detention in the United States*. https://immigrationforum.org/wp-content/uploads/2021/01/Immigration-Detention-Factsheet_FINAL.pdf

54. Loyo & Corrado, *Locked up but not forgotten.*
55. We detail the intensification of efforts to conceal or destroy information about immigration enforcement in general in Hiemstra, N., & Conlon, D. (2021). Reading between the (redacted) lines: Muddling through absent presences in public information requests on U.S. immigration detention. *ACME: An International Journal for Critical Geographies,* 20(6), 666–686, https://doi.org/10.14288/acme.v20i6.2090. In a 2017 article, Hiemstra identifies "periscoping" as an approach to circumvent barriers to information: Hiemstra, N. (2017). Periscoping as a Feminist Methodological Approach for Researching the Seemingly Hidden. *Professional Geographer,* 69(2), 329–336, https://doi.org/10.1080/00330124.2016.1208514. Other useful publications on researching immigration include: Maillet, P., Mountz, A., & Williams, K. (2017). Researching migration and enforcement in obscured places: practical, ethical and methodological challenges to fieldwork. *Social & Cultural Geography,* 18(7), 927–950. https://doi.org/10.1080/14649365.2016.1197963; Williams, J. M., & Coddington, K. (2021). Feminist periscoping in research on border enforcement and human rights. *Journal of Human Rights,* 20(1), 143–150, doi:10.1080/14754835.2020.1850243
56. The non-profit National Immigrant Justice Center (NIJC) provided critical guidance regarding wording and parameters of the requests, based on their own experience with FOIAs.
57. Center for Constitutional Rights (CCR). (2019, December 3). *Detention Watch Network (DWN)* v. *Immigration Customs and Enforcement (ICE) and Department of Homeland Security (DHS).* https://ccrjustice.org/home/what-we-do/our-cases/detention-watch-network-dwn-v-immigration-customs-and-enforcement-ice-and. However, a 2019 Supreme Court decision (not directly pertaining to detention: *Food Marketing Institute* v. *Argus Leader Media*) reversed decades of precedent to allow even broader use of Exemption 4, which is intended to protect "trade secrets" and a company's competitive position: Kirtley, J.E., Memmel, S., & Anderson, J. (2020). More "substantial harm" than good: Recrafting FOIA's exemption 4 after *Food Marketing Institute* v. *Argus Leader Media. Mitchell Hamline Law Review,* 46(3), 497–526, https://open.mitchellhamline.edu/mhlr/vol46/iss3/2

Chapter 2 "Meatballs that smell like fecal matter": When Bad Food is the Business Model

1. Office of Inspector General (OIG). (2019, February 13). *Issues requiring action at the Essex County Correctional Facility in Newark, New Jersey.* Department of Homeland Security (Report OIG-19-20). www.oig.dhs.gov/sites/default/files/assets/2019-02/OIG-19-20-Feb19.pdf. The report notes the review period for the inspection as July to September 2018.
2. OIG, *Issues requiring action at the Essex County Correctional Facility* (p. 6).

NOTES

3. Baker, J. (2019, October). HIG Capital's prison food and commissary store racket. *Private Equity Stakeholder Project.* https://pestakeholder.org/reports/report-hig-capitals-prison-food-and-commissary-store-racket/; Le, T. (2021, January). *Food service contractors in the US,* US industry (NAICS) report 72231. IBISWorld. IBISWorld.com.
4. Throughout this chapter, we reference documents that we analyzed in this project (many obtained through public records requests, on file with authors) related to food service contracting for each of these facilities, including Requests for Proposals, submitted bids, county decision-makers' deliberations and voting records, and contracts.
5. These statements are made on the Trinity Services Group website https://trinityservicesgroup.com/ and on employment website Indeed.com.
6. GD Correctional Services, LLC. (nd). Who we are. https://gdcorrections.com/about/
7. The information we have received in response to recent county information requests is less detailed. For example, in our 2021 and 2023 OPRAs to New Jersey counties, we did not receive information about how elected officials voted on submitted bids.
8. Ankney, D. (2020, January 8). Prisoners, guards, students protest Aramark. *Prison Legal News.* www.prisonlegalnews.org/news/2020/jan/8/prisoners-guards-students-protest-aramark/
9. Akinnibi, F. (2019, November 26). Prison food is latest target in campaign to divest holdings. *Bloomberg.* www.bnnbloomberg.ca/prison-food-is-the-latest-target-in-campaign-to-divest-holdings-1.1353688
10. The other top-tier industries in the sector are educational services; health care and social assistance; professional, scientific and technical services; concert and event promotion; and public administration. Le, *Food service contractors in the US.*
11. Le, *Food service contractors in the US* (p. 49).
12. Le, *Food service contractors in the US* (p. 14).
13. Le, *Food service contractors in the US* (p. 31).
14. Owens, H. B. (2018, October 15). The Batavian tours the Buffalo detention facility. *The Batavian.* www.thebatavian.com/howard-b-owens/the-batavian-tours-the-buffalo-detention-facility/522595
15. United States Department of Agriculture (USDA). (2015). *Dietary guidelines for Americans, 2015–2020,* 8th edition. www.dietaryguidelines.gov/sites/default/files/2019-05/2015-2020_Dietary_Guidelines.pdf
16. Little, K. (2015, June 26). McDonald's quarter pounder is getting bigger (really!). *CNBC.* www.cnbc.com/2015/06/26/mcdonalds-quarter-pounder-is-getting-bigger-really.html
17. Curcio, L., Mackler, C., & Mandel, M. (2012, November). *Expose and close: Hudson County Jail, New Jersey.* Detention Watch Network (p. 3). www.detentionwatchnetwork.org/sites/default/files/reports/DWN%20Expose%20and%20Close%20Hudson%20County.pdf

18. Freeman S., & Major, L. (2012, March). *Immigration incarceration: The expansion and failed reform of immigration detention in Essex County, NJ.* New York University School of Law Immigrant Rights Clinic in cooperation with New Jersey Advocates for Immigrant Detainees.
19. Human Rights First. (2018, February 27). *Ailing justice: New Jersey. Inadequate healthcare, indifference, and indefinite confinement in immigration detention.* https://humanrightsfirst.org/library/ailing-justice-new-jersey-inadequate-healthcare-indifference-and-indefinite-confinement-in-immigration-detention/ (p. 6).
20. OIG, *Issues requiring action at the Essex County Correctional Facility* (p. 6).
21. Freeman & Major, *Immigration incarceration*.
22. Human Rights First, *Ailing Justice: New Jersey* (p. 4).
23. Cho, E., Tidwell Cullen, T., & Long, C. (2020, April 30). *Justice free zones: U.S. immigration detention under the Trump administration.* ACLU, Human Rights Watch, National Immigrant Justice Center. www.aclu.org/report/justice-free-zones-us-immigration-detention-under-trump-administration; Curcio et al., *Expose and close: Hudson County jail*; Detention Watch Network. (2016, December). *A toxic relationship: Private prisons and U.S. immigration detention.* www.detentionwatchnetwork.org/sites/default/files/reports/A%20Toxic%20Relationship_DWN.pdf
24. Curcio et al., *Expose and close: Hudson County Jail* (p. 3).
25. Marlow, M. A., Luna-Gierke, R. E., Griffin, P. M., & Vieira, A. R. (2017). Foodborne disease outbreaks in correctional institutions-United States, 1998–2014. *American Journal of Public Health, 107*(7), 1150–1156. https://doi.org/10.2105/AJPH.2017.303816
26. Freeman & Major, *Immigration incarceration* (p. 23).
27. OIG, *Issues requiring action at the Essex County Correctional Facility* (p. 6).
28. Expected practices were laid out in great detail in the 2011 National Detention Standards. But they were removed in the pared-down 2019 NDS.
29. Human Rights First, *Ailing justice: New Jersey* (p. 4).
30. OIG, *Issues requiring action at the Essex County Correction facility* (pp. 4–5).
31. Freeman & Major, *Immigration incarceration*.
32. Human Rights First, *Ailing justice: New Jersey* (p. 4).
33. Human Rights First, *Ailing justice: New Jersey* (p. 4).
34. Katz, M. (2020, December 2). ICE detention issues in three NJ Counties. *WNYC* [audio report]. www.wnyc.org/story/ice-detainees-hunger-strike-nj/
35. Other issues include understaffing, insufficient teaching of basic food safety protocols to staff, and lack of oversight, corruption and negligence: Fassler, J. & Brown, C. (2017, December 27). Prison food is making U.S. inmates disproportionately sick. *The Atlantic.* www.theatlantic.com/health/archive/2017/12/prison-food-sickness-america/549179/
36. Fassler & Brown, Prison food is making U.S. inmates disproportionately sick.

NOTES

Chapter 3 "Cost Containment" and Litigation: The Institutionalization of Medical Neglect in Detention

1. Tosh, S. R., Berg, U. D., & Leon, K. S. (2021). Migrant detention and COVID-19: Pandemic responses in four New Jersey detention centers. *Journal on Migration and Human Security, 9*(1), 49–62, https://doi.org/10.1177/23315024211003855
2. Salant, J. D. (2020, April 10). NJ has more immigrant detainees with the coronavirus than any other state. *NJ.com*. www.nj.com/coronavirus/2020/04/nj-has-more-immigrant-detainees-with-the-coronavirus-than-any-other-state.html
3. Hooks, G. & Libal, B. (2020, December). *Hotbeds of infection: How ICE detention contributed to the spread of COVID-19 in the United States.* Detention Watch Network.
4. Hooks & Libal, *Hotbeds of infection.*
5. New York Lawyers for the Public Interest (NYLPI). (2017, February). *Detained and denied: Healthcare access in immigration detention.* www.immigrationresearch.org/report/other/detained-and-denied-healthcare-access-immigration-detention
6. Terp, S., Ahmed, S., Burner, E., Ross, M., Grassini, M., Fischer, B., & Parmar, P. (2021). Deaths in Immigration and Customs Enforcement (ICE) detention: FY2018–2020. *AIMS Public Health, 8*(1), 81–89. doi: 10.3934/publichealth.2021006; Buchanan, C., Ahmed, S., Nwadiuko, J., Dekker, A. M., Zeidan, A., Bitrán, E., Urich, T., Fischer, B., Burner, E. R. E., Parmar, P., & Terp, S. (2024). Deaths in Immigration and Customs Enforcement (ICE) detention: A fiscal year (FY) 2021–2023 update. *AIMS Public Health, 11*(1), 223–235. doi: 10.3934/publichealth.2024011
7. Adequate medical care for prisoners is guaranteed under the Eighth Amendment of the U.S. Supreme Court, which prohibits "cruel and unusual punishment" of prisoners, and was reinforced in a landmark 1976 U.S. Supreme Court decision *Estelle v. Gamble.* Adequate medical care for detained immigrants, technically held in *administrative* and not punitive detention, is protected under the Fifth Amendment, which disallows punishment of people without due process; Human Rights Watch (HRW) & Community Initiatives for Visiting Immigrants in Confinement (CIVIC). (2017, May 8). *Systemic indifference: Dangerous & substandard medical care in US immigration detention.* www.hrw.org/report/2017/05/08/systemic-indifference/dangerous-substandard-medical-care-us-immigration-detention. There are fears, however, that the current Supreme Court's originalist turn may threaten this right: Alsan, M., Yang, C. S., Jolin, J. R., Tu, L., & Rich, J. D. (2023). Health care in U.S. correctional facilities—A limited and threatened constitutional right. *New England Journal of Medicine, 388*(9), 847–852, doi: 10.1056/NEJMms2211252.
8. The agreements include the International Covenant on Civil and Political Rights, the Convention Against Torture, the Standard Minimum Rules for

the Treatment of Prisoners, and the Body of Principles for the Protection of All Persons under Any Form of Detention or Imprisonment; HRW & CIVIC, *Systemic indifference.*
9. NYLPI, *Detained and denied*; HRW. (2009). *Detained and dismissed: Women's struggles to obtain health care in United States detention.* www.hrw.org/report/2009/03/17/detained-and-dismissed/womens-struggles-obtain-health-care-united-states; Human Rights First (HRF). (2018, February). *Ailing justice: New Jersey. Inadequate healthcare, indifference, and indefinite confinement in immigration detention.* https://humanrightsfirst.org/wp-content/uploads/2022/04/Ailing-Justice-NJ.pdf
10. HRW & CIVIC, *Systemic indifference.*
11. Office of Detention Oversight. (2019). *Compliance Inspection: Essex County Correctional Facility Newark, New Jersey.* ICE (p. 7).
12. HRW & CIVIC, *Systemic indifference* (p. 66).
13. Curcio, L., Joshi, A., Mackler, C., & Mandel, M. (2012, November). *Expose and close: Hudson County Jail, New Jersey.* Detention Watch Network. www.detentionwatchnetwork.org/sites/default/files/reports/DWN%20Expose%20and%20Close%20Hudson%20County.pdf
14. HRF, *Ailing justice: New Jersey* (p. 7).
15. HRW & CIVIC, *Systemic indifference.* See also, HRW, *Detained and dismissed.*
16. Cho, E., Cullen, T. T., & Long, C. (2020, April). *Justice-free zones: U.S. immigration detention under the Trump administration.* ACLU, Human Rights Watch, National Immigrant Justice Center, https://immigrantjustice.org/research-items/report-justice-free-zones-us-immigration-detention-under-trump-administration; Kelly, G. (2022, April 5). Allegations of ICE mistreatment of detainees. *Investigative Post.* www.investigativepost.org/2022/04/05/allegations-of-ice-mistreatment-of-detainees/
17. HRW & CIVIC, *Systemic indifference* (p. 58).
18. HRW, *Detained and dismissed.*
19. Ellis, B., & Hicken, M. (2019, June 25). Please help me before it's too late. *CNN.* www.cnn.com/interactive/2019/06/us/jail-health-care-ccs-invs/
20. HRW, *Detained and dismissed*; NYLPI, *Detained and denied.*
21. NYLPI, *Detained and denied.*
22. HRF, *Ailing justice: New Jersey.* (p. 1); See also: HRW, *Detained and dismissed*; NYLPI, *Detained and denied*; Cho et al., *Justice-free zones*; Curcio et al., *Expose and close: Hudson County Jail, New Jersey*; Katz, M. (2021, April 28) New Jersey county ends lucrative and controversial jailing of ICE detainees. *WNYC.* https://gothamist.com/news/new-jersey-county-ends-lucrative-and-controversial-jailing-ice-detainees
23. Kelly, Allegations of ICE mistreatment of detainees.
24. HRF, *Ailing justice: New Jersey* (p. 7).
25. HRF, *Ailing justice: New Jersey* (p. 6).
26. HRF, *Ailing justice: New Jersey* (p. 7).

27. HRW & CIVIC, *Systemic indifference* (p. 61); Cho et al., *Justice-free zones*; Office of Inspector General (OIG). (2021, October 29). *Many factors hinder ICE's ability to maintain adequate medical staffing at detention facilities.* Department of Homeland Security. www.oig.dhs.gov/sites/default/files/assets/2021-11/OIG-22-03-Oct21.pdf
28. Freed Wessler, S. (2016, June 28). "This man will almost certainly die." *The Nation.* www.thenation.com/article/archive/privatized-immigrant-prison-deaths/
29. Ellis & Hicken, Please help me before it's too late.
30. HRW & CIVIC, *Systemic indifference*; OIG, *Many factors hinder ICE's ability to maintain adequate medical staffing at detention facilities.*
31. HRW & CIVIC, *Systemic indifference.*
32. NYLPI, *Detained and denied.*
33. HRF, *Ailing justice: New Jersey.*
34. Florida Immigrant Advocacy Center (FIAC). (2009, February). *Dying for decent care: Bad medicine in immigration custody.* https://aijustice.org/wp-content/uploads/2020/05/DyingForDecentCare.pdf; HRW, *Detained and dismissed*; HRW & CIVIC, *Systemic indifference*; HRF, *Ailing justice: New Jersey*; Ellman, N. (2019, October 21). *Immigration detention is dangerous for women's health and rights.* Center for American Progress. www.americanprogress.org/article/immigration-detention-dangerous-womens-health-rights/; Office of Inspector General. (2016, July 21). *ICE still struggles to hire and retain staff for mental health cases in immigration detention.* U.S. Department of Homeland Security. www.oig.dhs.gov/assets/VR/FY16/OIG-16-113-VR-Jul16.pdf; Office of Inspector General. (2011, March 28). *Management of mental health cases in immigration detention.* U.S. Department of Homeland Security. www.oig.dhs.gov/assets/Mgmt/OIG_11-62_Mar11.pdf
35. FIAC, *Dying for decent care*; HRF, *Ailing justice: New Jersey*; Alvarado, M., et al. (2019, December 19). Deaths in custody. Sexual violence. Hunger strikes. What we uncovered inside ICE facilities across the US. *Clarion Ledger.* www.clarionledger.com/in-depth/news/nation/2019/12/19/ice-asylum-under-trump-exclusive-look-us-immigration-detention/4381404002/
36. HRW & CIVIC, *Systemic indifference* (pp. 73–75).
37. HRW & CIVIC, *Systemic indifference*; HRF, *Ailing justice: New Jersey*; Cho et al., *Justice-free zones*; Erfani, P., Chin, E. T., Lee, C. H., Uppal, N., & Peeler, K .R. (2021). Suicide rates of migrants in United States immigration detention (2010–2020). *AIMS Public Health, 8*(3), 416–420. doi:10.3934/publichealth.2021031
38. Cho et al., *Justice-free zones* (p. 7); Erfani et al., Suicide rates of migrants in United States immigration detention (2010–2020).
39. HRF, *Ailing justice: New Jersey* (p. 2).
40. HRW & CIVIC, *Systemic indifference* (p. 75).
41. HRF, *Ailing justice: New Jersey.*

42. Ellman, *Immigration detention is dangerous for women's health and rights*; Committee on Homeland Security and Governmental Affairs. (2022, November 15). *Medical mistreatment of women in ICE detention*. U.S. Senate. www.hsgac.senate.gov/wp-content/uploads/imo/media/doc/2022-11-15%20PSI%20Staff%20Report%20-%20Medical%20Mistreatment%20of%20Women%20in%20ICE%20Detention.pdf
43. HRW, *Detained and dismissed*; Ellman, *Immigration detention is dangerous for women's health and rights*.
44. Committee on Homeland Security and Governmental Affairs, *Medical mistreatment of women in ICE detention*.
45. Shahshahani, A. N. & Ardalan, S. (2021, September 16). No justice, no freedom: Medical abuse in private prisons. *Womensenews.org*. https://womensenews.org/2021/09/no-justice-no-freedom-medical-abuse-in-private-prisons/; Ellman, *Immigration detention is dangerous for women's health and rights*; Committee on Homeland Security and Governmental Affairs, *Medical mistreatment of women in ICE detention*.
46. HRW, *Detained and dismissed*; Ellman, *Immigration detention is dangerous for women's health and rights*; Committee on Homeland Security and Governmental Affairs, *Medical mistreatment of women in ICE detention*.
47. HRW, *Detained and dismissed*.
48. HRF, *Ailing justice: New Jersey* (p. 4); HRW, *Detained and dismissed*.
49. Ellman, *Immigration detention is dangerous for women's health and rights*; HRW. (2016, March 23). *Do you see how much I'm suffering here?: Abuse against transgender women in US immigration detention*. www.hrw.org/report/2016/03/24/do-you-see-how-much-im-suffering-here/abuse-against-transgender-women-us
50. HRW. (2010, August 25). *Detained and at risk: Sexual abuse and harassment in United States immigration detention*. www.hrw.org/report/2010/08/25/detained-and-risk/sexual-abuse-and-harassment-united-states-immigration-detention; Detention Watch Network (2016). *A toxic relationship: Private prisons and U.S. immigration detention*. www.detentionwatchnetwork.org/sites/default/files/reports/A%20Toxic%20Relationship_DWN.pdf; Cullen, T. T. (2018, March 13). *ICE released its most comprehensive immigration detention data yet. It's alarming*. National Immigrant Justice Center. https://immigrantjustice.org/staff/blog/ice-released-its-most-comprehensive-immigration-detention-data-yet; Olivares, J., and Washington, J. (2022, July 13). "The worst day of my life": ICE jail nurse sexually assaulted migrant women, complaint letter says. *The Intercept*. https://theintercept.com/2022/07/13/ice-stewart-detention-sexual-misconduct/; Hargrove, D. (2022, August 8). Three women sue over sexual assault and retaliation at Otay Mesa Detention Center. *CBS8.com*. www.cbs8.com/article/news/investigations/alleged-sexual-abuse-and-retaliation-by-corecivic-guards-at-otay-mesa-detention-facility-in-san-diego/509-2e401b30-6414-400a-8b79-a5c96dede801

51. Ybarra, M. (2021). Site fight! Towards the abolition of immigrant detention on Tacoma's Tar Pits (and everywhere else). *Antipode, 53*(1), 36–55, https://doi.org/10.1111/anti.12610
52. Curcio et al., *Expose and close: Hudson County Jail, New Jersey* (p. 2).
53. Office of Inspector General. (2019, February 13). *Issues requiring action at the Essex County Correctional Facility in Newark, New Jersey.* Department of Homeland Security (p. 7).
54. Cho et al., *Justice-free zones.*
55. HRF, *Ailing justice: New Jersey.*
56. Curcio et al., *Expose and close: Hudson County Jail, New Jersey*; HRF, *Ailing justice: New Jersey*; Human Rights First. (2016, November). *Detention of asylum seekers in New Jersey.* https://humanrightsfirst.org/wp-content/uploads/2017/04/hrf-detention-asylum-seekers-nj-nov2016.pdf
57. Dow, J. (2020, December 30). PIX11 goes inside controversial Bergen County Jail housing ICE detainees. *PIX11.* https://pix11.com/news/local-news/new-jersey/pix11-goes-inside-controversial-bergen-county-jail-housing-ice-detainees/; Katz, M. (2021, January 29). ICE says Bergen County Jail detention center is overcrowded, but at-risk detainees still aren't getting released. *Gothamist.com.* https://gothamist.com/news/ice-says-bergen-county-jail-detention-center-is-overcrowded-but-at-risk-detainees-still-arent-getting-released; Tosh, Berg, & Leon, Migrant detention and COVID-19.
58. Cho et al., *Justice-free zones*; Katz, *ICE says Bergen County Jail detention center is overcrowded.*
59. Tosh, Berg, & Leon, Migrant detention and COVID-19 (p. 5); NYLPI, *Detained and denied*; NYLPI (2019, May 30). Family member of man who bled to death in immigration custody sues Hudson over medical care. https://nylpi.org/family-of-man-who-bled-to-death-in-immigration-custody-sues-hudson-county-over-medical-care/; Adely, H. (2017, July 27). Investigation: Medical neglect at Hudson County jail alleged in death of detainee. *Northjersey.com.* www.northjersey.com/story/news/watchdog/2017/07/27/hudson-county-prison-where-immigrant-died-has-history-complaints/492177001/; Immigrant Advocates Response Collaborative. (2019). *Behind bars in the Empire State: An assessment of the immigration detention of New Yorkers.* www.nyic.org/2/wp-content/uploads/2019/03/State-of-Immigration-Detention-of-NYers-v5.pdf
60. For example, Bernstein, N. (2010, January 9). Officials hid truth of immigrant deaths in jail. *New York Times.* www.nytimes.com/2010/01/10/us/10detain.html/; FIAC, *Dying for decent care: Bad medicine in immigration custody*; Takei, C., Small, M., Wu, C., & Chan, J. (2016, February 24). *Fatal neglect: How ICE ignores deaths in detention.* ACLU, DWN, NIJC; HRW & CIVIC, *Systemic indifference*; Long, C., Cullen, T., Rachko, T, & Ohta, R. (2018, June 20). *Code red: The fatal consequences of dangerously substandard medical care in immigration detention.* HRW, ACLU, NIJC,

DWN. www.hrw.org/report/2018/06/20/code-red/fatal-consequences-dangerously-substandard-medical-care-immigration; Ellis & Hicken, Please help me before it's too late; Cho et al., *Justice-free zones*; Aleaziz, H. (2020, September 24). A Congressional oversight committee found that ICE detainees died after receiving poor medical care. *BuzzFeed News*. www.buzzfeednews.com/article/hamedaleaziz/ice-detainees-medical-care-congressional-report; Office of Inspector General. (2023, February 1). ICE and CBP deaths in custody during FY 2021. U.S. Department of Homeland Security. www.oig.dhs.gov/sites/default/files/assets/2023-02/OIG-23-12-Feb23.pdf; Immigration and Customs Enforcement (ICE). (2024). *Detainee Death Reporting*. www.ice.gov/detain/detainee-death-reporting.

61. Terp et al., Deaths in Immigration and Customs Enforcement (ICE) detention: FY2018–2020; Buchanan et al., Deaths in Immigration and Customs Enforcement (ICE) detention: A fiscal year (FY) 2021–2023 update.

62. For example, as of January 5, 2022, there were eleven detainee deaths of COVID-19 confirmed by ICE. However, experts believe that deaths resulting from the contraction of COVID-19 in ICE detention centers are significantly under-reported. There are several known cases of detainees seriously ill with COVID-19 who were released, to die soon after in a hospital: Murdza, K. (2021, March 26). *How many ICE-related COVID-19 deaths have gone unreported?* Immigration Impact. https://immigrationimpact.com/2021/03/26/unreported-covid-deaths-ice/#.YdhAY2jMI2w

63. Takei et al., *Fatal neglect: How ICE ignores deaths in detention.*

64. HRW & CIVIC, *Systemic indifference: Dangerous & substandard medical care in US immigration detention.* See also Long et al., *Code red: The fatal consequences of dangerously substandard medical care in immigration detention.*

65. The National Commission on Correctional Health Care estimates that of the jails it accredits, 70 percent contract out their medical care; McLeod, M. (2019, September 12). The private option. *The Atlantic*. www.theatlantic.com/politics/archive/2019/09/private-equitys-grip-on-jail-health-care/597871/

66. The fourth county jail in our study, in Bergen County, New Jersey, is a real anomaly among U.S. jails in how it currently deals with medical care. In 2017, Bergen County dropped its contract with Corizon. The county now directly employs all medical personnel, and contracts out piecemeal for particular services.

67. Zoom Info. (n.d.). CFG Health Systems. https://www.zoominfo.com/c/cfg-health-systems-llc/16796868

68. Ellis & Hicken, Please help me before it's too late; Baker, J. (2019, October). HIG Capital's prison food and commissary store racket. Private Equity Stakeholder Project. https://pestakeholder.org/wp-content/uploads/2019/10/HIG-Capital-Prison-Food-Commissary-PESP-103019.pdf; McLeod, The private option.

69. Herner, H. (2024, November 13). Wellpath files for bankruptcy. *Nashvillepost.com.* www.nashvillepost.com/business/health_care/wellpath-files-for-bankruptcy/article_7895932e-a1fc-11ef-aecd-1f11839db5c1.html
70. Zeitlinger, R. (2024, April 1). Hudson County defies state comptroller's order, approves $13.5 million contract for jail medical services. *NJ.com.* www.nj.com/hudson/2024/04/hudson-county-defies-state-comptrollers-order-approves-135-million-contract-for-jail-medical-services.html
71. Bellamy, L. (2024, April 16). Orange County continues to use controversial medical provider at jail as it prepares new request for proposals. *Times Union.* www.timesunion.com/hudsonvalley/news/article/orange-county-jail-wellpath-correct-care-19403303.php
72. *CFG Health Systems L.L.C. v. County of Hudson.* DOCKET NO. A-3943-10T3. (NJ Superior, July 19, 2012). https://law.justia.com/cases/new-jersey/appellate-division-unpublished/2012/a3943-10.html
73. *CFG Health Systems L.L.C. v. County of Essex.* DOCKET NO. A-5101-06T5. (NJ Superior, September 18, 2007). https://law.justia.com/cases/new-jersey/appellate-division-unpublished/2007/a5154-06-opn.html
74. Ryan, J. (2008, January 25). Judge orders Essex to switch medical firms for jail. *NJ.com.* www.nj.com/news/2008/01/judge_orders_essex_county_to_r.html
75. Reutter, D. M. (2022, March 1). Wellpath founder and CEO pleads guilty to federal bribery charges. *Prison Legal News.* www.prisonlegalnews.org/news/2022/mar/1/wellpath-founder-and-ceo-pleads-guilty-federal-bribery-charges/; Reutter, D. M. (2020, March 3). Major prison health care companies funnel campaign contributions to sheriffs, get rewards. *Prison Legal News.* www.prisonlegalnews.org/news/2020/mar/3/major-prison-health-care-companies-funnel-campaign-contributions-sheriffs-get-rewards/
76. Harrison campaign: 'Illicit' pay-for-play details emerge regarding Wellpath's corruption. (2020, May 18). *InsiderNJ.com.* https://www.insidernj.com/press-release/harrison-campaign-illicit-pay-play-details-emerge-regarding-wellpaths-corruption/
77. For example, in its 2011 bid, CFG's CEO, Les Paschall, listed five political donations (each of $250 and $600), made to Essex County officials between 2008 and 2010, including a total of $900 made to Joseph DiVincenzo. In a 2015 disclosure, Paschall listed a $2,600 donation in 2011 to DiVincenzo. Paschall also noted political contributions to county officials Aimee Belgard and Donald Norcross in 2014. Other medical company owners have also given political donations to Essex County decision-makers. For instance, bid disclosure statements show that in 2014 Correctional Medical Care (CMC) owner Maria Carpio contributed $2,600 to Joseph DiVincenzo's campaign. Though such efforts didn't land the desired contracts, they indicate that playing the influence game is a component of competing for contracts. In 2017, new stricter pay-to-play laws were implemented,

paradoxically making it *more* difficult to track political contributions. Companies now make sure that their donation disclosures show $0, and route donations through third parties.
78. *CFG Health Systems L.L.C. v. County of Hudson.* DOCKET NO. A-3943-10T3 (July 19, 2012); Star-Ledger Editorial Board. (2010, January 23). Hudson County freeholders should drop jail contract appeal. *NJ.com*. www.nj.com/njv_editorial_page/2010/01/hudson_county_should_drop_medi.html; Hayes, M. (2009, December 3). Judge questions Hudson county's "rush" to award prison contract. *NJ.com*. www.nj.com/hudson/2009/12/judge_questions_hudson_countys.html#:~:text=A%20superior%20court%20judge%20today%20questioned%20why%20the,the%20report%20of%20an%20expert%20it%20had%20hired
79. Correctional Medical Care lost the Orange County Correctional Facility's contract despite being one of the lowest bidders, when the county's bid evaluation team excluded the company from considerations due to complaints received—and deaths—at other jails served by the company. The company was started in 2001 by Maria Carpio and her husband, Emre Umar, neither of them medically trained professionals. By 2008, the company was providing health services for 13 New York state jails and a total of 32 facilities in six states. Between 2009 and 2012, six inmates in these facilities died due to lack of appropriate medical care, and in 2014, the New York State Attorney General Eric Schneiderman sued Correctional Medical Care for failure to provide proper medical services: Reutter, D. (2016, September 2). Correctional Medical Care illegally practiced medicine in New York. *Prison Legal News*. www.prisonlegalnews.org/news/2016/sep/2/correctional-medical-care-illegally-practiced-medicine-new-york/; Office of the New York State Attorney General. (2014, September 25). A.G. Schneiderman announces settlement with health care company that provided substandard service to jail inmates in 13 NY Counties. https://ag.ny.gov/press-release/2014/ag-schneiderman-announces-settlement-health-care-company-provided-substandared/
80. NYLPI, *Detained and denied*; Wessler, "This man will almost certainly die."
81. HRW & CIVIC, *Systemic indifference* (p. 23).
82. Ellis and Hicken, Please help me before it's too late; See also, Ellis, B. and Hicken, M. (2023, December 19). Senators raise alarm about nation's largest prison health care provider. *CNN*. www.cnn.com/2023/12/19/us/wellpath-senators-investigation-invs/index.html. See also, Fenne, M. (2022, November). *Private equity firms rebrand prison healthcare companies, but care issues continue*. Private Equity Stakeholder Project. https://pestakeholder.org/wp-content/uploads/2022/11/Wellpath_HIG_12-2022.pdf
83. Ellis and Hicken, Please help me before it's too late.
84. McLeod, The private option.
85. Lungariello, M. (2019, April 12). Controversies swirl as Westchester County Jail considers new health care provider. *Lohud.com*. www.lohud.

com/story/news/local/westchester/2019/04/12/westchester-county-jail-health-care-correct-care-correct-care-solutions-wellpath-tennessee-mcnulty/3237201002/
86. Alvarado, M. (2018, July 14). How an inmate's death led to changes at the Hudson County jail. *Northjersey.com.* www.northjersey.com/story/news/new-jersey/2018/07/14/how-inmates-death-led-changes-hudson-county-nj-jail/773708002/
87. McLeod, The private option.
88. Baker, HIG Capital's prison food and commissary store racket.
89. Ellis & Hicken, Please help me before it's too late.
90. Ankney, D. (2021, March 1). Private medical contractor Wellpath pays $4.5 million in death of mentally ill jail detainee after judge finds it destroyed evidence. *Prison Legal News.* www.prisonlegalnews.org/news/2021/mar/1/private-medical-contractor-wellpath-pays-45-million-death-mentally-ill-jail-detainee-after-judge-finds-it-destroyed-evidence/
91. U.S. ICE. (2024). ICE Health Service Corps. www.ice.gov/detain/ice-health-service-corps
92. Molina, N. (2011). Borders, laborers, and racialized medicalization Mexican immigration and US public health practices in the 20th century. *American Journal of Public Health, 101*(6), 1024–1031. doi: 10.2105/AJPH.2010.300056
93. U.S. ICE. (2024, December 19). *ICE releases fiscal year 2024 annual report.* www.ice.gov/news/releases/ice-releases-fiscal-year-2024-annual-report
94. According to the IHSC 2020 report, the IHSC had about 1,700 positions. This includes 569 Public Health Service officers and 211 civil servants, so roughly 780 positions in the IHSC workforce are government/public employees. But that means that the remaining IHSC workforce, or about 920 people, is comprised of "contract health professionals."
95. HRW, *Detained and dismissed.*
96. HRW & CIVIC, *Systemic indifference.*
97. HRW & CIVIC, *Systemic indifference*; Cho et al., *Justice-free zones.*
98. HRF, *Ailing justice: New Jersey* (p. 6).
99. HRW, *Detained and dismissed.*
100. HRW & CIVIC, *Systemic indifference* (p. 70); Cho et al., *Justice-free zones*; Office for Civil Rights and Civil Liberties. (2021, April 28). *Memorandum: ICE Health Services Corps (IHSC) medical/mental health care and oversight.* www.dhs.gov/sites/default/files/2023-09/21_0428_crcl_rec_memo_to_ice_ihsc_medical_mental_health_care_oversight_redacted_508.pdf

Chapter 4 Starved for Profit: How Migrants Become Captive Consumers and Coerced Workers

1. Conlon, D. & Hiemstra, N. (2014). Examining the everyday microeconomies of migrant detention in the United States. *Geographica Helvetica, 69*, 335–344, https://doi.org/10.5194/gh-69-335-2014 (p. 341).

2. Office of Detention Oversight (ODO). (2010). *Quality assurance review. Enforcement and removal operations New York field office, Bergen County Jail – 30 November–2 December*. Department of Homeland Security (p. 18).
3. Curcio, L., Joshi, A., Mackler, C., & Mandel, M. (2012, November). *Expose and close: Hudson County Jail, New Jersey*. Detention Watch Network (p. 3).
4. Office of Inspector General (OIG). (2019, February 13). *Issues requiring action at the Essex County Correctional Facility in Newark, New Jersey*. Department of Homeland Security. (Report OIG-19-20) (p. 6).
5. Interview, July 8, 2013.
6. Herrera, J. (2020, April 30). In ICE detention, forced to pay for soap. *The Nation*. www.thenation.com/article/politics/coronavirus-ice-detention-soap/
7. Herrera, In ICE detention, forced to pay for soap.
8. Lind, D. (2020, March 23). ICE detainee says migrants are going on a hunger strike for soap. *ProPublica*. www.propublica.org/article/ice-detainee-says-migrants-are-going-on-a-hunger-strike-for-soap
9. Interview, July 8, 2013.
10. We examined commissary sales receipts for the Buffalo detention center from 2013 and from Orange County Correctional Facility from 2019.
11. Conlin, M. and Cooke, K. (2019, January 18). $11 toothpaste: Immigrants pay big for basics at private ICE lock-ups. *Reuters Euronews*. www.euronews.com/2019/01/18/11-toothpaste-immigrants-pay-big-for-basics-at-private-ice-lock-ups
12. Detailed information about commissary contracts for detention facilities at Buffalo and Elizabeth was not made available to us. County governments responded fully to our information requests for documents pertaining to the county jails. In contrast, it is much more difficult to obtain such documents via federal information requests, pertaining to the commissaries at Buffalo FDC (owned by the federal government) and Elizabeth Detention Center (owned by CoreCivic).
13. Baker, J. (2019, October). HIG Capital's prison food and commissary store racket. *Private Equity Stakeholder Project*. https://pestakeholder.org/reports/report-hig-capitals-prison-food-and-commissary-store-racket/
14. Requarth, T. (2019, May 13). How private equity is turning public prisons into big profits. *The Nation*. www.thenation.com/article/archive/prison-privatization-private-equity-hig/
15. Requarth, How private equity is turning public prisons.
16. Requarth, How private equity is turning public prisons.
17. H.I.G. Capital (n.d) hig.com/about/
18. Gupta, A. & Howell, S. (2023, September). The role of private equity in the U.S. economy, and whether and how favorable tax policies for the sector need to be reformed. *Washington Center for Equitable Growth*. www.equitablegrowth.org. See also Gornall, W., Gredil, O., Howell, S. T., Liu, X. & Sockin, J. (2021, December 24). Do employees cheer for private equity?

The heterogeneous effects of buyouts on job quality. *SSRN*. http://dx.doi.org/10.2139/ssrn.3912230

19. Media reporting on private equity firms' deleterious impacts include: Covert, B. (2018, July/August). The demise of Toys 'R' Us Is a warning. *The Atlantic*. www.theatlantic.com/magazine/archive/2018/07/toys-r-us-bankruptcy-private-equity/561758/; Greenhouse, S. (2021, July 18) Wisconsin workers fight factory move to Mexico: "anxiety is through the roof". *Guardian*. www.theguardian.com/us-news/2021/jul/18/hufcor-factory-janesivlle-wisconsin-opengate-capital. For research related to job security and private equity firms, see Gornall et al., *Do employees cheer for private equity?*

20. Gupta & Howell, The role of private equity in the U.S. economy.

21. Phalippou, L. (2020). An inconvenient fact: Private equity returns & the billionaire factory. *University of Oxford, Said Business School*, working paper. http://dx.doi.org/10.2139/ssrn.3623820; Fleischer, V. (2008). Two and twenty: Taxing partnership profits in private equity funds. *University of Colorado Law Legal Studies Research Paper* No. 06-27. https://ssrn.com/abstract=892440

22. Guyton, J., Langetieg, P., Reck, D., Risch, M., & Zucman, G. (2021). Tax evasion at the top of the income distribution: Theory and evidence. *National Bureau of Economic Research*, working paper 28542. www.nber.org/papers/w28542

23. Gupta & Howell, The role of private equity in the US economy (p. 2).

24. *Open Secrets*. (2024). Industry Profile: Private Equity & Investment Firms. www.opensecrets.org/federal-lobbying/industries/summary?id=F2600; Drucker & Hakim, *Private inequity*; Open Secrets. (2024). HIG Capital. www.opensecrets.org/orgs/hig-capital/summary?id=d000034458

25. Of course, that is not how H.I.G. sees it. A managing director at H.I.G., Jeff Zanarini, dismissed the idea that the company's approach has profoundly reshaped services provided in U.S. prisons and detention facilities. "He [Zanarini] noted that HIG has invested in hundreds of companies," reported Requarth in *The Nation*, "only a small fraction of which have ever provided correctional services." Zanarini further noted the relatively small size and scope of H.I.G. ownership of companies including Keefe, TKC Holdings, and Wellpath, mean "it is accurate to say that H.I.G. plays 'no role whatsoever in shaping the nation's jails and prisons'"; Requarth, How private equity is turning public prisons.

26. Aramark won the food service contract for Orange County Correctional Facility in 2022.

27. Baker, HIG Capital's prison food and commissary store racket.

28. Hiemstra, N. & Conlon, D. (2016). Captive consumers and coerced labourers: Intimate economies and the expanding US detention regime. In D. Conlon and N. Hiemstra (eds.). *Intimate economies of immigration detention: Critical perspectives*. (pp. 123–139). Routledge.

29. Moreno, L. (2012, July 27). For-profit immigration detention center underpays detainee workers, overcharges for services. *Cuéntame Immigration*. https://mycuentame-bravenew.nationbuilder.com/you_won_t_beleive_how_underpaid_workers_in_this_for_profit_immigration_detention_center_are_paid
30. Interview, March 27 2009; Hiemstra, *Detain and deport* (p. 97).
31. Conlon & Hiemstra, Examining the everyday micro-economies.
32. Office of Inspector General (OIG). (2023, September 5). *Results of an unannounced inspection of ICE's Caroline detention facility, Bowling Green, Virginia*. Department of Homeland Security. (Report OIG-23-51) (p. 5).
33. OIG, *Results of unannounced inspection—Caroline detention facility* (p. 24).
34. OIG, *Results of unannounced inspection—Caroline detention facility* (p. 13).
35. Interview, June 29, 2013.
36. Fernandes, D. (2007). *Targeted: Homeland security and the business of immigration*. Seven Stories Press; Moreno, For-profit immigration detention center underpays detainee workers.
37. Conlin & Cooke, $11 toothpaste: Immigrants pay big for basics at private ICE lock-ups.
38. ACLU. (2021, June 22). *Behind closed doors: Abuse & retaliation against hunger strikers in U.S. immigration detention*. www.aclu.org/publications/report-behind-closed-doors-abuse-retaliation-against-hunger-strikers-us-immigration-detention
39. Stevens, J. (2021). The political economy of work in ICE custody: Theorizing mass incarceration and for-profit prisons. In E. Hatton (ed.). *Labor and punishment: Work in and out of prison*. (pp. 86–132). University of California Press. https://doi.org/10.2307/j.ctv1npx3mx
40. Pauly, M. (2018, April 18). Immigrant detainees claim they were forced to clean bathrooms to pay for their own toilet paper. *Mother Jones*. www.motherjones.com/politics/2018/04/immigrant-detainees-claim-they-were-forced-to-clean-bathrooms-to-pay-for-their-own-toilet-paper/
41. *Menocal v. The GEO Group, Inc.*, Case no. 1:14-cv-02887. (U.S. District Court, Colorado, October 22, 2014). https://deportationresearchclinic.org/MenocalvGEO-Complaint-10-22-2014.pdf
42. Pauly, Immigrant detainees claim they were forced to clean bathrooms.
43. *Menocal v. The GEO Group Inc.*, Civil Action No. 1:14-cv-02887-JLK. 113 F.Supp.3d1125 (U.S. District Court, Colorado, July 6, 2015).
44. For a detailed synopsis and discussion of this and other detention labor lawsuits, see Stevens, The political economy of work in ICE custody.
45. *Menocal v. The GEO Group Inc.*, Case no. 1:14-cv-02887-JLK. (U.S. District Court, Colorado, March 13, 2017). https://deportationresearchclinic.org/App-1-GEOPetition-2017-3-13.pdf
46. Until 2019, the Northwest ICE Processing Center (NWIPC) was known as the Northwest Detention Center (NWDC).
47. Deng, G. (2023, December 22). Immigration facility can't pay detainees $1 a day for labor, WA Supreme Court rules. *Spokesman-Review*. www.

spokesman.com/stories/2023/dec/22/immigration-facility-cant-pay-detainees-1-a-day-fo/
48. Deng, Immigration facility can't pay detainees $1 a day.
49. Deng, G. (2024, January 24). State inspectors denied entry to privately-run immigration detention center in Tacoma. *Washington State Standard*. washingtonstatestandard.com/2024/01/24/state-inspectors-denied-entry-to-privately-run-immigration-detention-center-in-tacoma/
50. Washington State law includes an exemption from minimum wage regulations for "inmates of state, county, or municipal corrections or detention facilities." See Deng, Immigration facility can't pay detainees $1 a day.
51. Krell, A. (2023, December 22). Does WA minimum wage law apply to immigration detainees in Tacoma? Supreme court rules. *The Columbian*. www.columbian.com/news/2023/dec/22/does-wa-minimum-wage-law-apply-to-immigration-detainees-in-tacoma-supreme-court-rules/
52. Deng, Immigration facility can't pay detainees $1 a day.
53. Krell, Does WA minimum wage law apply.
54. Krell, Does WA minimum wage law apply.
55. *Nwauzor v The GEO Group, Inc.*, Case no 21-36025 (9th Cir. January 16, 2025). www.govinfo.gov/app/details/USCOURTS-ca9-21-36025/USCOURTS-ca9-21-36025-0/context
56. RTT News (2025, January 16). GEO Group to appeal Ninth Circuit ruling in Nwauzor case. *RTT News*. www.nasdaq.com/articles/geo-group-appeal-ninth-circuit-ruling-nwauzor-case
57. Worker Justice Center of New York. (2020, September 4). Immigrants detained at Buffalo Federal Detention Center due federal contractor over $1-per-day work program. Press Release. www.wjcny.org/
58. On labor rights as detailed in the NY Const. art III, § 24; for relevant NY Labor law, see NY Const. art XIX, § 652. www.nysenate.gov/legislation/laws/; for documents related to the Buffalo lawsuit see Stevens, J. (2024). *Deportation Research Clinic*. https://deportationresearchclinic.org/ and *Yeend and Phimasone v. Akima Global Services, LLC*, Case no: 1:20-cv-01281-TJM-CFH. (U.S. Supreme Court of New York, September 3, 2020). https://deportationresearchclinic.org/DRC-INS-ICE-FacilityContracts-Reports.html
59. Heaney, J. (2020, September 17). Working for $1 a day. *Investigative Post*. www.investigativepost.org/2020/09/17/working-for-1-a-day/
60. Pauly, M. (2017, April 3). How a private prison company used detained immigrants for free labor. *Mother Jones*. www.motherjones.com/politics/2017/04/geo-forced-labor-lawsuit/
61. U.S. Const. art. I, § 8, clause 17. https://constitution.congress.gov/browse/article-1/section-8/clause-17/
62. See *Yeend and Phimasone v. Akima Global Services, LLC*, Case no: 1:20-cv-01281-TJM-CFH. (U.S. District Court, New York, November 30,

2020) (Notice of Motion to Remand). https://deportationresearchclinic. org/Batavia/Doc18_NoticeofMotionto_12-01-2020.pdf
63. McDonnell Nieto Del Rio, G. (2023, August 29). ICE can renew Elizabeth detention contract after NJ judge ruling. *Documented.* https://documentedny. com/2023/08/29/ice-new-jersey-corecivic-elizabeth-detention/
64. *GEO Group Inc., and United States of America v. Newsom; Bonta, and State of California*, No. 20-56172 (9th Cir. September 26, 2022) https://cdn.ca9. uscourts.gov/datastore/opinions/2022/09/26/20-56172.pdf
65. Wiessner, D. (2022, September 27). GEO Group wins legal challenge to California ban on private immigrant prisons. *Reuters.* www.reuters.com/ legal/geo-group-wins-legal-challenge-california-private-immigrant-prisons-2022-09-26/; Wiessner, D. (2021, June 5). Biden admin. seeking to overcome Calif. Ban on private detention. *Reuters.* www.reuters.com/legal/ litigation/biden-admin-seeking-overcome-calif-ban-private-detention-2021-06-04/
66. Castillo, A. (2023, June 28). California tried and failed to ban for-profit ICE detention centers. What does that mean for other states? *Los Angeles Times.* www.latimes.com/politics/story/2023-06-28/california-private-detention-ban-overturned-future
67. *GEO Group Inc. and United States of America v. Newsom; Bonta, and State of California*, No. 20-56172 (p. 3).
68. *GEO Group Inc. and United States of America v. Newsom; Bonta, and State of California*, No. 20-56172 (p. 3).
69. Weill-Greenberg, E. (2023, September 18). Gavin Newsom can sign a bill to end price-gouging in California prisons. *The Appeal.* https://theappeal.org/ price-gouging-in-california-prisons-newsom-signature/; see also SB 474. Chapter 609 (October 8, 2023) (passed). https://legiscan.com/CA/text/ SB474/2023
70. Lyle, M. (2023, May 10). Lawmakers urged to rein in prison costs that put "backdoor tax" on inmates' families. *Nevada Current.* https://nevadacurrent. com/2023/05/10/lawmakers-urged-to-rein-in-prison-costs-that-put-backdoor-tax-on-inmates-families/

Chapter 5 The Accountability Industry: Rubber-stamping Bad Care

1. American Immigration Council. (2022, May 16). *Oversight of immigration detention: An overview.* www.americanimmigrationcouncil.org/research/ oversight-immigration-detention-overview
2. U.S. Immigration and Customs Enforcement (ICE). (2019). *2019 National Detention Standards for non-dedicated facilities.* www.ice.gov/detain/ detention-management/2019
3. Cho, E. H. (2020, January 14). The Trump administration weakens standards for ICE detention facilities. *ACLU.* www.aclu.org/news/immigrants-rights/ the-trump-administration-weakens-standards-for-ice-detention-facilities

NOTES

4. Cullen, T. T. (2018, March 13). ICE released its most comprehensive immigration detention data yet. It's alarming. National Immigrant Justice Center. https://immigrantjustice.org/staff/blog/ice-released-its-most-comprehensive-immigration-detention-data-yet
5. The 2018 report notes that ICE claims that all ICE facilities are inspected according to one of the three ICE standards (2000 NDS, 2008 PBNDS, or 2011 PBNDS), with 63 percent of them evaluated by the most detailed 2011 standards; Cullen, ICE released its most comprehensive immigration detention data yet.
6. Office of Inspector General. (2018, June 26). *ICE's inspections and monitoring of detention facilities do not lead to sustained compliance or systemic improvements.* Department of Homeland Security. www.oig.dhs.gov/reports/2018/ices-inspections-and-monitoring-detention-facilities-do-not-lead-sustained-compliance; U.S. House of Representatives Committee on Homeland Security. (2020, September 21). *ICE detention facilities: Failing to meet basic standards of care.* https://democrats-homeland.house.gov/activities/other-events/ice-detention-facilities-failing-to-meet-basic-standards-of-care
7. The Nakamoto Group, Inc. is owned by Jennifer Nakamoto, a Japanese-American woman who in defense of her company's work with ICE has proclaimed that her grandparents' detention in internment camps during World War II shapes her company's mission. Critics accuse her of twisting this family history, along with her business being woman- and minority-owned, as a distraction tactic from the poor performance of the company: Noguchi, Y. (2019, July 17). "No Meaningful Oversight": ICE contractor overlooked problems at detention centers. *National Public Radio.* www.npr.org/2019/07/17/741181529/no-meaningful-oversight-ice-contractor-overlooked-problems-at-detention-centers; *Rafu Shimpo.* Nakamoto group criticized for role in immigrant detention. (2019, October 2). https://rafu.com/2019/10/nakamoto-group-criticized-for-role-in-immigrant-detention/
8. Office of Inspector General, *ICE's inspections and monitoring of detention facilities do not lead to sustained compliance or systemic improvements.*
9. U.S. Immigration and Customs Enforcement. (2022, March 23). *Office of Detention Oversight inspections: Fiscal year 2021 report to Congress.* chrome-extension://efaidnbmnnnibpcajpcglclefindmkaj/https://www.dhs.gov/sites/default/files/2022-05/ICE%20-%20Office%20of%20Detention%20Oversight%20Inspections.pdf
10. National Immigrant Justice Center (NIJC). (2023, November 28). *Beyond repair: ICE's abusive detention inspection and oversight system.* https://immigrantjustice.org/research-items/policy-brief-beyond-repair-ices-abusive-detention-inspection-and-oversight-system
11. Beginning in 2018, legislation required that ICE make all inspection reports (along with a range of other types of documents) available to the public via

the ICE FOIA library. Prior to this, we obtained inspection reports through our own information requests, and by drawing on the information requests of others (such as organizations like the NIJC).

12. The rating systems have varied slightly throughout the years, so the rating terms used vary according to when the inspection was conducted.
13. National Immigrant Justice Center (NIJC) & Detention Watch Network (DWN). (2015, October 22). *Lives in peril: How ineffective inspections make ICE complicit in detention center abuse.* https://immigrantjustice.org/lives-peril-how-ineffective-inspections-make-ice-complicit-detention-center-abuse (p. 4).
14. NIJC & DWN, *Lives in peril*; Cullen, ICE released its most comprehensive immigration detention data yet.
15. Office of Inspector General. (2019, February 13). *Issues requiring action at the Essex County Correctional Facility in Newark, New Jersey.* Department of Homeland Security. (Report OIG-19-20).
16. For example: Office of Inspector General. (2006, December). *Treatment of immigration detainees housed at Immigration and Customs Enforcement facilities.* Department of Homeland Security. (Report OIG-07-01); Office of Inspector General. *ICE's inspections and monitoring of detention facilities do not lead to sustained compliance or systemic improvements*; Office of Inspector General. (2019, January 29). *ICE does not fully use contracting tools to hold detention facility contractors accountable for failing to meet performance standards.* Department of Homeland Security. (Report OIG-19-18).
17. U.S. Government Accountability Office (GAO). (2020, August 19). *Immigration detention: ICE should enhance its use of facility oversight data and management of detainee complaints.* www.gao.gov/products/gao-20-596; U.S. GAO. (2021, January 13). *Immigration detention: Actions needed to improve planning, documentation, and oversight of detention facility contracts.* www.gao.gov/products/gao-21-149; U.S. GAO. (2023, January 9). *Immigration detention: ICE can improve oversight and management.* www.gao.gov/products/gao-23-106350
18. Warren, E. (2019, April 17). Warren, colleagues demand answers from ICE following investigation of for-profit contractors running immigration detention facilities. Office of Senator Elizabeth Warren. www.warren.senate.gov/oversight/letters/warren-colleagues-demand-answers-from-ice-following-investigation-of-for-profit-contractors-running-immigration-detention-facilities
19. U.S. House of Representatives Committee on Homeland Security. (2019, September 26). *Oversight of ICE detention facilities: Is DHS doing enough?*; U.S. House of Representatives Committee on Homeland Security, *ICE detention facilities: Failing to meet basic standards of care*; Office of Inspector General. (2022, November 15). *Medical mistreatment of women*

in ICE Detention. Testimony of Dr. Joseph V. Cuffari. Committee on Senate Homeland Security and Governmental Affairs. United States Senate.
20. NIJC & DWN, *Lives in peril*; Detention Watch Network (2016). *A toxic relationship*, www.detentionwatchnetwork.org/sites/default/files/reports/A%20Toxic%20Relationship_DWN.pdf; Cho, E., Taurel, P., & Shah, A. (2021). *ICE's detention inspection program is systemically flawed and has not improved*. ACLU. www.aclu.org/documents/aclu-white-paper-ices-detention-inspection-program-systemically-flawed-and-has-not-improved-0; NIJC, *Beyond repair*.
21. Office of Inspector General, *ICE's inspections and monitoring of detention facilities do not lead to sustained compliance or systemic improvements* (p. 7, note 12).
22. Gaynor, A. (2022, August 1). Nakamoto Group accused of rubber-stamping ICE facility inspections. *Prison Legal News*. www.prisonlegalnews.org/news/2022/aug/1/nakamoto-group-accused-rubber-stamping-ice-facility-inspections/
23. Office of Inspector General, *ICE's inspections and monitoring of detention facilities do not lead to sustained compliance or systemic improvements*; Cho, Taurel, & Shah, *ICE's detention inspection program is systemically flawed and has not improved*.
24. Office of Inspector General, *ICE's inspections and monitoring of detention facilities do not lead to sustained compliance or systemic improvements* (p. 6).
25. Takei, C., Small, M., Wu, C., & Chan, J. (2016, February 24). *Fatal neglect: How ICE ignores deaths in detention*. American Civil Liberties Union, Detention Watch Network, National Immigrant Justice Center (p. 6).
26. Takei et al., *Fatal neglect* (p. 18).
27. U.S. House of Representatives Committee on Homeland Security, *Oversight of ICE detention facilities: Is DHS doing enough?* (p. 12).
28. NIJC, *Beyond repair*.
29. Cho, Taurel, & Shah, *ICE's detention inspection program is systemically flawed and has not improved*; American Immigration Council, *Oversight of immigration detention: An overview*.
30. Office of Inspector General, *ICE's inspections and monitoring of detention facilities do not lead to sustained compliance or systemic improvements*; U.S. House of Representatives Committee on Homeland Security, *Oversight of ICE detention facilities: Is DHS doing enough?*; U.S. House of Representatives Committee on Homeland Security, *ICE detention facilities: Failing to meet basic standards of care*.
31. Ellis, B., & Hicken, M. (2019, June 25). Help me before it's too late. *CNN*. www.cnn.com/interactive/2019/06/us/jail-health-care-ccs-invs/
32. Cho, E., Tidwell Cullen, T., & Long, C. (2020, April 29). *Justice-free zones: U.S. immigration detention under the Trump administration*. American Civil Liberties Union, Human Rights Watch, and National Immigrant Justice

Center. https://immigrantjustice.org/research-items/report-justice-free-zones-us-immigration-detention-under-trump-administration.
33. Cho et al., *Justice-free zones*.
34. Cho et al., *Justice-free zones*.
35. Salant, J. D. (2020, April 10). NJ has more immigrant detainees with the coronavirus than any other state. *NJ.com*. www.nj.com/coronavirus/2020/04/nj-has-more-immigrant-detainees-with-the-coronavirus-than-any-other-state.html; Hooks, G. & Libal, B. (2020, December). *Hotbeds of infection: How ICE detention contributed to the spread of COVID-19 in the United States*. Detention Watch Network; Tosh, S. R., Berg, U. D., & Leon, K. S. (2021). Migrant detention and COVID-19: Pandemic responses in four New Jersey detention centers. *Journal on Migration and Human Security*, 9(1), 49–62, doi/10.1177/23315024211003855.
36. Office of Inspector General, *ICE's inspections and monitoring of detention facilities do not lead to sustained compliance or systemic improvements* (p. 4); See also, Freed Wessler, S. (2016, January 26). "This Man Will Almost Certainly Die." *The Nation*. www.thenation.com/article/archive/privatized-immigrant-prison-deaths/; U.S. House of Representatives Committee on Homeland Security, *Oversight of ICE detention facilities: Is DHS doing enough?*; U.S. House of Representatives Committee on Homeland Security, *ICE detention facilities: Failing to meet basic standards of care*.
37. U.S. GAO, *Immigration detention: Actions needed to improve planning, documentation, and oversight of detention facility contracts*.
38. U.S. GAO, *Immigration detention: ICE can improve oversight and management* (p. 1).
39. U.S. GAO, *Immigration detention: ICE can improve oversight and management*; NIJC, *Beyond repair*.
40. Noguchi, "No Meaningful Oversight": ICE contractor overlooked problems at detention centers.
41. U.S. GAO, *Immigration detention: Actions needed to improve planning, documentation, and oversight of detention facility contracts*.
42. Office of Inspector General, *ICE's inspections and monitoring of detention facilities do not lead to sustained compliance or systemic improvements*; U.S. House of Representatives Committee on Homeland Security, *Oversight of ICE detention facilities: Is DHS doing enough?*; U.S. GAO, *Immigration detention: Actions needed to improve planning, documentation, and oversight of detention facility contracts*.
43. U.S. House of Representatives Committee on Homeland Security, *Oversight of ICE detention facilities: Is DHS doing enough?* (p. 2); Office of Inspector General, *ICE's inspections and monitoring of detention facilities do not lead to sustained compliance or systemic improvements*.
44. Cho et al., *Justice-free zones* (p. 5).

45. Bernal, R. (2023, February 16). ICE unable to stamp out abuse allegations at detention centers. *The Hill*. https://thehill.com/latino/3860354-ice-unable-to-stamp-out-abuse-allegations-at-detention-centers/
46. U.S. GAO, *Immigration detention: ICE should enhance its use of facility oversight data and management of detainee complaints*; American Immigration Council, *Oversight of immigration detention: An overview*.
47. Cho et al., *Justice-free zones* (p. 8).
48. Office of Inspector General, *ICE's inspections and monitoring of detention facilities do not lead to sustained compliance or systemic improvements* (pp. 8–9); Cho, Taurel, & Shah, *ICE's detention inspection program is systemically flawed and has not improved*.
49. Office of Inspector General, *Issues requiring action at the Essex County Correctional Facility in Newark, New Jersey*.
50. Human Rights First (HRF). (2018, February 27). *Ailing justice: New Jersey. Inadequate healthcare, indifference, and indefinite confinement in immigration detention*. https://humanrightsfirst.org/wp-content/uploads/2022/04/Ailing-Justice-NJ.pdf
51. Warren, E. (2020, December). *The accreditation con: A broken prison and detention facility accreditation system that puts profits over people*. Office of Senator Elizabeth Warren.
52. Cho, The Trump administration weakens standards for ICE detention facilities.
53. American Correctional Association (ACA). (2025, January 10). *About us: Goals*. www.aca.org/ACA_Member/ACA/ACA_Member/AboutUs/AboutUs_Home.aspx?hkey=0c9cb058-e3d5-4bb0-ba7c-be29f9b34380
54. National Commission on Correctional Health Care. (2025, January 10). About us. https://www.ncchc.org/about-us/
55. New York Correct Care Medical Services / Wellpath 2021 contract and bid for Orange County Correctional Facility's medical services contract, on file with authors (pp. 201 and 234).
56. American Correctional Association. (2025, January 10). *Seeking accreditation*. www.aca.org/ACA_Member/ACA/ACA_Member/Standards_and_Accreditation/Seeking_Accreditation_Home.aspx?hkey=ed52ffa0-24e4-4575-9242-1aa9d7107e69
57. Friedmann, A. (2014, October 14). How the courts view ACA accreditation. *Prison Legal News*. www.prisonlegalnews.org/news/2014/oct/10/how-courts-view-aca-accreditation/
58. Commission on Accreditation for Law Enforcement Agencies, Inc. (CALEA). (2025, January 10). *Law enforcement accreditation: Cost*. www.calea.org/law-enforcement-accreditation-cost
59. Warren, *The accreditation con*.
60. Friedmann, How the courts view ACA accreditation.
61. Warren, *The accreditation con*.
62. Friedmann, How the courts view ACA accreditation.

63. Hunter, G. (2016, July 6). Betraying the promise of accreditation: Quis custodiet ipsos custodes? *Prison Legal News.* www.prisonlegalnews.org/news/2016/jul/6/betraying-promise-accreditation-quis-custodiet-ipsos-custodes/; Warren, *The accreditation con.*
64. Warren, *The accreditation con* (p. 2).
65. Friedmann, How the courts view ACA accreditation; Hunter. Betraying the promise of accreditation; Warren, *The accreditation con.*
66. Hunter, Betraying the promise of accreditation (p. 8); Friedmann. *How the courts view ACA accreditation.*
67. Hunter, Betraying the promise of accreditation.
68. Hunter, Betraying the promise of accreditation.
69. Friedmann, How the courts view ACA accreditation; Warren, *The accreditation con.*
70. Hunter, Betraying the promise of accreditation; Warren, *The accreditation con.*
71. Hunter, Betraying the promise of accreditation (p. 3).
72. Hunter, Betraying the promise of accreditation; Warren, *The accreditation con.*
73. Warren, *The accreditation con* (p. 7).
74. Warren, *The accreditation con.*
75. National Commission on Correctional Health Care. (2021, May 14). *CFG Health Systems' gift supports correctional health.* www.ncchc.org/cfg-health-systems-gift-supports-correctional-health/
76. The ACA's tax form 990 for period ending Sept 2021 (access through ProPublica), shows revenue from Accreditation contracts = $2,082,455; and revenue from conferences = $1,323,516; Warren, *The accreditation con* (p. 8).
77. American Correctional Association. (2024, August 1). *Conventions, Advertising, and Corporate Relations Department.* https://www.aca.org/ACA_Member/ACA/ACA_Member/Meetings/Meetings_Home.aspx
78. Warren, *The accreditation con.*
79. As listed in NCCHC's 2024 Marketing and Resource Guide: National Commission of Correctional Health Care. (2025, January 10). 2024 Marketing Guide. chrome-extension://efaidnbmnnnibpcajpcglclefindmkaj/https://www.ncchc.org/wp-content/uploads/2024-MARG_FILL-rev.pdf
80. American Correctional Association. (2025, January 10). 2025 Marketing Kit. https://user-3imepyw.cld.bz/American-Correctional-Association-Marketing-Kit-2025
81. Warren, *The accreditation con*; Hunter, Betraying the promise of accreditation.

Chapter 6 Breaking Unjust Detention Dependencies

1. The organization Freedom for Immigrants has an online, interactive map that allows one to geographically locate businesses with ICE contracts:

Freedom for Immigrants. (2025). *Mapping U.S. immigration detention.* www.freedomforimmigrants.org/map. See also, Worth Rises. (2022). *The prison industry corporate database.* https://data.worthrises.org/ (last updated October 2022).
2. Worth Rises. (2020). *The prison industry: Mapping private sector players.* https://worthrises.org/theprisonindustry2020; Worth Rises, *The prison industry corporate database.*
3. Worth Rises. (2018). *Immigration detention: An American business.* https://worthrises.org/immigration#block-yui_3_17_2_1_1529993566255_362753; Worth Rises, *The prison industry: Mapping private sector players*; Worth Rises, *The prison industry corporate database.*
4. Le, T. (2021, January). *Food service contractors in the US.* IBISWorld. US Industry (NAICS) Report 72231.
5. National Commission of Correctional Health Care. (2025, January 10). 2024 Marketing Guide. chrome-extension://efaidnbmnnnibpcajpcglclefindmkaj/https://www.ncchc.org/wp-content/uploads/2024-MARG_FILL-rev.pdf
6. Keefe Group, Inc. (2025, January 10). *Keefe Supply Company.* www.keefegroup.com/companies/keefe-supply-company/
7. Henderson, M. (2017, January 31). US prison commissary giants are set to merge. *San Quentin News.* https://sanquentinnews.com/us-prison-commissary-giants-merge/; Baker, J. (2019). *HIG Capital's prison food and commissary store racket.* Private Equity Stakeholder Project. https://pestakeholder.org/reports/report-hig-capitals-prison-food-and-commissary-store-racket/; Conlon, D., & Hiemstra, N. (2014). Examining the everyday micro-economies of immigrant detention in the United States. *Geographica Helvetica, 69,* 335–344. It is important to note here that this pairing of companies–food services and commissaries–can be seen as incentivizing the production of bad food so that inmates and detainees are driven to purchase extra food from commissaries.
8. Fenne, M. (2023, January 26). *PE-owned Wellpath continues to prioritize profit over care.* Private Equity Stakeholder Project. https://pestakeholder.org/news/pe-owned-wellpath-continues-to-prioritize-profit-over-care/
9. American Friends Service Committee (AFSC). (2024, July 12). *Investigate: Aramark.* https://investigate.afsc.org/company/aramark.
10. Cronin, K. (2021, November 9). Aramark and the international detention industry. University of Delaware's *The Review.* https://udreview.com/foreign-affairs-column-aramark-and-the-international-detention-industry/
11. Katz, M. (2018, August 16). Should New Jersey Democratic officials keep jailing immigrants for ICE? *WNYC.* www.wnyc.org/story/should-new-jersey-democratic-officials-keep-jailing-immigrants-ice/
12. Difilippo, D. (2024, November 22). Feds look to add immigration jails in New Jersey. *New Jersey Monitor.* https://newjerseymonitor.com/2024/11/22/feds-look-to-add-immigration-jails-in-new-jersey/; ACLU (2024,

November 22). ACLU FOIA litigation reveals new information regarding ICE plans to expand immigration detention in New Jersey. www.aclu.org/press-releases/aclu-foia-litigation-reveals-new-information-regarding-ices-plans-to-expand-immigration-detention-in-new-jersey; Nieto-Munoz, S. (2024, June 17). Immigrant advocates alarmed by prospect of new immigrant jail in Newark. *New Jersey Monitor.* https://newjerseymonitor.com/2024/06/17/immigrant-advocates-alarmed-by-prospect-of-new-immigrant-jail-in-newark/; Valenzuela, V. (2024, November 20) "Cruelty is built into the system": ICE set to open new immigration detention system in New Jersey. *Documented.* https://documentedny.com/2024/11/20/ice-detention-new-jersey-deportation-trump/

13. Katz, M. (2018, July 11). Under Trump, Democratic New Jersey counties cash in on detaining immigrants. *WNYC.* www.wnyc.org/story/under-trump-liberal-newjersey-counties-cash-in-detaining-immigrants/; Janoski, S. (2018, July 2). Bergen County will collect $12M for housing immigrant detainees. *Northjersey.com.* www.north jersey.com/story/news/bergen/2018/07/02/bergen-county-collect-housing-immigrant-detainees/585842002/

14. O'Dea, C. (2019, April 25). Protestors demand Essex County end contract to house ICE detainees. *NJ Spotlight.* www.njspotlight.com/2019/04/19-04-24-protestors-demand-essex-county-end-lucrative-contract-to-house-ice-detainees/

15. Quoted in Guerguerian, A. (2021, April 21). Cold as ICE: North Jersey counties rake in millions from the feds while holding immigrant detainees in subhuman conditions. *The Indypendent.* https://indypendent.org/2021/04/corruptandinbed/

16. Katz, Should New Jersey Democratic officials keep jailing immigrants for ICE?

17. Xian, M. (2021, September 30). A new immigrant detention center will open in former Clearfield County prison. *WESA.* www.wesa.fm/courts-justice/2021-09-30/a-new-immigrant-detention-center-will-open-in-former-clearfield-county-prison

18. Hernández, D. M. (2016). Surrogates and subcontractors: Flexibility and obscurity in U.S. immigrant detention. In N. Elia, D. M. Hernández, J. Kim, S. L. Redmond, D. Rodríguez, & S. E. See (eds.), *Critical ethnic studies: A reader* (pp. 303–325). Duke University Press; Martin, L. (2016). Discretion, contracting and commodification: privatisation of US immigration detention as a technology of government. In D. Conlon & N. Hiemstra (eds.), *Intimate economies of immigration detention: Critical perspectives* (pp. 32–50). Routledge; Hiemstra, N. & Conlon, D. (2017). Beyond privatization: Bureaucratization and the spatialities of immigration detention expansion. *Territory, Politics, Governance,* 5(3), 252-268. doi: 10.1080/21622671.2017.1284693.

19. Immigrant Legal Resource Center (ILRC), Ceres Policy Research Institute (Ceres), and Detention Watch Network (DWN). (2022, September). *If you build it, ICE will fill it: The link between detention capacity and ICE arrests.* www.detentionwatchnetwork.org/pressroom/reports/2022/if-you-build-it-ice-will-fill-it-link-between-detention-capacity-ice-arrests. See also, Misra, T. (2018, July 10). Where cities help detain immigrants. *Bloomberg.* www.bloomberg.com/news/articles/2018-07-10/where-u-s-counties-are-detaining-immigrants
20. AFSC. (2015, December). *The role of for-profit prison corporations in shaping U.S. immigrant detention and deportation.* chrome-extension://efaidnbmnnnibpcajpcglclefindmkaj/https://afsc.org/sites/default/files/documents/BedQuotaWhitePaper.pdf; Cohen, M. (2015, April 28). How for-profit prisons have come the biggest lobby no one is talking about. *Washington Post,* www.washingtonpost.com/posteverything/wp/2015/04/28/how-for-profit-prisons-have-become-the-biggest-lobby-no-one-is-talking-about/; DWN. (2015, June). *Banking on detention: Local lock-up quotas and the immigrant dragnet.* www.detentionwatchnetwork.org/pressroom/reports; DWN. (2016). *A toxic relationship: Private prisons and US immigration detention.* www.detentionwatchnetwork.org/pressroom/reports; Collingwood, L., Morin, J. L., & El-Khatib, S. O. (2018). Expanding carceral markets: Detention facilities, ICE contracts, and the financial interests of punitive immigration policy. *Race and Social Problems, 10,* 275–292. doi: 10.1007/s12552-018-9241-5; Medina, E. (2023, May 9). Bed mandates and corporate profits: Tracing the privatization and expansion of immigration detention in the United States. *The Flaw.* https://theflaw.org/articles/bed-mandates-and-corporate-profits/
21. AFSC, *The role of for-profit prison corporations in shaping U.S. immigrant detention and deportation*; DWN, *Banking on detention*; DWN, *A toxic relationship*; Medina, Bed mandates and corporate profits.
22. AFSC, *The role of for-profit prison corporations in shaping U.S. immigrant detention and deportation* (p. 4).
23. AFSC, *The role of for-profit prison corporations in shaping U.S. immigrant detention and deportation*; Cohen, How for-profit prisons have become the biggest lobby no one is talking about; DWN, *Banking on detention*; DWN, *A toxic relationship*; Medina, Bed mandates and corporate profits.
24. DWN, *A toxic relationship* (p. 11).
25. Collingwood et al., Expanding carceral markets; Morín, J., Torres, R., & Collingwood, L. (2021). Cosponsoring and cashing in: US House members' support for punitive immigration policy and financial payoffs from the private prison industry. *Business and Politics,* 23(4), 492–509. doi:10.1017/bap.2021.6
26. Morín et al., Cosponsoring and cashing in.
27. McCarty, D. (2022, June 21). Private prison industry shifts focus to immigrant detention centers, funding immigration hawks. *Open Secrets.*

org. www.opensecrets.org/news/2022/06/private-prison-industry-shifts-focus-to-immigrant-detention-centers-funding-immigration-hawks/
28. Guha, A. (2019, July 12). "Complicit" New Jersey Democrats face pressure to end ICE contracts. *Rewire.* https://rewire.news/article/2019/07/12/complicit-new-jersey-democrats-facepressure-to-end-ice-contracts/
29. Lee, E. (2011, December 21). Cronyism, political donations surround detention center in Newark, says report by immigrant advocates. *NJ.com.* www.nj.com/news/index.ssf/2011/12/essex_county_comes_under_fire.html; Wilwohl, J. (2011, August 17). Feds may reconsider county jail deal. *Newark NJ Patch.* http://newarknj.patch.com/groups/politics-and-elections/p/feds-reconsider-essex-county-jail-deal; Conlon & Hiemstra. Examining the everyday micro-economies of immigrant detention in the United States; Hiemstra & Conlon, Beyond privatization: Bureaucratization and the spatialities of immigration detention expansion.
30. Hunter, G. (2016, July 6). Betraying the promise of accreditation: Quis custodiet ipsos custodes? *Prison Legal News.* www.prisonlegalnews.org/news/2016/jul/6/betraying-promise-accreditation-quis-custodiet-ipsos-custodes/; Pauly, M. (2019, February 6). Mississippi's prison bribery scandal is in the past, but the state still hasn't learned its lesson. *Mother Jones.* www.motherjones.com/politics/2019/02/mississippi-corrections-corruption-bribery-private-prison-hustle/
31. AFSC, *The role of for-profit prison corporations in shaping U.S. immigrant detention and deportation*; DWN, *Banking on detention*; DWN, *A toxic relationship*; Medina, Bed mandates and corporate profits.
32. DWN, *A toxic relationship* (p. 11).
33. Cohen, How for-profit prisons have become the biggest lobby no one is talking about.
34. AFSC, *The role of for-profit prison corporations in shaping U.S. immigrant detention and deportation*; DWN, *A toxic relationship*; Warren, E. (2020, January 17). Warren leads colleagues investigating the revolving door between federal agencies and the private detention industry. Office of Senator Elizabeth Warren. www.warren.senate.gov/oversight/reports/warren-leads-colleagues-investigating-the-revolving-door-between-federal-agencies-and-the-private-detention-industry
35. Warren, Warren leads colleagues investigating the revolving door between federal agencies and the private detention industry.
36. Warren, E. (2019, June 6). Senator Warren, Representative Jayapal investigate former White House Chief of Staff General John Kelly's "cynical" and "unethical" decision to join the Board of Directors of federal contractor running the nation's largest detention center for migrant children. Office of Senator Elizabeth Warren. www.warren.senate.gov/oversight/letters/senator-warren-representative-jayapal-investigate-former-white-house-chief-of-staff-general-john-kellys-cynical-and-unethical-decision-to-

join-the-board-of-directors-of-federal-contractor-running-the-nations-largest-detention-center-for-migrant-children
37. Given the increasing climate of fearmongering and attacks against organizations and individuals, specific organization names have not been included.
38. Alvarado, M. (2020, November 24). Hudson County freeholders extend contract to house ICE detainees, drawing renewed scrutiny. *Northjersey.com*. www.northjersey.com/story/news/hudson/2020/11/24/hudson-county-nj-freeholders-extend-contract-house-ice-detainees/6407189002/
39. *The Chronicle*. (2019, July 10). Vigils for undocumented migrants planned. www.chroniclenewspaper.com/news/local-news/vigils-for-undocumented-migrants-planned-BQCN20190710190719994
40. Conlon, D. (2013). Hungering for freedom. In D. Moran, N. Gill & D. Conlon (eds.). *Carceral spaces: Mobility and agency in imprisonment and migrant detention* (pp. 133–148). Ashgate.
41. Freedom for Immigrants. (2020). *Hunger Strikes*. www.freedomforimmigrants.org/hunger-strikes.
42. Stein, M. I. (2019, April 19). Hunger strikes at ICE detention centers spread as parole, bond are denied. *NPR*. www.npr.org/2019/04/19/713910647/hunger-strikes-at-ice-detention-centers-spread-as-parole-bond-is-denied/
43. Alvarado, M. (2020, November 27). Detained immigrants at Bergen County Jail stage hunger strike, get support from protesters. *Northjersey.com*. https://www.northjersey.com/story/news/new-jersey/2020/11/27/ice-detainees-bergen-county-jail-hunger-strike-get-support/6398654002/; Goodman, A., and "Lautaro." (2021, February 17). Why I led a hunger strike against ICE in New Jersey. *The Counter*. https://thecounter.org/hunger-strike-against-ice-new-jersey-documented/; Lind, D. (2020, March 23). ICE detainee says migrants are going on a hunger strike for soap. *ProPublica*. www.propublica.org/article/ice-detainee-says-migrants-are-going-on-a-hunger-strike-for-soap.
44. Owens, H. B. (2021, February 25). ICE officials reject activists claims of unhealthy conditions at Buffalo Federal Detention Facility. *The Batavian*. www.thebatavian.com/howard-b-owens/ice-officials-reject-activists-claims-of-unhealthy-conditions-at-buffalo-federal; Guerguerian, A. (2022, August 25). Immigrants on hunger strike at Buffalo Federal Detention Facility speak out, assert rights. *The Indypendent*. https://indypendent.org/2022/08/immigrants-on-hunger-strike-at-buffalo-federal-detention-facility-speak-out-assert-rights/; Parra, D. (2023, April 5). Hunger-striking ICE detainees sue over conditions at NY's Orange County Jail. *City Limits*. https://citylimits.org/2023/04/05/hunger-striking-ice-detainees-sue-over-conditions-at-nys-orange-county-jail/; Rayman, G. (2022, February 17). Hunger strike among ICE detainees in upstate jail over conditions; Jail officials dispute allegations. *Daily News*. www.nydailynews.

com/2022/02/17/hunger-strike-among-ice-detainees-in-upstate-jail-over-conditions-jail-officials-dispute-allegations/

45. DWN. (2021). *State legislation bans on immigration detention.* www.detentionwatchnetwork.org/sites/default/files/State%20Legislation%20Bans%20on%20Immigration%C2%A0Detention_DWN_12.16.2021.pdf; Wolf, R. (2023, March 10). *States lead the way in banning immigration detention centers.* Immigration Impact. https://immigrationimpact.com/2023/03/10/state-bills-banning-immigration-detention-centers/

46. DWN, *State legislation bans on immigration detention.*

47. Castillo, A. (2023, June 28). California tried and failed to ban for-profit ICE detention centers. What does that mean for other states? *Los Angeles Times.* www.latimes.com/politics/story/2023-06-28/california-private-detention-ban-overturned-future

48. Alvarado, M. (2021, August 16). While Murphy waits to act, ICE extends detainee contract. *NJ Spotlight News.* www.njspotlightnews.org/2021/08/nj-ice-immigration-detainee-contract-extended-murphy-bill-unsigned/

49. Wiessner, D. (2023, August 29). New Jersey ban on immigrant detention blocked in lawsuit by CoreCivic. *US News & World Report.* www.usnews.com/news/top-news/articles/2023-08-29/new-jersey-ban-on-immigrant-detention-blocked-in-lawsuit-by-corecivic; Kaulessar, R. (2024, January 9). NJ says judge erred in allowing ICE detention center in Elizabeth to stay open. *Northjersey.com.* www.northjersey.com/story/news/new-jersey/2024/01/09/nj-appeals-ruling-allowing-ice-detention-center-open/72146999007/

50. Sanchez, T. (2019, March 6). An ICE jail in California may close soon. What will happen to its 400 detainees? *San Francisco Chronicle.* www.sfchronicle.com/bayarea/amp/An-ICE-jail-in-California-may-close-soon What-13665702.php

51. Atmonavage, J. (2021, June 30). Groups sue to stop ICE from transferring detainees hundreds of miles away from N.J. *NJ.com.* www.nj.com/news/2021/06/groups-sue-to-stop-ice-from-transferring-detainees-hundreds-of-miles-away-from-nj.html; Alvarado, M. (2021, July 8). They wanted ICE contracts stopped. Now detainees are being shipped to other states. *NJ Spotlight News.* www.njspotlightnews.org/2021/07/ice-detainees-nj-bergen-county-jail-hudson-county-jail-end-agreements-transfer-detainees-out-of-state/; McDonnell Nieto del Rio, G. (2021, October 25). ICE denies release requests, sending detained immigrants across the country. *Documented NY.* https://documentedny.com/2021/10/25/are-detained-immigrants-a-public-safety-threat-ice-says-yes-as-transfers-continue/

52. McDonnell Nieto del Rio, G. (2022, July 6). Detention transfers separate immigrants from legal representation. *Documented NY.* https://documentedny.com/2022/07/06/ice-immigration-legal-transfers/

53. Zawodny, D. (2022, July 28). Maryland lawmakers passed Dignity Not Detention to protect immigrants. So ICE detains them elsewhere. *Baltimore*

Brew. www.baltimorebrew.com/2022/07/28/maryland-lawmakers-passed-dignity-not-detention-to-protect-immigrants-so-ice-detains-them-elsewhere/
54. Quoted in Alvarado, They wanted ICE contracts stopped.
55. McDonnell Nieto del Rio, Detention transfers separate immigrants from legal representation.
56. O'Dea, C. (2019, April 25). Protestors demand Essex County end contract to house ICE detainees. *NJ Spotlight.* www.njspotlightnews.org/2019/04/19-04-24-protestors-demand-essex-county-end-lucrative-contract-to-house-ice-detainees/
57. Quoted in Katz, Should New Jersey Democratic officials keep jailing immigrants for ICE?
58. Quoted in Katz, Under Trump, Democratic New Jersey counties cash in on detaining immigrants.
59. Zhang, J., Kang-Brown, J., & Kotler, A. (2024, January). *People on electronic monitoring.* Vera Institute. www.vera.org/publications/people-on-electronic-monitoring
60. Mijente. (2022, May). *Tracked and trapped: Experiences from ICE digital prisons.* https://notechforice.com/digitalprisons/
61. Bhuiyan, J. (2022, March 7). Poor tech, opaque rules, exhausted staff: inside the private company surveilling US immigrants. *The Guardian.* www.theguardian.com/us-news/2022/mar/07/us-immigration-surveillance-ice-bi-isap
62. Mijente, *Tracked and trapped: Experiences from ICE digital prisons.*
63. DWN. (2024, February 6). *Biden's border funding: What's at stake.* www.detentionwatchnetwork.org/sites/default/files/2.6.24_Biden%20Border%20Funding_Explainer_DWN.pdf
64. ICE. (2023, December 29). *ICE Annual Report.* Department of Homeland Security. www.ice.gov/information-library/annual-report
65. Mijente, *Tracked and trapped: Experiences from ICE digital prisons*; Zhang et. al., *People on electronic monitoring.*
66. Mijente, *Tracked and trapped: Experiences from ICE digital prisons*; Zhang et. al., *People on electronic monitoring.*
67. Zhang et. al., *People on electronic monitoring* (p. 8).
68. Thompson, T. (1990, December 9). Electronically monitored house arrest far from perfect. *Washington Post.* www.washingtonpost.com/archive/local/1990/12/10/electronically-monitored-house-arrest-far-from-perfect/419acda2-06dc-4962-b912-c197b40a4a08/; Bhuiyan, Poor tech, opaque rules, exhausted staff.
69. *Business Wire.* (2011, February 11). The GEO Group closes $415 million acquisition of B.I. Incorporated. www.businesswire.com/news/home/20110211005372/en/The-GEO-Group-Closes-415-Million-Acquisition-of-B.I.-Incorporated

70. This proved especially timely when the Biden administration announced in 2021 a decision to phase out private prisons in the criminal justice system: Bhuiyan, Poor tech, opaque rules, exhausted staff.
71. Zhang et. al., *People on electronic monitoring.*
72. Bhuiyan, Poor tech, opaque rules, exhausted staff.
73. McCarty, Private prison industry shifts focus to immigrant detention centers, funding immigration hawks.
74. Bhuiyan, Poor tech, opaque rules, exhausted staff.
75. U.S. Government Accountability Office. (2022, June 22). *Alternatives to detention: ICE needs to better assess program performance and improve contract oversight.* www.gao.gov/products/gao-22-104529
76. TRAC. (2024). *Immigration detention quick facts.* https://tracreports.org/immigration/quickfacts/detention.html
77. Mijente, *Tracked and trapped: Experiences from ICE digital prisons.*
78. Schwenk, K. (2023, December 8). For private prison companies, surveilling immigrants is the next big windfall. *Jacobin.* https://jacobin.com/2023/12/private-prisons-lobbying-ice-surveillance-dhs-immigration
79. Quoted in Schwenk, For private prison companies, surveilling immigrants is the next big windfall.
80. Mijente, *Tracked and trapped: Experiences from ICE digital prisons*; Zhang et. al., *People on electronic monitoring.*
81. Aziz, U., Cape-Davenhill, L., & Conlon, D. (2024) Ruth Wilson Gilmore. In Gilmartin, M., Hubbard, P., Kitchin, R., & Roberts, S. (eds.) *Key Thinkers on Space and Place* (pp. 145–152). Sage.
82. Color of Change and Worth Rises. (2023, February 6). Policy blueprint for ending carceral profiteering. https://worthrises.org/pressreleases/policy-blueprint; Hiemstra, N., & Conlon, D. (2021). Reading between the (redacted) lines: Muddling through absent presences in public information requests on U.S. immigration detention. *ACME: An International Journal for Critical Geographies, 20*(6), 666–686. doi: 10.14288/acme.v20i6.2090
83. Gill, N., Conlon, D., Tyler, I., & Oeppen, C. (2014). The tactics of asylum and irregular migrant support groups: Disrupting bodily, technological, and neoliberal strategies of control. *Annals of the American Association of Geographers, 104*(2), 373–381. doi: 10.1080/00045608.2013.857544
84. Viera, G. (2023, October 27). *Communities not cages: A national movement to end ICE detention.* [Symposium presentation]. Elizabeth Detention Center: Past, Present, and Future. Rutgers University, NJ.
85. Weiberger, E. (2024, December 26) Incoming! *London Review of Books, 46*(24). www.lrb.co.uk/the-paper/v46/n24/eliot-weinberger/incoming
86. McLeod, M. (2019, September 12). The private option. *The Atlantic.* www.theatlantic.com/politics/archive/2019/09/private-equitys-grip-on-jail-health-care/597871/
87. Simon, M. (2019, September 20). GEO Group running out of banks as 100% of known banking partners say "no" to the private prison sector. *Forbes.com.* www.forbes.com/sites/morgansimon/2019/09/30/geo-group-runs-out-of-

NOTES

banks-as-100-of-banking-partners-say-no-to-the-private-prison-sector/?sh=5f8f17663298; Telford, T. & Merle, R. (2019, June 27). Bank of America cuts business ties with detention centers, private prisons. *Washington Post.* www.washingtonpost.com/business/2019/06/27/bank-america-cuts-business-ties-with-detention-centers-private-prisons/; Yancey-Bragg, N. (2019, June 27). Bank of America to cut ties with companies that help run immigrant detention centers, private prisons. *USA Today.* www.usatoday.com/story/money/2019/06/27/bank-america-cut-ties-detention-centers-private-prisons/1589221001/
88. Garrison, J. (2019, June 26). "Shut down the concentration camps": Wayfair employees walk out, hundreds protest. *USA Today.* www.usatoday.com/story/news/nation/2019/06/26/wayfair-walkout-hundreds-protest-sales-migrant-detention-centers/1569622001/
89. Yi, K. (2020, July 15). Landlord wants to cut ties with NJ Immigrant Detention Center. *WNYC.* www.wnyc.org/story/landlord-wants-cut-ties-nj-immigrant-detention-center/
90. For more on a justice focused anti-detention movement and abolitionist thinking more generally, see Gilmore, R. W. (2022) *Abolition Geography: Essays Towards Liberation.* Verso.
91. Libal, B. (2021, May). *Communities not cages: A just transition from immigration detention economies.* Detention Watch Network. www.detentionwatchnetwork.org/pressroom/reports/2021/communities-not-cages-just-transition-immigration-detention-economies

Afterword: Chaos and Cruelty in the First Month of the Second Trump Administration

All URLs in the Afterword were last accessed in February 2025.

1. Department of Homeland Security (2025, January 17). *U.S. Department of Homeland Security has taken unprecedented steps resulting in a border more secure than it was four years ago.* Fact Sheet. www.dhs.gov/archive/news/2025/01/17/fact-sheet-dhs-has-taken-unprecedented-steps-resulting-border-more-secure-it-was#:~:text=In%20the%20first%20half%20of,1%2C500%20for%2021%20consecutive%20days
2. American Immigration Council (2025, January 22). *After day one: A high-level analysis of Trump's first Executive Actions.* www.americanimmigrationcouncil.org/research/after-day-one-high-level-analysis-trumps-first-executive-actions (p. 1).
3. American Immigration Council (2025, January 22). *After day one: A high level analysis of Trump's first Executive Actions* (p. 2).
4. Warren, R. (2024, September 5). US undocumented population increased to 11.7 million in July 2023: Provision CMS estimates derived from CPS data. Center for Migration Studies. https://cmsny.org/us-undocumented-population-increased-in-july-2023-warren-090624/

5. CBP One is a mobile application introduced by Customs and Border Patrol (CBP) in 2020. In 2023, the app was expanded for use by migrants to facilitate control over scheduling of initial asylum appointments at the U.S.-Mexico border.
6. TRAC (2025, February 25). Little empirical evidence that arrests and removals are higher under Trump. tracreports.org/reports/754/
7. TRAC, Little empirical evidence that arrests and removals are higher under Trump.
8. Zanger, J., & McLogan, J. (2025, February 4). Nassau County police joining forces with ICE agents. Here's how officials say it will work. *CBSNews.com.* www.cbsnews.com/newyork/news/nassau-county-police-partnering-with-ice-agents/
9. Gibson, B. (2025, February 13). Trump's mass deportation plan hits its own wall. *Axios.* www.axios.com/2025/02/13/trump-immigration-deportation-obstacles
10. Sisak, M. (2025, February 7). Federal prisons being used to detain people arrested in Trump's immigration crackdown. *AP News.* https://apnews.com/article/immigration-federal-prisons-trump-25d676a6ebbff139ae04a75cd91be7e8
11. Montaya-Galvez, C. (2025, February 5). ICE releases some migrant detainees as its detention facilities reach 109% capacity. *CBS News.* www.cbsnews.com/news/ice-releases-some-migrant-detainees-detention-facilities-reach-109-percent-capacity/
12. Goswami, R. & Talcott, S. (2025, February 6). Trump team considers housing detained migrants in container offices. *Semafor.* www.semafor.com/article/02/06/2025/trump-administration-container-company-to-provide-temporary-migrant-housing
13. Ainsley, J. (2025, February 7). Trump administration preparing to restart immigrant family detention. *NBC News.* www.nbcwashington.com/news/politics/trump-administration-preparing-restart-immigrant-family-detention/3839437/?os=0SLw57pSD&ref=app
14. Opila, C. (2025, February 7). Sending migrants to Guantánamo Bay is a costly, abusive shift in immigration detention. *Immigration Impact.* https://immigrationimpact.com/2025/02/07/sending-migrants-guantanamo-bay-costly-abusive-detention/
15. Loyd, J.M. & Mountz, A. (2018). *Boats, borders, and bases: Race, the Cold War, and the rise of migration detention in the United States.* University of California Press.
16. Foster-Frau, S. (2025, February 8). Why lawyers worry migrants sent to Guantánamo are in a "legal black hole." *Washington Post.* www.washingtonpost.com/immigration/2025/02/08/guantanamo-migrants-trump-deportations-noem/
17. Woodward, A. (2025, February 21). Trump administration abruptly empties out Guantánamo prison of all immigrant detainees. *Independent.* www.

independent.co.uk/news/world/americas/us-politics/trump-guantanamo-bay-prison-immigrants-b2702448.html
18. Foster-Frau, Why lawyers worry migrants sent to Guantánamo are in a "legal black hole."
19. Hesson, T. (2025, February 1). ICE aims to lower US immigration detention standards to encourage more sheriffs to aid crackdown. *Reuters*. www.reuters.com/world/us/trump-administration-aims-lower-immigration-detention-standards-let-more-jails-2025-02-01/
20. National Immigrant Justice Center. (2025, January 31). Nonprofits sue the Department of Justice and Kristi Noem to restore legal access for immigrants facing deportation. https://immigrantjustice.org/press-releases/nonprofits-sue-department-justice-and-kristi-noem-restore-legal-access-immigrants; Complaint for Declaratory and Injunctive Relief. U.S. District Court for the District of Columbia. Case No. 1:25-cv-00298. https://amicacenter.org/app/uploads/2025/01/Complaint-for-Declaratory-and-Injunctive-Relief.pdf
21. Acevedo, N. & Dilanian, K. (2025, February 4). Rubio touts Bukele's "generous" offer to jail U.S. citizens in El Salvador, but experts say it's illegal. *NBC News*. www.nbcnews.com/news/latino/el-salvador-jail-us-nayib-bukele-marco-rubio-rcna190574
22. Turkewitz, J., Farnaz, F., Aleaziz, H., & Correal, A. (2025, February 19) Migrants deported to Panama under Trump plan, detained in remote jungle camp. *New York Times*. www.nytimes.com/2025/02/19/world/americas/us-migrants-panama-jungle-camp.html
23. Harrison, C. & Robertson, K. (2025, February 19) Tracking Trump and Latin America: Migration. *Americas Society/Council of the Americas (AS/COS)*. www.as-coa.org/articles/tracking-trump-and-latin-america-migration
24. Reports indicate that the resulting detention centers are even worse than in the United States, with violence, abuse, and appalling conditions: Hiemstra, N. (2019). Pushing the US-Mexico border south: United States' immigration policing throughout the Americas. *International Journal of Migration and Border Studies*. 5 (1/2): 44–63. doi: 10.1504/IJMBS.2019.099681
25. See Mountz, A. (2020). *The death of asylum: Hidden geographies of the enforcement archipelago*. University of Minnesota Press; Conlon, D. (2024). The spectacle of invisibility: Vanishing points and the spatialised legal violence of the U.K.'s expanding quasi-carceral geography of immigration control. *Geopolitics*, 1–32. doi: 10.1080/14650045.2024.2411328
26. Shaw, D. (2025, January 29). Prison company banking on ICE raids donated to Trump inauguration. *Sludge*. https://readsludge.com/2025/01/29/prison-company-banking-on-ice-raids-donated-to-trump-inauguration/
27. Schwellenbach, N. & Kladzyk, R. (2025, January 17). Private prison giant hired ICE detention chief. Project on Government Oversight. www.pogo.org/investigations/private-prison-giant-hired-ice-detention-chief
28. Schwellenbach & Kladzyk, Private prison giant hired ICE detention chief.

29. Heffernan, S. (2025, January 2022). Marshall Project: What will Trump's executive order on private prisons really do? www.themarshallproject.org/2025/01/22/trump-private-prisons-executive-order
30. Leary, A. (2016, August 24). Behind Marco Rubio, a powerful ally: Private prison operator Geo Group. *Tampa Bay Times*. www.tampabay.com/behind-marco-rubio-a-powerful-ally-private-prison-operator-geo-group/2290600/; McCarty, D. (2022, June 21). Private prison industry shifts focus to immigrant detention centers, funding immigration hawks. Open Secrets.org. www.opensecrets.org/news/2022/06/private-prison-industry-shifts-focus-to-immigrant-detention-centers-funding-immigration-hawks/
31. Kerr, D. (2025, February 6). US immigration is gaming Google to create a mirage of mass deportations. *The Guardian*. www.theguardian.com/us-news/2025/feb/06/ice-us-immigration-deportations-google
32. U.S. Immigration and Customs Enforcement. (2025, February 14). Detention statistics. www.ice.gov/detain/detention-management
33. TRAC, *Little empirical evidence immigration arrests and removals are higher*.
34. Montaya-Galvez, ICE releases some migrant detainees as its detention facilities reach 109% capacity.
35. Kocher, A. (2025, February 14). ICE's latest detention data shows growth of immigrants targeted with no criminal histories—exactly as predicted. Austin Kocher Substack. https://austinkocher.substack.com/p/ices-latest-detention-data-shows
36. Lee, M., & Groves, S. (2025, January 23). Immigrant detention beds may be maxed out as Trump promises mass deportations. *PBS News*. www.pbs.org/newshour/politics/immigrant-detention-beds-may-be-maxed-out-as-trump-promises-mass-deportations
37. Mascaro, L., Freking, K., & Brown, M. (2025, February 21). Senate Republicans approve budget framework over Democratic objections after all-night vote. *PBS News*. www.pbs.org/newshour/politics/senate-republicans-approve-budget-framework-over-democratic-objections-after-all-night-vote
38. Diamante, R. (2025, February 7). Trump administration pushes to expand migrant detention as congressional Republicans mull funding. *Spectrum News 1*. https://spectrumlocalnews.com/tx/south-texas-el-paso/news/2025/02/07/trump-texas-republicans-migrant-detention-funding
39. *CBS News*. (2025, February 5). Sheriffs say funds, space and staffing will hinder Trump administration requests to help ICE. www.cbsnews.com/video/sheriffs-say-funds-space-and-staffing-will-hinder-trump-administration-requests-to-help-ice/
40. New York City Bar. (2025, February 13). The Trump administration's early 2025 changes to immigration law. www.nycbar.org/reports/the-trump-administrations-early-2025-changes-to-immigration-law/; Just Security. (2025, February 23). Litigation tracker: Legal challenges to Trump

administration actions. www.justsecurity.org/107087/tracker-litigation-legal-challenges-trump-administration/

41. Nieto-Munoz, S. (2025, February 7). Amid ICE raids and deportation threats, N.J. Democrats are split on immigrant protection bill. *New Jersey Monitor.* https://newjerseymonitor.com/2025/02/07/amid-ice-raids-and-deportation-threats-n-j-democrats-are-split-on-immigrant-protection-bill/

42. Jones, R. (2021). *White borders: The history of race and immigration in the United States from Chinese exclusion to the Border Wall.* Beacon Press; Nevins, J. (2010). *Operation Gatekeeper and beyond: The war on "illegals" and the remaking of the U.S.-Mexico boundary.* Routledge.

43. While Trump suspended the entire U.S. refugee resettlement program on day one, another Trump executive order now allows white Afrikaaner "refugees" from South Africa. See Kocher, A. (2025, February 8). Saying the thing out loud: Trump's latest refugee order embraces white victimhood. Austin Kocher Substack. https://austinkocher.substack.com/p/saying-the-thing-out-loud-trumps

Index

t refers to a table

9/11: 15–16

Abbott, Governor Greg 159–60
Access Corrections 90
Access Securepak 90
accreditation agencies 8, 114–23
    conferences 121–2
    fees for 117–8
    marketing by 121–3
Adelanto Facility, California 87, 98
Advanced Tech Group (ATG) 90
advocacy, and anti-detention activism 97, 102–3, 133–4, 144, 145–6, 149, 155–6
Ahtna Technical Services 60
Akima Global Services (AGS) 25, 39, 49, 51, 65, 80
    lawsuits against 98, 100–1
Albania, funding of detention centers by Italy 6
Alternatives to Detention (ATD) 140–4
Amazon 124
American Civil Liberties Union (ACLU) 36, 109, 113, 128
American Correctional Association (ACA) 105, 107, 115–22
    marketing by 122–3
American Friends Service Committee 36
American Immigration Council 106
Amnesty International 149
anti-detention activism 127, 133–50
Anti-Drug Abuse Act (1988) 15
Antiterrorism and Effective Death Penalty Act (1996) 15
Aramark Corporation 27, 29, 40–5, 61, 92, 121, 124, 127
asylum seekers 14, 15, 127, 134, 153
Aurora Detention Facility, Colorado 97, 98
Australia
    detention centers in 5
    Pacific Solution 156

Bank of America 124, 148
Barclays Bank 148
Batavia Service Processing Center *see* Buffalo Service Processing Center

Bergen County Jail, NJ 21, 23, 26–7, 70, 87, 89, 128, 134
    COVID in 62
    food provision in 40, 43–4, 56–7, 61
    hunger strikes in 136
    IGSA agreement with ICE 32*t*
    medical care in 65
BI, Inc. (Behavioral Interventions) 142–3
Biden, Joseph 5, 18, 19–20, 101, 113, 137–8, 141, 151, 153, 160
Bloomberg 90
Bondi, Pam 158
Booker, Senator Cory 131
boycotts, and anti-detention activism 147, 162
Britain, proposal to send detainees to Rwanda 5–6, 156–7
Buffalo Service Processing Center, Batavia NY 21, 23, 25, 39, 79–80, 98, 127, 135, 139
    food provision in 39, 49, 51, 54
    hunger strikes in 136
    lawsuits against 100–1
    medical care in 65–6
Bukele, Nayib 156
Bush, George H.W. 15
Bush, George W. 16

Caliburn International 20, 133
California
    ban on private contracts 101–2, 135, 137–8
    BASIC Act (2023) 102, 147
California Department of Corrections 102
carceral facilities 10, 14–15, 19–20, 29–30, 70, 116–7
    lobbying by 10
    monitoring and surveillance in 141
CBM Managed Services 43–4
Center for Constitutional Rights (CCR) 33
Centers for Disease Control and Prevention (CDC) 55
Central America, migration to US from 14, 17
Centurion Health 120, 121
CFG Health Systems 27, 72–4, 78, 120
    bribery by 75

INDEX

children 20, 133, 147–8
  see also families
Chinese people and citizenship rights 12
Clearfield County, Pennsylvania 129
Clinton, Bill 15
Cold War 13
commissaries 7–8, 83–93, 126, 147
  commission rates in 88–9
  prices charges by 83, 87–8
Commission on Accreditation for Law Enforcement Agencies (CALEA) 116–7
complaints 35, 71, 104
  against GEO Group 98–100
  against violations of labor laws 100
  burying of 113–4
  food provision 38–6, 51–61, 90
  medical services 63–71, 81, 112
Congressional Budget Office 36
Contract Detention Facility (CDF) 23
CoreCivic company 3, 6, 20, 26, 39, 80, 96, 119, 121, 124, 128, 137–8
  divestment from 177
  donations to Trump campaign by 157
  lawsuits against 97–8
  lobbying by 11, 130–1
  lodges lawsuit against New Jersey 101
corporations *see* private companies
Correct Care Solutions (CCS later Wellpath) 29, 65–6, 72–3, 77, 78
Correctional Health Services (CHS) 73, 74
Correctional Medical Care (CMC) 73, 75–6, 119
Correctional Medical Group 73
Corrections Corporation of America (CCA later CoreCivic) 26, 33, 118–9, 130–1
CorrectRX Pharmacy Services 121
county jails 7, 72
  accreditation of 115
  deaths in 72
  medical care in 73–4
Courtesy Products 90, 127
COVID-19 pandemic 5, 18, 46, 56–7, 62–3, 70, 112, 136
Creative Corrections company 108
Cuba, migration to US from 14

Democratic Party 4, 12, 23, 161–2
Department of Homeland Security (DHS) 2, 16, 79, 132
  Office of the Inspector General (OIG) 38, 70, 81, 94–5, 108, 110
deportation 17, 19, 80–1, 152–3
detainees
  ankle shackles for 142
  commodification of 82, 89, 95, 97
  complaints by 38, 51–7, 67, 69, 113–4
  criminalizing of 2, 15
  electronic monitoring of 141–3
  hunger strikes by 136–7
  interviews with 37
  numbers of 3, 5, 10, 16t, 17–18, 158–9
  out-of-state transfer of 40, 138–9
  protests by 26, 135–6
  purchasing from commissaries by 83–8
  surveillance of 141–3
  use of prisons and military bases for 154
  work by 8, 11, 47, 83–4, 93–7, 147
  see also transgender detainees; voluntary work program; women detainees
detention bed quota 17, 130–1
detention centers
  conditions in 2–3, 70–1
  contracts for 24t
  deaths in 2–3,18, 63, 68, 71–2, 110–1, 119
  dependency of local economy on 2, 126–30, 157
  dismantling of 133, 144–50
  expansion of 10, 18, 113, 129, 153–4, 159
  law suits against 97–103
  sexual abuse in 69–70
  suicides in 68
  see also accreditation; detainees; inspections
detention system
  costs of 2, 10, 19, 20t, 159
  as deterrence 13–14, 17
  dismantling of 144–50
  divestment from 147–8
  financialization of 3, 6, 19, 21, 90
  indefinite detention 15
  infrastructure of 14–16, 90, 118, 143–4
  lobbying for 130–3
  outsourcing of 149, 154–6
  response to immigration 21, 214
  revenue from 1–3, 14, 95–6, 1023, 128–30
  see also Alternatives to Detention; anti-detention activism; deportation
Detention Watch Network (DWN) 33, 36, 62, 109, 150
Dignity Not Detention Bill (2021) 135
Divincenzo, County Executive Joseph 1, 75

El Salvador, offer to take US detainees 156
Elberon Development Group 26, 148

Elizabeth Contract Detention Facility, NJ 21, 23, 25–6, 70, 80, 96, 101, 111, 119, 135, 138
and anti-detention activism 148
Detainee Handbook (2013) 54
food provision in 39, 52–4, 57
hunger strikes in 136
medical care in 64, 66–71
Ellis Island Immigration Station 12, 79
Enforcement and Removal Operations (ERO) 108–11
enslaved people 12
Epps, Christopher (former Commissioner Mississippi Department of Corrections) 132
Esmor Correctional Services 25–6
Essex County Correctional Facility, NJ 1, 21, 23, 27, 72, 74–5, 87–9, 94, 115, 128
anti-detention activism in 134
conditions in 70–1
Detainee Handbook (2013) 93
food provision in 38–44, 52–3, 55–7, 60, 85
hunger strikes in 136
medical care in 64, 66–8, 72, 74–5, 109

Fair Labor Standards Act (1990) 93
families, separation of 17–18,133–4#
Federal Bureau of Prisons 115, 132
federal government, detention policies of 2, 8, 19, 26, 48–9, 92, 98–9, 101–3, 137–8
Fidelity Bank 124
Fleishmann, Congressman Chuck 131
Folkston Processing Center 131
food provision 7, 38–61
calorie requirements 49–50
contaminated food 55–7
insufficient quantities of 50–1, 83–7
Food Service Administrator (FSA) 48
food supply companies 7, 39–61, 125
contracts for 40t, 47
food for employees 58–9
prices charged per meal 44t
Free, Andrew (attorney) 100
Freedom for Immigrants 36, 136
Freedom of Information Act (FOIA) 30–1, 33
Freedom of Information Law, NY (FOIL) 34

GD Correctional Services (GDCS) 28, 40–3, 49, 58, 60
gender, and medical care 68–9

GEO Group 3, 6, 20, 33, 97, 121, 124, 128, 135, 137–8, 142–3, 148
and ATD 142–4
divestment from 147
donations to Trump campaign by 157
lawsuits against 97–101
lobbying by 11, 130–2, 135, 137
Global Detention Project 5, 149
Global Tel*Link 27, 28–9, 132
Government Accountability Office (GAO) 109, 112–3, 143
Guantánamo Bay 154–5

Haiti, migration to US from 14
H.I.G. Capital 45, 72–3, 90–2, 127, 132
Homan, Tom 155
Homeland Security Act (2003) 16
Hudson County Correctional Facility, NJ 21, 23, 27–9, 86–9, 128
deaths in 71, 78
food provision in 40, 47, 49–50, 52–4, 56–8, 85–6
hunger strikes in 136
medical care in 63, 65–6, 67–71, 73–5, 104
work by detainees in 83, 94
Human Rights First 36, 52, 53, 56–7, 66–8, 81, 115
Human Rights Watch 36, 69, 81, 149
hunger strikes 97, 134–6

IBISWorld 45–6, 125
Illegal Immigration Reform and Immigrant Responsibility Act (1996) 15
immigration, as an election issue 5, 19, 151
Immigration and Customs Enforcement (ICE) 1, 16, 113
Enforcement and Removal Operations (ERO) 108–11
Office of Detention Oversight (ODO) 51, 104, 108–12
Office of Professional Responsibility 108
requests for information from 30–1
Immigration and Enforcement Health Service Corps (IHSC) 7, 25–6, 63, 65, 79–82
Immigration and Nationality Act (1965) 13
Immigration and Naturalization Service (INS) 14, 28, 107
Immigration Reform and Control Act (1986) 15
information
access to 29–37, 145
redaction of 31, 32t, 34

INDEX

Inmate Calling Solutions (ICS) 90
inspections 35, 38, 60–1, 104, 107–14
Intelligence Reform and Terrorism Prevention Act (2004) 16
Intensive Supervision Appearance Program (ISAP) 141–4
Intergovernmental Service Agreement (IGSA) 23, 27–8, 137
International Detention Coalition 149
International Refugee Assistance Project 155
Italy, funding of detention centers in Albania 6

Japanese people, internment of 12
Jefferson County Jail, Texas 85
J.P. Morgan Chase 124, 148

Keefe Commissary Network (KCN) 26–9, 84, 88–90, 92, 132
Keefe Group 45, 90, 121, 124, 126–7
Kelly, General John 20, 133
Kemp, Governor Brian 131
Kennedy, Amy and Patrick 75, 132
Kirsch, Judge Robert 101
Krome Service Processing Center 25

Labor Law Wage Determination 96
labor laws, violation of 97–103
Laken Riley Act (2025) 152, 159
Laredo Detention Center, Texas 97–8, 106
Latin America 13
lobbying 11, 15–16, 46, 92, 120, 130–2, 161

Management and Training Corporation (MTC) 131–2, 137
Massachusetts 102
McCarthy, Representative Kevin 131
medical care 7, 62–82
    violation of standards in 111–2
medical service providers 72–82, 73t, 125–6
    litigation by 74–6
mental health care 67–8
Mexicans, repatriation of 12
Mexico, migration to US from 14
MGT of America Inc. 110
Microsoft 124
Mississippi Department of Corrections 132
Moran, Senator Jerry 131
Moshannon Valley Processing Center 129, 139
Murphy, Phil 101

Nakamoto Group 108–11
Nassau County 153

National Commission on Correctional Health Care (NCCHC) 115–23
    Marketing and Resource Guide (2023) 121–2, 125–6
National Detention Standards (NDS) 8, 105–7, 112, 114, 136, 155
    and food standards 48–9, 52–4, 57, 59, 61
    Performance-Based NDS (PBNDS) 106
    violations of 8, 60–1, 69, 78, 83–4, 94, 107–9, 112–3, 115
National Immigrant Justice Center (NIJC) 34–5, 36, 107, 109
National Sheriff's Association (NSA) 116
Native Americans 12
Nevada 102
New Jersey 18–19, 21, 22map, 128
    anti-detention activism in 134
    bail reform laws (2017) 46, 129
    ban on detention center contracts (2021) 23, 26, 101, 128, 135, 138, 140
New York 21
    anti-detention activism in 135
    ban on detention center contracts (2021) 135
    detention centers in 22map
Northrop Grumman Corporation 124
Northwest ICE Processing Center (NWIPC) 99

Obama, Barack 17, 139, 156
Office of Detention Oversight (ODO) 51, 104, 108–12
Office of the Immigration Detention Ombudsman 114
Open Public Records Act, NJ (OPRA) 34
Orange County Correctional Facility, NY 21, 23, 28–9, 86, 89, 112, 116–7, 118–9, 135, 139
    food provision in 40–1, 54, 92
    hunger strikes in 136
    medical care in 68, 72–6
    work by detainees in 83
Otay Mesa Detention Center 98

Panama, as staging point for deportations 156
Patriot Act (2001) 16
Portview Properties 26
Prevention Through Deterrence strategy 15
Prison Legal News report (2016) 119–20
prisons *see* carceral facilities
private companies 10–11, 19, 72, 137–8
    bribery and corruption in 75–6, 120

contracts with guaranteed minimums for 17, 25, 27, 33
divestment from 147–8
donations to Trump campaign by 157
favoritism in awarding contracts to 76–7, 82, 131
lawsuits against 97–103
lobbying by 11, 130–3
sponsorship by 121
see also revolving door
private equity companies 91–2
Private Equity Stakeholder Project 78, 89
private prison industry, profits in 14–15
Project on Government Oversight 157
public record requests 30–5, 52, 86

Quality Choice Health Care 73, 75–6

racism 16, 19, 133, 161
and national identity 12
Reagan, Ronald 14–15
Republican Party 4, 12, 23, 131, 159, 161–2
Requarth, Tim 90–1
Requests for Proposals (RFP) 42, 50–1, 74, 76, 88, 116, 154
revolving door between private companies and government 20, 119–20, 132–3, 157–8
Rubio, Senator Marco 131, 132, 156, 158

Sandweg, John (former acting director of ICE) 139
Secure Communities Program 17
Service Contract Act 96
Service Processing Centers (SPC) 23
slaves *see* enslaved people
SmartLINK 141–3
Stanley Black & Decker 124
state government 84, 102, 157, 160
Stewart Detention Center, Georgia 97, 131
STG International (STGi) 80

T. Don Hutto Residential Center 98
Texas, offer of jail space for detainees 159–60
TKC Holdings 45, 90, 92, 127
Trafficking Victims Protection Act (TVPA) 98
transgender detainees 69
Transnational Records Access Clearinghouse (TRAC) 35, 158–9

Transparency and Human Rights Project 35
Treatment Authorization Requests (TAR) 80
Trinity Services Group 25, 40–1, 45, 90, 92, 124, 127
Trump, Donald 5
1st term 17–18, 101, 106, 113, 134, 136, 137–8, 147
2nd term 19, 147, 148, 151–61
legal challenges to 160

Umar, Emre (Correctional Health Care) 119
United States
citizenship of 12, 161
birthright citizenship 152, 160
national identity of 12–13, 16, 161
non-white immigrants in 13, 16
United States Marshals Service (USMS) 27–8
US/Mexico border 10, 14, 18, 21, 151

Vainieri, Commissioner Anthony 127–8, 140
Valley Metro Barbosa Group (VMBG) 25, 51
Vanguard Bank 124
VF Corporation 124
Voluntary Work Program (VWP) 83–4, 93–6, 105

Wackenhut Corporation (later GEO Group) 14
Warren, Senator Elizabeth 109, 116
Warren Report 117–8, 120
Washington State General Attorney's Office 99–100
Wayfair company employee protests 148
Wellpath company 7, 28–9, 72–3, 90, 111, 116, 119, 121, 124, 127
bribery by 75
lobbying by 132
Wells Fargo Bank 124, 148
Westchester Jail, NY 78
Wexford Health company 121
Women detainees, medical care for 68–9

xenophobia 133

YesCare 120–1
York County Prison, Pennsylvania 129